TALENT IS AN ASSET THE STORY OF

SPARKS

For my darling Flora and dear Jack
May 2005. One in, one out

TALENT IS AN ASSET THE STORY OF
SPARKS

DARYL EASLEA

OMNIBUS PRESS

LONDON / NEW YORK / PARIS / SYDNEY / COPENHAGEN / BERLIN / MADRID / TOKYO

Cover designed by Fresh Lemon
Picture research by Jacqui Black

ISBN: 978.1.84772.781.7
Order No: OP52866

Exclusive Distributors
Music Sales Limited,
14/15 Berners Street,
London, W1T 3LJ.

Music Sales Corporation,
257 Park Avenue South,
New York, NY 10010, USA.

Macmillan Distribution Services,
56 Parkwest Drive
Derrimut, Vic 3030,
Australia.

Every effort has been made to trace the copyright holders of the photographs in this book but one or two were unreachable. We would be grateful if the photographers concerned would contact us.

Typeset by: Phoenix Photosetting, Chatham, Kent
Printed by: Gutenberg Press Ltd, Malta

A catalogue record for this book is available from the British Library.

Visit Omnibus Press on the web at www.omnibuspress.com

Contents

Contents

Introduction

No Ulterior Motives?

Novelty 1 *the quality of being new and intriguing.* **2** *something new and strange.* **3** *a small, cheap and usually kitsch toy or souvenir. 14c: from French* novelté

Chambers 21st Century Dictionary

"By nature, Sparks' music isn't apt to appeal to much of a middle ground. Its childishness and its makers' looks, looks, looks ensure its hold on the young, and its wry wit and perverto tinge should continue to captivate fringe types of all ages."

Richard Cromelin, *Phonograph Record*, 1975

"The people who have the most trouble dealing with what we've been doing are the ones who analyse so much, the 'older' rock fans. They tend to outguess our motives, and there are no ulterior motives."

Russell Mael, 1983.

"Well, screw the past."

Ron Mael 2006

O ver its 40 year history, the flagship UK BBC TV music programme *Top Of The Pops* had its fair share of 'moments', when viewers experienced some sort of defining event. These usually coincided with a degree of early maturity and rebellion on the part of the observer. In some, this may have occurred in their early teens, some younger, watching pop as the twisted cartoon it often resembles.

While David Bowie hugging Mick Ronson during 'Starman' in 1972, or Johnny Rotten singing 'Pretty Vacant' in 1977 are often cited, this author had his moment when, on May 9, 1974, five quirky individuals seemed to leap through the screen singing 'This Town Ain't Big Enough For Both Of Us'.

On an edition of the show that also featured in the studio easy listening crooner Vince Hill, soft toys The Wombles and boogie labourers Status Quo, stock still in front of us was a man rolling his eyes, bolted to the ground, exaggeratedly hitting his electric keyboard. He had slicked-back hair and a moustache. To his side, there was another man who looked vaguely similar, with curly flowing hair and what looked like a short dress on. A kimono, perhaps. Behind them were a fairly standard team of players from the day with their wide lapels, centre partings and flares. But it wasn't about them; it was all about the two men out front.

They looked like 'before' and 'after' pictures of an American small-town accountant who could take it no longer and had dropped out. However it was the size of the keyboard player's moustache that made it all the more noteworthy. Covering no more than an inch underneath his nose, this facial hair seemed exceptionally familiar to everyone who was watching. It had been seen somewhere before; some thought perhaps of Oliver Hardy or Charlie Chaplin, to whom it was intended as tribute. Some thought of Stephen Lewis, Inspector Blake from the recently finished yet still hugely popular ITV comedy series *On The Buses*. But most, if not all, people thought of one person only – Adolf Hitler.

And in 1974, the impact of the Second World War still cast something of a long shadow over Britain. Although it had been over for nearly 30 years, watching this spectacle was a generation whose parents had either fought in or had been born during the war. To find Hitler playing the piano on one of the BBC's prominent programmes was enough to send some older viewers into apoplexy.

'This Town Ain't Big Enough For Both Of Us' became the soundtrack to that early summer and beyond; trips to the funfair, to town, to the park, presenting a macabre netherworld that stood apart from a chart that was frankly full of enough weirdos already. But even among the four-eyed vaudeville of Elton John, the mirrored-topper of Noddy Holder, the sinister Bacofoil of Gary Glitter and the androgyny of David Bowie, it still seemed bizarre. Ron Mael – the wearer of this moustache – looked something like the public information films warning of things youngsters did not yet quite understand: about men offering sweets and taking you for a ride in their cars.

And the other one, Ron's younger brother, Russell, looked beautiful. It was as if he slept in a vat of moisturiser and lived a life being permanently startled in soft focus. Although it seemed nothing could be taken at face value; there was something about the speed of his delivery combined with a mixture of anxiety and supreme confidence that added to an overall unease.

It was about the clothes and the colour and the time. The taste of the exotic controlled and presented and beamed into the UK's living rooms. That Sparks were at their zenith in a Britain recovering from three-day weeks and the unrelenting grimness and relative poverty of the mid-Seventies comes now as little surprise. Lives were enlivened and brightened by the peacock people who would appear in our homes once a week. Aspirational values, cheap tailoring and the bizarre mingled together.

The long backwash of the moon landing of 1969 and the space films that followed, combined with a full-scale embracing of retro with the popularity of movies such as *American Graffiti* and *The Great Gatsby*, produced a generation of men (and it was mainly men as performers) who dressed like the future yet sounded like the past. Sparks were faintly straight compared to some acts but they had a man who looked like Adolf Hitler playing the piano, they looked striking, unusual, frightening, and they had made an impression, having scored the biggest hit single of their career.

The more we learned about this group, the more we, if not liked them, were intrigued. Ron wrote the songs and Russell sang them; they'd been in a group called Sparks before, but not this one; the pair supposedly had all sorts of connections to the American aristocracy; the Kennedys were fans; the Rainiers let them use their holiday home in Monaco; they were indeed the children of Doris Day.

Many people had a similar moment: teenage fan John Taylor, who six years later would form his own group called Duran Duran, felt equally strongly: "Remember *Bedazzled* with Peter Cook and Dudley Moore? They're on that *Top Of The Pops*-style programme and Moore as Stanley Moon comes out and says 'I love you, I love you', the crowd goes crazy and then Peter Cook as the devil comes out and goes 'I hate you, I hate you'. Well, Sparks was like watching both characters at the same time. Russell is so seductive and upfront, while Ron is holding everything back. It's a very strong presentation."

This strong presentation became a national obsession over the summer of 1974. The duo's performances were enough to get them on the radar of one of the groups they had so admired as teenagers in Los Angeles: The Beatles. Although it is highly unlikely that John Lennon ever said the oft-quoted 'Christ! There's Hitler on the telly!' while watching the programme. Or if he even said it at all; Beatles experts Pete Nash and Mark Lewisohn both suggest that it is apocryphal. This was a yarn begun by Sparks' first English bass player, Martin Gordon, while reviewing a later concert of theirs for *Mojo* magazine in 1995. Lennon would have been a US resident for three years by that point. However, it is wholly possible he *may* have caught Sparks on a US TV special in 1974 when they performed 'Something For The Girl With Everything'. Introduced by Keith Moon with a little help from ex-Beatle Ringo Starr, Sparks definitely registered with Paul McCartney, who was sufficiently aware of the group's existence and impact to dress up as Ron Mael for his 1980 video for 'Coming Up'.

Sparks kept appearing on *Top Of The Pops* for the next 18 months. Further singles came and went and Ron Mael's stare seemed to burn brighter and brighter into the telly. Then gradually, Sparks disappeared. When I finally picked up their first four British albums in 1978 in a record shop bargain bin, I might as well have been buying some big band swing as they were already long forgotten. But those records! They sounded fresh and very relevant to the current new wave scene.

And then, Sparks went disco. At a time when everyone from The Rolling Stones to Dolly Parton was sashaying down the nightclub, they produced an album called *No. 1 In Heaven*. Its lead single, 'The Number One Song In Heaven', saw them back on *Top Of The Pops*. They were now performing alongside artists such as The Damned and The Monks. Hitler now had a bit of a perm. It was delightful to have them back.

Apart from a period of British radio silence in the Eighties, Sparks continue to be a fixture on the scene. Since the mid-Nineties, Sparks have been regulars to the UK, culminating in their ground-breaking *21 Nights* series of London shows in which they played all of their albums in chronological order over May and June of 2008.

When you look at Sparks' peers from their 1974 breakthrough, they are either disgraced (Gary Glitter), discarded (The Rubettes), disbanded (Slade), dead (lead singers from Mud and Sweet), have become institutions (Elton John) or at a level where they no longer need to record (David Bowie). For an act still to be consistently making music – just listen to the otherworldliness of their 22nd album, *The Seduction Of Ingmar Bergman*, released in November 2009 – that sounds as strange and otherworldly while remaining often unashamedly commercial three decades on, is nothing short of remarkable. So let me remark upon it. At some length.

It is not that easy to try and find the true story of Sparks. Larry Dupont, a character who played a large role in their early career and remains a friend, is fully aware how protective Sparks are of their past. "I respect their desire to maintain their image but it's a shame as their history is extraordinarily interesting. They had so much perseverance. That group was rejected so much in their early days, they stuck a big piece of paper on the wall of their rehearsal room and wrote every rejection on it. The list became so long but it never seemed to stop them from going out and getting another audition." Sparks have had their share of dazzling moments and less than successful interludes, but one thing is very much certain: their tenacity, resilience and ability to capitalise on an opportunity is forever remarkable.

Simply put, Sparks are one of the most essential art-pop groups of all time. In fact, as time passes, they are almost the sole, long-lasting definers and purveyors of the genre. As Richard Cromelin wrote as early as 1975, "[they] continue to captivate fringe types of all ages". *Talent Is An Asset:*

The Story Of Sparks will dispel several myths that surround the group and bluntly not care very much about the others. Although there are those who fear it is likely to be a collection of half truths, quotes from folks that don't know the brothers or their real history, and nonsense about their ages, sexuality and Doris Day, there are others who want to know the story, even if parts of it are well-trodden, because frankly, it is one of the most interesting in pop.

When Ron and Russell Mael relocated to Britain in 1973, they hit the pop world as Sparks and looked like oddballs, even in the context of the glam rock movement that welcomed them. Soon defined by their weird and wonderful 1974 number two single, 'This Town Ain't Big Enough For Both Of Us', from the *Kimono My House* album, Sparks have gone on to release 22 albums over four decades, each record inhabiting a bizarre world of its own. Their songs are peppered with puns and pop culture nods, as well as nostalgia and jokey images, all mixed up in a kaleidoscope of musical references ranging from rock to glam to disco.

It's all about context. Had Sparks come from New York or London, it may have made perfect sense. But they didn't. They came from Los Angeles. And from a time when the love vibe was so strong and laid back, they cut the same, strange outsider figures that they remain over 40 years later.

The cowboy analogy of their greatest hit (and indeed a comparison they have returned to at various times over their career) is wholly appropriate. Ron and Russell Mael have lived on pop's outskirts since the late Sixties; they may have occasionally made a foray into the centre of town, but that has usually been brief, often dazzling. But, this blaze of glory soon dies down and we are on to the next gunfight.

Although they have been a great influence on a generation of performers, Sparks' impact has not struck a similar mass-appeal chord as fellow-travellers such as David Bowie or Roxy Music. Yet their first wave of success and the complete, discrete world they offered can be seen as feeding into punk. And 1974's 'Amateur Hour', both in sound and ideology, seems to predict the movement by at least a couple of years.

Sparks' Giorgio Moroder-produced phase can be seen as a direct precursor to the great UK synth duos and bands of the Eighties. By the

21st century, their music was so ornate and unusual that it seemed simply too ahead of itself to influence *anyone.*

Defy categorisation and you will always have a funny old time of it. "The missing link between the androgynous menace of The Rolling Stones and the cool histrionics of The Associates. The Archies meet Zappa via Crimson and Purple. Bubblegum metal with a dash of prog," is author Paul Lester's attempt. Sparks came and went in the world of mass appeal. "Maybe because it was such a complete world that once you had a couple of doses of it that was enough," writer Jon Savage suggests. "And it would've been easier to see them as a novelty act." Novelty is a strange word, yet very relevant to Sparks when considering the word's definitions (see above). Their detractors could easily dismiss them as cheap and kitsch but Sparks constantly strive to remain intriguing and strange. They are archetypal old school pop stars, still awaiting their next break, the next curtain call.

Sparks have been there or thereabouts – *Saturday Night Live,* the Whisky A Go Go, Max's Kansas City, the Marquee, and the El Mocambo. They have been known to the great and the good. For a group that appeared as if from nowhere in 1974, they had already worked with music industry legends such as Bob Dylan's manager, Albert Grossman, Todd Rundgren, an Electric Prune (Jim Lowe), Derek Taylor and were managed by John Hewlett, an ex-member of John's Children who had learned his craft from one of the most successful figures of British Sixties pop, Simon Napier-Bell. That they were signed to Island and produced by Muff Winwood, a man who had come from another brother act, The Spencer Davis Group, meant their pedigree was already pretty special.

Brothers in pop are a strange and mixed blessing. Ray and Dave Davies; Noel and Liam Gallagher – you do not think of happy campers when you think of them. "You wonder how you'd spend your entire life in the company of your brother," writer Ira Robbins posits. "I know that doesn't sound odd, but it's like you've chosen to spend your entire professional existence reliant on somebody that you were raised with."

It is the remarkable blend of two great eccentrics that makes Sparks' pop so unpalatable for some: in a review I wrote in 2002 of *Lil' Beethoven,* I used the expression "musical Marmite". For those who love, it is an always-giving world of untold riches. Tony Visconti lays a lot of this at the door of Russell and his realisation of Ron's concepts: "I'd never heard a lead singer sound like him before. It's somewhere between Tiny Tim and Robert Plant. He's got such an unusual voice. He's got a real signature sound in his vocals but you wouldn't hear any Americans with a guy like that in the group. There wouldn't be a lead singer like that. He sounds like he comes from some upper-crust British family."

Perhaps Sparks never got over their education: UCLA in the febrile Sixties, drinking in film studies instead of dope and booze, learning about French *nouvelle vague*. Film is very much part of Sparks' make-up: it plays a huge role in everything they've done and film studies have coursed throughout their writing, most visibly on 'This Town Ain't Big Enough For Both Of Us', based on the clichés spouted in a Western. The *Lil' Beethoven* trilogy (*Lil' Beethoven*, *Hello Young Lovers* and *Exotic Creatures Of The Deep*) are all mini-movies in themselves.

Sparks' first radio drama is an imaginary visit to Hollywood by Ingmar Bergman, one of their all-time favourite directors. Russell is wearing a Hollywood T-shirt on the cover of their second album, *A Woofer In Tweeter's Clothing*. Alain Delon, Jean-Paul Belmondo, Clint Eastwood, Donald Duck, Lassie, Mickey Mouse, Meryl Streep, Toshiro Mifune, Paul Newman, Grace Kelly, Roman Polanski, Ronald Colman, Sergei Eisentein, Tsui Hark and Warren Beatty all populate Ron Mael's narrative. One of their great disappointments to date has been their failure to realise their ambitions to make a film, *Mai The Psychic Girl*.

Ron Mael was one of the first writers to develop proper irony in a pop song. Strange subjects of masculinity, white women, art galleries and things like this. There have always been many different meanings; Sparks were singing more songs about buildings and food while David Byrne was still at college.

Talent Is An Asset is an exploration of Sparks' extraordinary career drawing on hours of new interviews and research. It comes as close as possible to pinning down the quicksilver nature of two gifted musicians who have gone out of their way to remain unpredictable and elusive, forever entrenched behind a glittering gallery of jokes, impersonations and musical eccentricities.

The duo are fiercely protective of their privacy; they tell all yet say little. They have a sort of southern gentleman air about them of incredible politeness and grace. Their inner circle also operates with a ring of politely tightly fitted steel – the very height of civility, but divulging very little. Like the inscrutable nature of Sparks' music, this has attracted fans for years.

So, let us embark on this journey that takes us from the Los Angeles suburbs in the Fifties to Sweden in the Noughties, taking in several world capitals, 22 albums, 33 or so band members and at least six managers. We skirt on glam, punk, disco and we hardly stand still. *Talent Is An Asset* is a fascinating tale from a pair of fascinating Maels.

Chapter One

It's A Sparks Show Tonight!

"The story of Sparks is also the story of an overnight sensation, six years in the making."

Joseph Fleury, 1975

"Knowing less about us is probably better for the mythology. You know, like 'What the hell is going on with those guys?' I like that."

Russell Mael, 2008

So much mystery surrounds Ron and Russell Mael's upbringing that it is worth noting all the various possibilities that have been put forward over the years about their origins. It would, for example, be fascinating if their name was assumed. Or that they had been child models. Or actors. People who seek to correct these myths often carry a sanctimonious air that only *they* know the correct answers to the myriad web of questions that the brothers and their work seem to provoke.

The Maels' ability to fox is well-known; one of the most enduring myths is that they are the children of Doris Day. This was a gag that originated in 1974 in *Flashes*, the Sparks fan club magazine, and perpetuated in the 2002 edition of *The Encyclopaedia of Popular Music* and included as fact in a 2003 *Record Collector* article by this author. That their name appears to subvert the masculine to misspell 'Mael' has also given writers an opportunity to discuss how the pair's image toys with male stereotypes and manly American icons.

So let's deal with the 'D' word straight away. To cope with the constant bombardment of similar questions presented by journalists over the years, "We started making up these ... lies," Ron Mael told *The Times* in 2003. "We're Doris Day's sons. That is hyperbole I guess," Russell told *Plan B* magazine in 2007 in response to the question "Please quote your favourite hyperbole about your band." Amusing because, of course, no one but themselves created it.

It would have been fascinating if Doris Day *had* been their mother, as it was an apposite choice for them to pick; an actress with a strong image, so widely associated with purity and chastity that people believed her public image was the reality and public image is always a *very* significant factor when looking at Sparks.

However, my apologies to all those who wish to trundle on the rumour mill; Mael *is* Ron and Russell's family name and, let's face it, it is a pretty unusual one, dating back to the fifth century and of Celtic origin. Once popular in Ireland and Wales, as well as Brittany, the name meant 'king', 'chief' or 'prince' and grew in usage after St. Mael, who accompanied St. Cadfan on his travels through Wales before reaching his destination on Bardsey Island off the Lleyn Peninsula, where he eked out his days living as a hermit.

Ronald David Mael was born on August 12, 1945 in Culver City, California to Meyer and Miriam Mael. Younger brother Russell Craig Mael arrived on October 5, 1948 in Santa Monica, California. The brothers are three years older than many of their biographies have suggested. Lying about your age is hardly a pop crime, and if ever a group were showbiz enough to have shaved off a few years, Sparks certainly qualified. For all their quirkiness and left-of-centre nature, Sparks are the epitome of *showbiz*.

The brothers grew up in the affluent, largely residential area of Pacific Palisades, Los Angeles. Located between Brentwood to the east, Malibu to the west and Santa Monica to the south east, 'where the mountains meet the sea', Pacific Palisades also contains the western end of Sunset Boulevard. The Maels first lived on Washington Boulevard before moving to a house on Galloway Street on a grid of streets off West Sunset Boulevard. The area has several popular culture references: its local high school was the setting of Brian De Palma's 1976 chiller, *Carrie*, and the long-running James Garner TV detective vehicle, *The Rockford Files*, was filmed there.

The America the brothers grew up in was prosperous, triumphant, yet deeply troubled. It had recently successfully fought a war on two fronts and by ending a period of isolationism, had taken its place as a superpower in world hegemony. Less than five years later, the United States had seen the advance of Communism in Eastern Europe and China; the Soviets develop their own atomic weaponry; and was facing very real concerns about internal security. Wisconsin Senator Joseph McCarthy had sprung up to exploit the prevailing mood of fear and uncertainty with his activities on the House Un-American Activities Committee.

While the idyllic surroundings of Pacific Palisades shielded the Mael household from what was going on, the rampant imperialism of the US combined with a reinforcement of decent moral values would give the Maels both a reference point and source material across the years.

One of the Mael brothers' earliest public appearances was captured in a newspaper cutting from 1954. It finds the brothers in Native American dress at the fourth annual Fiesta La Ballona festival in Culver City. Fiesta La Ballona days began in 1951 as a week-long celebration of the region's early settlers. People would go to events dressed up as Native American Indians, rancheros, señoritas, cowboys and cowgirls. "Cowboy and Indian costumes held a bright spotlight in the Fiesta La Ballona Kiddies' Parade," the paper harks. "Winners in this division, left to right are: Russell Mael, 5; Ronnie Mael, 9." Both in face paint and holding weaponry, the brothers are unmistakable and their enthusiastic participation demonstrates their early willingness to put on a show.

The story about being child models and actors was another product of the Mael spin. Or was it? Again, there are interviews suggesting they were in the *Sears* catalogue, and although the brothers denounced the tales to Michael Bracewell in *The Times* in 2003, they were *still* regaling journalists with stories of their modelling career in 2006.

3

"It wasn't really child acting," Ron told *Record Collector* in 2003. "We did some catalogue modelling things. It was more standing in front of a camera and smiling more than Shakespeare."

"There's nothing to show for our hard-earned hours spent out there," Russell added. They have said that their mother was a "typical Hollywood mom" who pushed them into modelling, but that she was also a teacher and a librarian. Perhaps she was all three. What is indisputable is how big a fan Miriam was of her children (and remains to this day).

Music was already on the agenda in the Mael household. Ron took piano lessons from the age of six to nine, while their father was a keen follower of both film and popular music. "Our father bought us 'Hound Dog' by Elvis and 'Long Tall Sally' by Little Richard, so they were the first records we owned," Ron told *The Guardian* in 2002. "I don't know what his inspiration was for doing that … they weren't the kind of records you usually bought as educational tools for your child." Russell's first record was 'Breathless' by Jerry Lee Lewis. "I thought [Jerry Lee] was amazing," Russell said. "I still listen to that record now and I just get as big a buzz; it's not nostalgic in the slightest."

However, the Maels' childhood idyll ended abruptly when Meyer, a painter and graphic designer for the *Hollywood Citizen*, died in February 1957 at the age of 40. "It was a heart condition," Ron later told *Mojo*. "I was 11 when he died. It was very sudden and unexpected. There was no build up. He was so young and … it just wasn't like what happened in movies or books. I really learned a big lesson, that things can happen totally out of the blue and there isn't a rational order to things."

Miriam did her best to cope. "She seemed to roll with it, as they say," Russell said. "I guess because she had been married to an artist, she kind of understood what we were up to, having aspirations towards being musicians." Miriam kept her children entertained not only by playing music, but by taking them to countless movie shows. A strong work ethic was instilled from an early age with Ron selling ice-cream to supplement his studies. "I know the two of them worked really hard," future Urban Renewal Project member Ronna Frank says. "Their father died and their mother strove to put them through college. They were both really nice people."

After a period of "rolling with it", bringing up two boys single-handedly, Miriam remarried, but the bond that Ron and Russell had with their stepfather, Oscar 'Rogie' Rogenson, was variable. "They had this weird relationship; they treated him civilly but they never really were easy with [Rogie]," original Sparks bassist Jim Mankey recalls. "Maybe over time they found it easier but they were having that problem that many young people have when the father goes and the new one comes along. They liked the guy, they just didn't really seem to accept him."

"By the time I was on the scene, they already had a very long history with him and yet there was definitely a tension whenever [Rogie] was around," Mankey continues. "It's like an after-school special. 'You must get over it, your father's gone, your mother wants this new guy and it makes her happy and you guys can move on if you don't like it.' It undoubtedly shaped their lives."

Despite such testimonies, there is little to suggest that the tension was too great. Rogie and Miriam doted on the boys, who became inseparable; Ronnie, as he was known (and still is by those close to him) kept a protective eye on his younger sibling and the two began to retreat into a world of art and dreams. "It's common for mathematical geniuses' creativity to flare up and it burns away at an early age," Mankey recalls. "They were already old before their years when they started and they've still got it."

The Rogenson family ran what at best could be called a head shop, or otherwise, a novelty shop in Pacific Palisades. The Gilded Prune was a small store with a huge glass window, whose stock would often overflow home.

"Their house was just full to the brim," Mankey laughs. "It was stuffed full of weird items that made you laugh when you saw them: plastic rubber lips around; books full of fart jokes; kitchy-doodads. 'Oh look a piece of soap that you sing into like a microphone' – whatever! I think Rogie probably did sell some bongs and cigarette papers, too. As far as I ✓ know, he was the one that brought in all those novelty items, although possibly their mother had something to do with that. Miriam was a really funny person."

It's clear that the brothers' strong sense of humour and warped way of looking at situations came from the sense of play infused in them by their mother. Future Sparks' drummer Harley Feinstein remembers it with affection: "They had all kinds of crazy stuff in there. Their house was also full of newspapers stuffed halfway to the ceiling; they didn't throw anything away."

In a rare acknowledgment of his family, Ron Mael told Nick Kent in a 1974 *NME* interview that 'Pop' Mael was "one of them guys who hangs around Century City in the tall buildings there, importing garbage – posters, newer trendy stuff like you get from Habitat – nouveau semi riche, y'know?" Surrounded by oddities, it's little wonder that the music that the Maels would go on to record became odd. A later picture of the group, taken by friend Larry Dupont in their Pacific Palisades living room, hints at the bric-a-brac filling their abode. To Ron's left there is a bobbing head model of Paul McCartney, between his legs there is a plate with Franklin Delano Roosevelt on it. Figurines and cuddly toys abound.

However one should not get the wrong impression by such kitsch possessions as Miriam and Rogie were lovers of high culture too, a love they instilled in the boys and something that was to blossom further when, in 1964, Ron went from Palisades High School to one of the most prestigious universities in America, the University of California at Los Angeles (UCLA), to study graphic design. One of the first friends Ron made at UCLA was industrial design student Larry Dupont. Their love of collecting gave them a strong bond.

"Ron is a collector like me," Dupont says. "One of our professors, John Newhart, used to work for [designer] Charles Eames. Eames was an antique toy collector, and now he's somewhat considered just a couple of steps away from Da Vinci. Because he worked on film, Newhart was an influence on us; he exposed me way back then to toys. Over a period of time we went crazy collecting stuff." While Russell was often too busy playing sport, collecting obsessed Ron. "I collect things; it's like a disease," Ron said in 2003. "I collect sports figurines ... Beatles trading cards. When I was little, I used to go to all the automobile shows because I loved cars. And so I've got a collection of all the new automobile launch brochures going right back."

After finishing at Palisades High on Bowdoin Street, Russell followed Ron to UCLA in 1966 to study theatre, arts and film making. Unfortunately, the fruits of Russell's labours were never to be seen, as he told Mark Leviton in 1983. "When I got to UCLA I was in theater arts, undergraduate film work. They flunked me on my first film, actually. One professor thought it was like early Polanski, but the rest gave me an 'F.' It's the same old story as our musical career – we're either considered brilliant or get an 'F' in work habits."

The drive and ambition that Russell and his older brother shared was already apparent to Larry Dupont. "I think Ron was far more determined to make the thing work but you put the two of them together and they were both unwavering. I did an awful lot of stuff with Ron and Russ together. Ron and Russ always came as a package."

Much has been made over the years of the fact that the Mael brothers have never wed; there have been relationships that simply got in the way of their principal concern – making music. "Neither of us is married – we're too busy having a good time," Russell said in *BAM Magazine* in 1983. "On the surface, maybe we look less 'rock 'n' roll' than the average group, but on the other hand we're more 'rock 'n' roll' than those pictures of Led Zeppelin on the farm with their wives and kids, Rock 'n' roll lifestyles mean you have a wife and then cheat on her, so rather than do that, we're honest and stay unmarried. I don't know anybody in any other band who's as un-tied down as the two of us. We dislike homey things – for ourselves anyway."

"We have friends who have families," Ron told *The Word* magazine in February 2006. "I get it vicariously; having a traditional family would be a real restriction on what we do."

Like so many American teenagers of their generation, Ron and Russell were stopped in their tracks by The Beatles' February 1964 appearance on *The Ed Sullivan Show*. On August 20 that year, they saw The Beatles perform at the Las Vegas Convention Hall and the following year, Ron and Russell, accompanied by Miriam, saw the Fab Four at the Hollywood Bowl. Strongly influenced by music and popular culture, the brothers absorbed whatever they heard whether it be listening to Motown on Boss Radio KHJ and KRLA, watching The Supremes on *The Ed Sullivan Show*, or collecting singles from rock'n'roll through to surf music. They also strove to see as many shows as possible and can be clearly seen in the audience during The Ronettes' appearance in *The Big*

TNT Show, a prototype concert movie filmed in Los Angeles' Moulin Rouge Club on November 29, 1965, featuring Ray Charles, Petula Clark and The Byrds among others.

Although the Maels had a shared love of The Beach Boys, it was British music that was to influence them most; as the Sixties progressed, their Anglophile tastes expanded into the sort of psychedelic-influenced mod pop that usurped Merseybeat. "'Tattoo' by The Who – we used to listen to that and think we wanted to be as cool as that," Russell said in 2003. "'Waterloo Sunset' ... not only did we like it musically, but it was speaking of this utopian England." Within a matter of years the brothers would be in London. "We came over and went to Waterloo Bridge and Waterloo Station – it's not quite as romantic as it was on the record!"

However there was one single, 'Happenings Ten Years Time Ago' by The Yardbirds, that really hit the spot. Produced by Simon Napier-Bell and released in October 1966, it was three minutes of surreal, psychedelic aural imagery. Ron and Russell would listen to it and marvel at its wonder and it was to become something of a touchstone for their early work.

The brothers would later become evangelical about their tastes and were happy to share them, as Jim Mankey recalls. "Ron and Russ were the equivalent of how The Beatles were in Liverpool; how they took the latest records from sailors that came in to port. In Ron and Russ' case, it was all the freaks and disreputable types that they met in their stepfather's shop who would share their musical desires."

The exuberance and optimism of LA in the mid-Sixties has been well-documented. "LA was fun, full of music and clubs and also hopeful feelings," Ronna Frank recalls. "UCLA was perfect for the Maels; it was a place where they could indulge their art and find other like-minded souls."

Although they have since suggested that they were passing through university waiting for something better to come along, Ron and Russell threw themselves into college life and their cultural dabblings became grander. Later on, fellow travellers such as Harley Feinstein would benefit from their wisdom: "I was just starting off in college and I was looking for people to learn from. They were really up on new wave, European cinema, photographers like Diane Arbus. I had never been to Fellini and Godard movies. We went to see Bergman movies together; they introduced me to that whole world – a real cultural education."

Ronna Meyer, a student at California State University of Northridge in the San Fernando Valley, was married to Ron's best friend, Fred Frank. "It was great fun. Ron was a year ahead of me, and Russ was a year or two behind," Ronna recalls. "I'd met Ron when I was at Fairfax High School through my husband. They were also in the same fraternity at UCLA, so I went to lots and lots of fraternity parties. We went on hayrides in West LA as part of the fraternity parties. Ron Mael was on the hay wagon, too."

Ron, Fred and Ronna were inseparable during Ron's early years at UCLA. Ron was best man at Fred and Ronna's wedding in 1966 and nearly married Fred himself, as Ronna recalled. "At our wedding, the person who married us asked if Ron 'Mael' instead of Ronna 'Meyer' would take Fred to be their husband. Oops!"

Ronna also got to know Ron's kid brother, whom she recalls as "poetic. His hairstyle and face resembled Jim Morrison." She considered Ron to be the more serious of the two, very much into art, and heavily into silk-screening T-shirts.

With their shared tastes and loves, it was inevitable that the brothers, as most teenage Americans had done after seeing *A Hard Day's Night*, should take the logical step from being music lovers to music makers and form a band. But right from their earliest recordings there seemed to be little straight pop in their repertoire. Although other names such as The Bel Air Blues Project, Moonbaker Abbey and Farmer's Market have been mentioned, Ron and Russell Mael's first proper group was called Urban Renewal Project, featuring Fred Frank on guitar and Ronna on drums.

"We used to practise in the gym at Palisades High School," Frank, who had previously played in The Loafers, says. "In the later stages, there was a young boy, aged 13, who played drums. There was also a college-aged guy who played bass." The group's look, as future Sparks publicist, fan club chief and finally manager, Joseph Fleury, later described it, was "rather Beefheart in appearance – Ron with his vest and ten-gallon hat, while Russell donned short, ear-length hair."

The closest Urban Renewal Project came to the big time was when they entered a couple of Battle Of The Bands competitions. The first was

9

at the Los Angeles Sports Arena in 1967. Due to financial and technical constraints, Urban Renewal Project had to go through a single amplifier for the heats. "It was amazing," Frank recalls. "The arena was filled with so much sound, you couldn't hear anything specific. It was very exciting. We were very hopeful back then, and played Booker T and the MGs' 'Green Onions', with me on snare drum." The cacophony was fairly unpleasant and the band failed to progress any further. Reportedly, another act competing that day was Taj Mahal.

Another Battle Of The Bands occurred at the Hollywood Wilshire YMCA. This time, only two groups showed up, and the other outfit were not in sporting mode, "pulling out leads to the speakers". Piqued by this display of bad form, Urban Renewal Project played, as Russell told *Sounds* in 1970, "our most obnoxious song in retaliation". It was then they realised that the band members were all playing in different keys. "We played a lot of Rolling Stones stuff, and music from that era," Frank recalls.

Although their music was not dissimilar to what thousands of other bands were into, there was a strong streak of individuality and darkness running through the brothers even then. A session at Fidelity Recording Studio at 6315 Yucca, Hollywood, marked the recorded debut of the Maels.

Ronna Frank: "We recorded a song onto a 45 called 'Computer Girl' in a studio; Russ wrote lyrics and Ron wrote the music. Russ sang lead, I played piano, Fred played guitar, and I can't remember what Ron actually did on it. My part was to say 'This is a recording,' throughout the piece." Frank also recollects the four band members being in a small room facing the sound booth next to a grand piano.

A test acetate exists of 'Computer Girl', along with three other cuts – 'A Quick Thought', 'The Windmill' and 'As You Like It'. 'Computer Girl', later given away with the superb Japanese volume, *Sparks Guide Book*, is quite remarkable and demonstrates how the brothers started as they meant to continue. Its subject matter was about a man who forms a relationship with a female who is a computer. Alongside Ronna Frank's repeated 'This is a recording' intonations, reminiscent of later English eccentrics like the Flying Lizards, Russell sings about placing an IBM card in her stomach to get a date over Ronna's snare, with her husband's tremolo-laden guitar floating in the background. It's all rather odd and the influence of The Velvet Underground is unmistakeable.

"We couldn't figure out way back then that we were singing about computers, when there weren't computers *per se*, so we can't figure out how we got the metaphor of a 'Computer Girl' into a lyric," Russell explained in the BBC documentary *This Town Ain't Big Enough For Both Of Us – The Story Of Sparks* in 2007. "There you go, ahead of the game again."

The band's third appearance – at an Industrial Design Conference at UCLA – was a less than illustrious proposition. The participants wanted something far more straight-ahead, and the only time the group could play was while the delegates were eating. It was not a huge success. "Anything they could do to make a buck, they were willing to do," Larry Dupont recalls. "Someone got the band this job and it was the worst combination of venue and band you could possibly imagine."

The spectre of being called up to fight in the Vietnam War would hang over the Mael brothers for the next few years. On June 23, 1967, the pair, along with Dupont and early friend and occasional band associate Harold Zellman, attended the 10,000-strong anti-war demonstration centred on the Century Plaza Hotel. US President Lyndon Johnson was attending a fundraising dinner for the Democratic Party when a coalition of groups opposing the war converged on Century City. Muhammad Ali delivered the gathering's keynote speech.

"Everyone was there," Dupont recalls. "It was one of the first decent sized anti-war demonstrations in Los Angeles. The kind of people who went out to protest were people coming out of work at the end of the day in business suits, and mothers with children. The protests hadn't been taken over by the younger, more boisterous crowd yet." The police, who had been anticipating a smaller crowd, did not have the event especially well-organised. The march came to a halt when some radicals began a sit-down protest in the road. "The crowd was strung out across this bridge with another major cross street underneath and it was going no place," Dupont remembers. "We couldn't tell what the hell was going on. I got on Ron's shoulders; even though there was some guy up there with a bullhorn shouting into the crowd, we couldn't hear a thing he was saying. The police tried to push the crowd back with half the people still moving forward. A riot broke out with the cops pounding people and everybody scattering in all directions."

Johnson rarely campaigned publicly after this, and the demonstration could be seen as the first step on the route to his withdrawal from running for a second term of presidential office the following year. Although Zellman and Dupont went to further demonstrations, this was the only one at which the Maels were present.*

Urban Renewal Project sputtered out, as Fred Frank was unable to dodge the draft.

Ronna Frank: "We kept playing together, and played around areas of Los Angeles at different clubs. Fred was drafted in 1968. We had already begun working to earn a living and Ron and Russ wanted to pursue just the band. So we drifted apart from the others."

Things changed into a higher gear musically when the brothers met Earle Mankey. As Fleury said in the 1975 release *2 Originals Of Sparks*, "The brothers placed a 'guitarist wanted' ad in a local music shop, and wound up with a rounded Gene Clark haircut and shades." Which was cool, as Clark's former group, The Byrds, were just about acceptable on the Mael radar. "We detested folk music because it was cerebral and sedate and we had no time for that," Ron told *The Guardian* in 2002. "But The Byrds were OK because they electrified it and they had English hairstyles."

Born in 1947, Washington native and UCLA engineering graduate Mankey was something of a whizz-kid. He was a technically accomplished guitarist and knew how the recording process worked. "Earle was really talented at recording – just on a reel-to-reel tape player," Russell said in 2003. "He could do whatever you wanted; playing things backwards, speeding up vocals. It was a very different attitude to a lot of LA bands at that time. Mostly new bands went out and played their stuff in front of a public and assessed how it fared. We never went that route. It became almost the same issue as we are facing today – 'How best do you present something that you've recorded?'"

---

* Despite their political motivation, it would take some 39 years before Ron and Russell would record their first explicit protest song as Sparks, '(Baby, Baby) Can I Invade Your Country?'

"We were doing things like 'sampling' one note from a classical record
– long before 'sampling' was even a term," Ron added. "We didn't have
to worry about what anyone thought, because no one was hearing it.
We were just doing things we thought sounded cool. We've been in that
position a few times since – the first stuff was 'pure studio'."

A new band, Halfnelson – named after a one-handed wrestling hold –
was born. Larry Dupont, who had by now graduated and was working as
a photographer at UCLA, was a constant presence, taping things on his
recorder. He also inveigled the band into another art project.

Larry Dupont: "Halfnelson worked on the music for a 16mm film a
friend and I were making in college about the Goodyear blimp. We went
off and got all the gear and ultimately made a movie in a UCLA basement.
My dark room became our editing room." Although Halfnelson added
the original music, the soundtrack expanded to something rather grander,
as Dupont confirmed. "Eventually we discovered organs and symphony
orchestras and used that. We showed the film to several people at various
different stages."

While the film was never finished, the project showed the Maels'
willingness to experiment. With Mankey's involvement, a 12-track
demo was recorded with bass player 'Surly' Ralph Oswald and drummer
John Mendelsohn now part of the group. Russell played bass on a lot
of the recording, while Ron mainly played organ. To show this was
a real proposition, Mike Berns, a drummer from local band Rabbit
Mackay, became Halfnelson's manager. As a player, according to Harley
Feinstein, he was into "rootsy, bluesy stuff, a million miles away from
what Halfnelson wanted to do". However, Berns had connections in the
LA music scene and provided the finance for their demo.

After the tape was recorded, the line-up seemed to flake away. Oswald
and Mendelsohn went off to form Christopher Milk (and later Arthur
Treacher's Fish and Chips). Mendelsohn found notoriety as an outspoken
rock critic for *Rolling Stone* magazine. He later wrote in his 1995
autobiography, *I, Caramba (Confessions of An Antkiller)*, "I joined a group
called Halfnelson, later renamed Sparks. Two years before, the singer and
I, the only two longhaired boys in sight, had sneaked suspicious glances
at one another in Italian 101. They wanted to be precious and adorable,
as they wrongly imagined The Kinks to be, while I, a Who fan, wanted

to be intimidating. I was soon asked not to be in the group any more." As the band needed a drummer, Berns would sit in wherever possible.

With the demo, which was to be artfully packaged to look like a 'proper' album – its tracks being 'Chile Farm Farney', 'Johnny's Adventure', 'Roger', 'Arts And Crafts Spectacular', 'Landlady', 'The Animals At Jason's Bar And Grill', 'Big Rock Candy Mountain', 'Millie', 'Saccharin And the War', 'Join The Firm', 'Jane Church' and 'The Factory' – Halfnelson were set to knock the Los Angeles music scene dead.

Chapter Two

Californian Folk Songs: Halfnelson

"Mostly, Sparks are somewhere else entirely. American Bandstand *will never hold them. Instead, someone will have to resurrect* Ready, Steady, Go!*"*

Bearsville biography, 1971

"There's no telling what kind of people they really are underneath all their arty trappings."

Jim Mankey, 2009

Halfnelson's demo recording, which later, erroneously, came to be known as *A Woofer In Tweeter's Clothing*, was almost finished. However, a proper band was needed, and a new rhythm section was essential, as well as a place to rehearse. Russell was in Ace Music in Santa Monica when he spotted a 'drummer needs band' card.

"I spoke to Russ on the phone – Ron, he and Earle came over to my house and auditioned me," Harley Feinstein remembers. "We didn't do anything [to start with] and then we started taking pictures, they were readying me to be part of the group. We became pretty good friends

15

right away. They were immersed in this demo, which they were then mixing, which they thought was going to be an album."

At 19 Feinstein had no pop pedigree to speak of. He had been playing drums for around four years, and had been in the junior high school band at Emerson High in Westwood. "I would hang out with my friends, get drunk and jam, but I had very little in the way of drumming skills." However, with his cheekbones and shock of curly hair, Feinstein fitted in with the Maels' idea of how a band should look; no beard, not a scrap of fat, somewhere between the more photogenic members of the early Who and Kinks. "At first, there wasn't much for me to do apart from be in photographs and make it look like we were a band."

There was some tension between manager and drummer Mike Berns and new boy Feinstein, as Berns had been sitting in on early rehearsals with the group. "He *really* wanted to be Halfnelson's drummer," says Feinstein. "He was more of a bluesy, folky sort of guy, very different from a cultural and musical point of view. He looked like Charles Manson, with long hair and long beard – a cool-looking guy, but Ron and Russ were completely fascinated with the Mod look of England."

Berns was ultimately happier being the wheeler dealer.

Larry Dupont: "In Hollywood when people meet people, they pat them on the shoulder and the first question they ask themselves is 'Who is this person and what can they do for me?' and secondly 'What are their weaknesses?' I don't know if Ron and Russ were consciously using Mike Berns; certainly Mike Berns was consciously using the band. If people are consciously using each other to some end, then there's really nothing nefarious in that."

Halfnelson would rehearse wherever they could. "We were definitely a band," Feinstein confirms. "Ron or Russ would come to rehearsals with an acoustic guitar and strum out a basic melody and some words and then we would develop it. There was no doubt there was hierarchy in who was in control of the group: Ron and Russ were the leaders because of the amount of influence they had. Earle was right behind them. I was the lowest man on the totem pole."

Feinstein was not in that position for long. Although Russell added some bass here and there, the group needed to find a full-time bass player. Earle Mankey asked his younger sibling to join. "Jim came along," says Feinstein. "Although he was pretty quiet, we had a bond."

Halfnelson now had a unique selling point of having two sets of brothers in the band.

Jim Mankey: "It was not really so much of an issue for us. It did seem to be of interest to people that there were brothers, for whatever that means, probably nothing! Ron and Russ had an ESP going on between them but Earle and I have a smooth, working relationship. Not *quite* the same as ESP."

Having just turned 19, Jim Mankey, like Feinstein, had little experience and again, seemed beyond the Californian stereotype of a musician. Influenced by Lee Stephens of Blue Cheer, Jim had played in a high school garage band called 3Day Blues and having recently bought his first motorcycle, he would bike down from East LA to Halfnelson rehearsals in Satsuma. "I was like the guy in a T-shirt who emulated my grungy rock idols. Ron and Russell had a lot of colourful friends and I think I was less colourful than most of them, in fact. They placed me in the 'slimy T-shirt' school of rock'n'roll – which I was."

Jim's first impressions of the Mael brothers were indelible: "Ron had an afro, in keeping with the times I suppose. It was a shock to me to meet such strange and driven people. They knew what they wanted to do and they did it, whereas me… I was just a 'let it happen or whatever happens I'll just hang out and experience it' kind of a guy."

Jim and Harley both got on; as well as seeking the natural affinity that a rhythm section should have, they were united in that they were both the newcomers and outsiders, sharing a traditional rock'n'roll wing against the more cerebral Earle, Ron and Russell.

Jim Mankey: "Harley's the funniest guy. He's the nicest guy you'll ever know. He was just loads of fun. We were always out partying and picking up girls, stuff like that."

Vietnam was still an issue, and the fear of the call-up was still prevalent, especially as the draft had turned into a lottery system in 1969, parts of which were broadcast live on US TV. This reactivated a system first used in the Second World War, based on a number-selection structure relating to the potential conscript's date of birth. To turn something so serious into little more than prime-time TV added to the overall resentment of the war. Having already participated in a major anti-Vietnam demonstration, there was no question about the Mael brothers' feelings on the war. Avoiding the draft became paramount.

Larry Dupont: "Ron and I were both playing these rather big games trying to keep from being called up. We both went in on the same day for a medical. We were also going to the same free lawyer who advised us on how to not get drafted. I had damaged my stomach having chickenpox when I was 16, and that was enough to get me out. People were doing insane things like jumping up and down on their bare feet to damage them. I even thought about going in for a CAT scan to make it appear that I had a brain tumour."

Such extreme actions were taken as par for the course at the time, while students were staying in education to avoid the draft. However, both Ron and Russell were now out of college.

Larry Dupont: "Ron was rather down in the dumps because he couldn't get out [of the draft]. He was getting very good legal advice from a little operation at the bookstore Papa Bach on Santa Monica Boulevard. Ron's tactic ultimately was to repeatedly keep appealing, which resulted in choking them in their own paperwork. Eventually his file kept moving further and further back in the draw and it got fatter and fatter and fatter. That was how Ron got out.

"I don't remember if Russell got out because by the time his number came up, the whole thing had quietened down. There was definitely a very palpable cloud hanging over everybody's heads about what you were going to do if you were actually drafted and had to go."

With most educated white middle class males performing stunts to evade the call-up, the majority who were drafted were poor, especially in the African-American community. The spectre of Vietnam would be in the background for the first two years of the Seventies, but fortunately, unlike Ron's old friend Fred Frank from Urban Renewal Project, all the members of Halfnelson avoided having to fight a senseless war.

The Halfnelson regime was simple: practice. Nothing was to get in the way of it. Although Feinstein and Jim Mankey liked to party and had an eye for the ladies, the primary focus was Halfnelson. And there was one golden rule for rehearsals – no jamming.

Jim Mankey: "We never got stoned or anything. Nobody in that band was the slightest bit into that kind of thing. Pretty unusual for the time I must say. Ron and Russell were fine role models for a young man like me. They were incredibly focused."

Harley Feinstein: "I never knew Ron to have a girlfriend. Russ had various girlfriends, but the brothers were much more intent on building their careers as musicians rather than living the hedonistic lives of rock'n'roll stars."

The Maels ensured that the new recruits were listening to the right music: "I learned about Syd Barrett from them and *The Madcap Laughs* was a favourite of mine," Jim Mankey says. "They told me about Pink Floyd. I heard *The Piper At The Gates of Dawn* and The Move, although I never really got into them as much as Ron and Russell did. They would introduce me to things they liked because they loved to share their references. It was a useful education for me. They were trying to make me think less about The Doors and more about The Kinks."

Harley Feinstein: "They were very different to your average guys who would get together and play music. They were not only quirky from a musical point of view, but they struck me as being very intelligent."

The Maels had an evangelical belief in listening to music that wasn't prescribed by the West Coast powers that be and, in 1970, it took quite some effort to seek out some of the records the brothers were listening to. It's amazing because they never became freaks themselves. They were too busy absorbing it all.

The group needed a permanent rehearsal space. "We tried practising at other people's houses but we were stopped as we were loud and pretty grating," Harley Feinstein recalls. They eventually found a suitable alternative, located on an anonymous industrial estate in the San Fernando Valley, close to where Cerwin Vega made speakers, through Warren Fleischman, the uncle of a bass player named Neil who had originally auditioned for Halfnelson.

Jim Mankey: "It was a small factory in Hollywood that manufactured beds for dogs. Some crazy band rehearsed upstairs; they had horse in the title and they played George Harrison songs."

Having a proper rehearsal facility committed Halfnelson to improving, as they gathered at what the group christened the 'Doggie Bed Factory'.

Harley Feinstein: "There was the factory part, where all the workers from south of the border would knock together these doggie beds, and an unused room that became our studio." It also became a convenient rendezvous for the drummer's amorous activities. "I was only 20, living with my parents – I used to meet girls there."

The group would practise twice a week, and Mike Berns would bring as many people down as possible to see them play. Larry Dupont would frequently attend, making tapes and taking photos.

Harley Feinstein: "We would dress the place. We had a papier mâché boat we put together. We stayed up until 3am out in the middle of the street in this rough neighbourhood, with all these lights. Larry was our in-house recording engineer, photographer and artist – he set up the lights in the street, like a movie set in this industrial estate. Ron and Russ had a lot of respect for Larry's views. He would give a lot of input for everything – what we should do, where we should play, how we should set up the instruments; and later, what the album covers should look like. Larry played an important role in the group."

"Something was abundantly clear," Dupont recalls. "Jim was a great guitarist – a better guitarist than Earle. Earle realised that too, which was what kept Jim as bassist."

Berns brought a variety of music business types down to view the group including Jack Nitzsche (who heard not a note of music because of a power failure), while around 100 copies of the demo were circulated around LA scenesters in an attempt to convince record company types into believing it was a finished master. Many of the A&R guys, rooted in a peaceful post-Woodstock vibe, as fan and future manager Joseph Fleury noted, "believed Halfnelson to be, on the strength of their music, a bunch of deranged acid heads after one too many sugar cubes."

Record companies weren't exactly banging down the door. A copy of the demo was sent to Frank Zappa's Straight Records and further afield to The Beatles' Apple label in London. Russ Regan at UNI politely (and presciently) suggested that Halfnelson were "two years ahead of their time". The group found an ally in LA writer Katherine Orloff, who was quick to show her support and wrote a three-column feature for the British *Sounds* newspaper in October 1970. Orloff, who went on to become a successful Hollywood publicist for many years, recalls the piece with affection.

Although unclear as to who brought Halfnelson to her attention, Orloff remembers that "they were pitched to me as 'the band that practises in a doggie bunk bed factory.' It was too delicious to pass up because I got to go to a doggie bunk bed factory. It was everything it promised to be." With its faux-gloomy opening paragraph culminating in the line, "How about discovering a group that is a total failure?", the feature served as a wonderful calling card for the group.*

With such lines as "[they] haven't made a cent, except once when Earle found a dime under the organ," it told the tale of the band struggling to survive despite having originality, wit and flair. Orloff compared Halfnelson to The Kinks and The Bonzo Dog Band, while suggesting that musically they were "well, weird. In other words, without consciously trying, their sound and manner is very English. They could be an immensely popular performing band." Mike Berns called it straight in the article: "This group is going to make it. I'm tired of being called a lunatic."

Berns would be called a lunatic for a while longer.

Aware of the indifference surrounding Halfnelson, Earle Mankey persuaded the brothers to cut another demo, this time comprising four tracks – 'Wonder Girl', 'Fa La Fa Lee', 'High C' and 'Slowboat' – which subsequently become known as *Folk Songs From California*: an in-joke regarding the Mael brothers' hatred of the genre.

The demo found its way to musician and producer Todd Rundgren. By coincidence, the Mael brothers were known to Rundgren through his then-girlfriend Miss Christine from Frank Zappa protégés the GTOs (Girls Together Outrageously), who had also been seeing Russell.

---

* Although it has been said that Katherine Orloff was a friend of Halfnelson's, she had no prior knowledge of them, and this interview was the only time they met (although she has continued to keep an eye on Sparks' career).

Jim Mankey: "She was very nice... and outrageous, beautiful, frightening. With someone like Christine, if you wanted to measure up in her eyes then you needed to have a very strong fashion sense. She was a colourful figure."

Rundgren had become something of an alternative celebrity by 1970. He'd made three albums as the leader of Philadelphia pop-psych act Nazz (who had named themselves after 'The Nazz Are Blue', a track by Mael favourites The Yardbirds) and was set on a solo career, initially under the name Runt. Like many others on the LA scene, he was bemused upon hearing the demo, but unlike those, he was convinced there was something there. Berns set up another showcase gig and Rundgren asked his friend and engineer Thaddeus James Lowe to join him out in the San Fernando Valley.

Lowe had been the vocalist in legendary West Coast garage punk-psychedelic band The Electric Prunes. "Todd played me a demo of the band doing 'Roger'," Lowe recalls. "He asked if I wanted to get involved. The stuff sounded real Tinkertoy with pots and pans crashing but with a spike through it lyrically. I thought they were very interesting. So, this showcase was set up at the 'Doggie Bed Factory.' Needless to say I had never been in a 'Doggie Bed Factory' before. At least not that I remember."

All the rehearsals the band had been doing paid off. Rundgren and Lowe were impressed with what they saw and heard. "We rehearsed to be heard," Jim Mankey says. "Only someone who was a real hard worker and focused could practise as much as we did. When people came to see, it filled us with dread because none of us thought we could really play that well. We rehearsed seemingly forever and then, amazingly enough, the band actually got a record deal, which was quite exciting for a little punk like me."

Although the majority of the music business could not fathom Halfnelson's appeal, Rundgren's persistence paid off. Having the ear of his manager, Albert Grossman, he convinced the latter to sign the band to his new Bearsville label. "Albert trusted Todd as well," said Lowe, "and Todd liked the band and saw potential."

Grossman was a music industry legend. Born of Russian Jewish ancestry in Chicago in 1926, he'd given up a career with the Chicago

Housing Authority to become involved in managing the nascent folk scene after seeing Bob Gibson perform. He set up a club, the Gate of Horn in Chicago, and soon joined forces with the team behind the Newport Jazz Festival and set up the Newport Folk Festival. Although seen by the folk movement as one who thought in purely commercial terms only, by the Sixties Grossman was overseeing the careers of artists such as John Lee Hooker, Odetta, Richie Havens, Gordon Lightfoot, Janis Joplin and Rundgren himself. These, however, were satellites to his main artist, Bob Dylan, whom Grossman managed between 1962 and 1970, having a profound influence on his career. His wife, Sally, even appeared on the sleeve of Dylan's 1965 album *Bringing It All Back Home*, photographed at the Grossman home in Woodstock.

Grossman opened the Bearsville Recording Studios in upstate New York in 1969, with the label following a year later. Although independent, Bearsville was part of the larger Warner Brothers group of companies. "There was a time when Warners, which distributed Bearsville, was a very ambitiously artistic label," US rock critic and long-time Sparks champion Ira Robbins says: "In the late Sixties and early Seventies, it was a label that really championed art and despite where it came from and what it would later become, for a long time it was a label that really coddled and supported and promoted art in a wonderful way."

Halfnelson signed to Bearsville in late 1970. As Robbins points out, "Beefheart and Zappa were through Warner Brothers, so it wasn't that odd for Halfnelson to be on Warner Brothers. It wasn't so much that they were a hard band to push, it's just that they had a very limited audience."

Now it was a case of identifying that limited audience and selling the band to them. Grossman suggested that Halfnelson needed a better manager as Feinstein recalls. "Around the time we got signed, we were influenced to get a heavier manager, and Mike got cut out – he financed the demo, got us signed and then he was gone."

Larry Dupont: "They really had no place to go with Mike. Mike did not understand the group. He wasn't a good manager. One day, it was over."

In his place came Roy Silver, a manager of the old school and a wise Hollywood business type, who seemed to be sufficiently under the radar for a lot of people to later question his existence. Silver was a

23

straight-talking character who sat behind an enormous desk and who had, among other things, founded the Tetragrammaton record label with his artist Bill Cosby. Silver achieved notoriety for being Bob Dylan's first manager before signing him away to Albert Grossman in 1962 for the then substantial sum of $10,000, which financed his management company. By the end of the Sixties, Silver, whom Dupont describes as "extreme Hollywood", had masterminded Cosby's career, alongside slightly more eccentric turns such as Tiny Tim, as well as releasing John Lennon and Yoko Ono's controversial *Two Virgins* album (when Capitol in the US refused to distribute it due to the nude sleeve) and signing Deep Purple for the US.

Jim Mankey: "Silver cultivated an image of being a powerful, intimidating manager. He had a magnificent office and he would bark at us; he intimidated us all – he was good at that. The only other rock act he had at the time was [the all-female rock band] Fanny, who had some popularity in England. We knew they were big because we went to a party with the girls and Mick Jagger came to see them."

Harley Feinstein: "[Halfnelson] played several gigs that had been arranged by Mike Berns. Our first was at the Lindy Opera House on Wilshire Boulevard. We had to demonstrate a new PA that somebody had developed – so it was full of people that had some business involvement with the guy who had invented it. We blasted our songs through it. Then we played an LA nightclub, Gregar, and there was nobody there – it was literally empty. We played a little coffee house on Stoner Avenue; we played a handful of gigs and nobody came to see them."

The first show at which people responded enthusiastically to Halfnelson was a gig at Bishop Amat Memorial High School on Fairgrove Avenue in La Puente, East LA, found for them by Jim Mankey. They performed Tomorrow's 'My White Bicycle', one of two Sixties cover versions in their early set (the other being The Equals' UK hit, 'Baby Come Back'), and the kids began stomping their feet. Another gig at Reading Civic Auditorium in upstate California got a great response, too.

The stage show was shaping into something wholeheartedly unusual. Ron would wear eyeliner, with his lips and eyes contorting, glowering at his brother's traditional rock star flouncing. While Jim stood stock still,

24

his brother Earle would, as Joseph Fleury said, "wear glitter suits and attempt to be everyone's favourite English poof guitarist".

Halfnelson's debut album, which drew on some of the demos, was produced by Rundgren at ID Studios, a small independent facility on La Brea Avenue. Thanks to his Electric Prunes pedigree, it would appear James Lowe was the logical choice to engineer.

However, as Lowe admits, "I didn't go around telling people I had been in the band at that point. I was still ashamed we hadn't become The Beatles, so I just shut up about it. I don't think the [guys in Halfnelson] even knew. I had engineered a number of Nazz, Runt and Todd records at that point so I was probably just recommended as Todd's engineer."

Even though they were continually playing and rehearsing, the band were obviously novices in the studio.

James Lowe: "They didn't have any real 'method' they brought to the first record. They were very cooperative and were willing to try things and be what a group that is being 'produced' should be – willing. Most songs were approached in group force as the band could play this odd material live. 'High C' was the first thing we recorded and I jammed some limited drums up there in the headphones and they went for the drama. I remember hearing their demo and thinking we were going to have to do a bunch of overdubs, but we didn't."

Rundgren acted as a sounding board, building on the work that Ron, Russell and Earle had done while offering encouragement. "We later realised that not all record producers do that," Russell said. "A&R people then get involved. There is no reason for A&R people to exist; people that are paid to take what you have and smooth down the rough edges and get rid of any character that may be involved to make it palatable. We were so spoiled working with Todd – we didn't know what a producer does."

Rundgren tried to apply some of the blanket harmonies for which he became renowned on the recordings, but was met with band rejection and cries of "slick ballads" from the studio floor.

"Todd encouraged us to be as eccentric as we could be musically and he pushed us to be better," Ron said in 2003, "but he wasn't altering what we were doing."

Jim wasn't sure if Rundgren – who gained a reputation as an exacting man in the studio – rated him as a player. "Todd was good to me. I don't think he particularly admired my ability. I got the impression he would've been happier if I'd just left and didn't come back." However, the producer took the young bass player under his wing. "He would buy me dinner because I couldn't afford it and maybe occasionally we'd take some psychedelic drugs. He was good to me."

Harley Feinstein: "It was mind-blowingly stimulating to all of us – the act of recording was fascinating. I loved it. Back then, going to a recording studio and making a record was a huge deal; we felt very lucky, fortunate to have that opportunity – now, everybody records. We were just walking on a cloud, couldn't believe how lucky we were."

"I could never see someone like Todd sign a band like us and release a record like that now," Ron said in 2003. "I don't think people would have such patience with us today." In 1971, patience was certainly what was needed with Halfnelson.

Featuring songs that Rundgren suggested "would not relate to the outside world", *Halfnelson* was released in the autumn, full of brittle, intricate pop and containing so much treble it makes your speakers contract. It did, as Russell said, "retain the essence of our 'living room' demos".

"The album was incredible," Joseph Fleury wrote. "Every song was a strange little gem, and immediately catchy and tuneful. The point is, the more you hear the songs, the less accessible you think they will become." Critic Ned Raggett's assessment of opening track 'Wonder Girl' is spot on. Raggett argues that with Ron's tinkling piano and Russell's vocal acrobatics, the track, with its "ever-so-slightly-weird lyrics about love that couldn't quite be taken at face value", saw the Maels establish themselves so perfectly "that arguably the rest of the brothers' long career has been a continual refinement from that basic formula".

'Fa La Fa Lee', sung by a cold-suffering Russell, is a giddy piece of pop, albeit one that Ron described in 1975 as "incest at the roller-rink". The fairly indecipherable Russell-written 'Roger' ("my first major composition of any stature") became a key track from the demo and the one that made ears turn, featuring a guitar sound not dissimilar to 'Love You' from Syd Barrett's *The Madcap Laughs*.

'High C', one of the band's most well-received live songs, was the first track to be recorded for the album and shows quite how outside the scene they were. Writing about imaginary characters has since become commonplace after various British songwriters the Maels admired such as Ray Davies, Pete Townshend and Roy Wood introduced the practice back in the mid-Sixties. However, to sing about an opera singer who is having issues reaching high C marks out Sparks' unique selling points of novelty and strangeness.

'Fletcher Honorama', which took around 20 takes to complete, and was later covered by R Stevie Moore, is remarkable. It shows the indirect influence of The Doors on the group in the menacing, somnambulant backing to Russell's swampy vocals. On certain listens, one can hear this track and believe that Sparks never actually bettered it. It is "about a celebration being thrown for an old man named Fletcher just before his death", Ron said in 1975. "His friends didn't want to wait until he died to get together." The repeated detuned piano riff in the instrumental break adds spice to the proceedings. The Beach Boys provide a reference point on 'Simple Ballet'. It took Russell seven takes to get the 'oh no' before the ornate instrumental.

The Ron and Russell co-write 'Slowboat' is perilously close to being a Sparks ballad. "This was written around the time of 'Bridge Over Troubled Water' and 'Let It Be'," [both 1970] Ron said in 1975. "The reason for this one not being accepted can only be attributed to a lack of backing by the record company." Russell thought that it should have been a single. Hearing it today, it seems out of place on this or any Sparks record, featuring acoustic guitar and a guitar solo straight out of an AOR manual. It's also rather lovely. Russell would perform this on stage from a papier mâché boat on wheels, dressed in his sailor's suit.

As if to underline their own disgust at a straightforward love song being on the album, the riposte came with the Earle Mankey-penned 'Biology 2', featuring the guitarist and his then wife, Alisha, and one of the few tracks from the album to get radio play. 'Saccharin And The War', another Russell song, further emphasises the democracy of the early albums. Russell believed that this song, about weight reduction – something of a lifelong Mael obsession – was better on the original demo tape. 'Big Bands', a rewrite of 'Summer Days' from the Urban

Renewal Project repertoire, is, as Ron said, "a medley or, to be more blunt about it, a song composed of about six parts spliced together that we couldn't play straight through from start to end. A typical 'set-up-that-final-rave-up song' song." Its lyrical references to Herbert Hoover were later sardonically downplayed by Ron, who explained, "This was when American references could be extensively used since our audience, though small, was mostly American."

'(No More) Mr Nice Guys', a storming rocker featuring the guitar of its co-writer Jim Mankey, contains the seeds of the approach Sparks would soon take. Amended to the singular, Alice Cooper borrowed the title for his 1973 hit single. "Well, at least somebody was to make a buck out of it," Russell said in 1975. "'Nice Guys' met with resounding approval by the six waitresses and sparse 'tour bus' audiences that caught our regular Whisky A Go Go shows in LA." *

Despite its frangible, askance pop, *Halfnelson* seemed to lack any commercial sensibility. It was released in a sleeve with a Sixties catalogue model – whom some initially believed to be Grace Kelly – sitting in a car, while the band looked on. "The *Halfnelson* cover was Ron's idea but they reached a point where something else was needed," Larry Dupont recalls. "I thought colour-tinting would be best, so I took the photographs for that and then the whole thing was pieced together and then I ended up colouring it."

"I'm impressed by how developed our musical direction was on *Halfnelson*," Ron later mused. "There was a sense of trying to both play within the rules of what constitutes pop music and also seeing what happens when you find those rules too confusing."

After *Halfnelson* had been out for a short while, Roy Silver, concerned for his charges, arranged a meeting with Albert Grossman at the Chateau Marmont in Los Angeles. He presented them with a proposition.

Harley Feinstein: "Albert told us his plans for the group. He thought we had a real chance of making it. He told us to picture a telephone

* Cooper later recorded another song with a title borrowed from Sparks, 'I Like Girls' from his 1982 album, *Zipper Catches Skin*.

pole. The pole has been standing there for many years and people keep going up to it and tacking up notes to it about their groups; every single square inch of that pole has a nail in. 'My goal as the owner of the record company is to find the inch of space that isn't covered and put you into it'. And then the name change was discussed."

Ron later wrote in *Profile* how they set about the change. Grossman thought the name Halfnelson was "too weird. Too esoteric. Too wrestling." With his years in the business and an eye for a good turn, the bear-like Grossman had just the name. "Sparks Brothers! Get it? Wild and wacky like The Marx Brothers, but since that name had already been taken, a perfectly acceptable alternative. A great quantity of silence greeted this announcement."

Harley Feinstein: "We weren't that hot on the name Halfnelson, we were fine with changing the name. Several other names had been bandied about in the past. It was very difficult for us to get one to agree on. One of the names we had considered was 'Chinese People'. We were all into WC Fields and there was a line from his film *International House*, where he was concerned about the amount of people from China around, so he exclaims loudly, 'Ah! Chinese people!'"

Jim Mankey: "If there was any dissension about the name change, it would only have come from Ron; he was the man in charge. He thought the new name was laughable and not very creative and he was right. Halfnelson was kind of an odd name, too. A name that evoked sweaty wrestlers was not what we were about. Ron and Russ had kind of a bad attitude towards authority and they didn't like the likes of Albert Grossman giving them suggestions on how they should act or write their music."

They were also concerned that the surviving members of The Marx Brothers – Groucho, Gummo and Zeppo – would be angry. The band compromised and shortened the name simply to Sparks, although they were The Sparks Brothers long enough for Warner Brothers to put an ad in the music trade welcoming them to the label.

The *Halfnelson* album was rechristened simply *Sparks*, with the group standing against a red-brick wall, coloured by Larry Dupont. "That was 100% Ron's idea," Dupont says. "I do seem to remember that at the time Ron had a brick fetish and I think he had at one point tried to make brick pants out of plastic bricks to wear on stage, which didn't work very well."

To coincide with the re-release, the album's most commercial track, 'Wonder Girl', was put out as a single, and on July 29, 1972, Sparks performed it, with '(No More) Mr Nice Guys', on *American Bandstand*. Genial host Dick Clark commented on their appearance; indeed, the pictures of them with Clark, who sports a grown-out straight's haircut of the early Seventies in suit and tie with Ron in his psycho John Oates phase with eye make-up and Beatle pendant, are slightly unnerving. 'Wonder Girl' gave Sparks a taste of national fame as the single rose to 92 in the *Cash Box* chart, and nearly made it into the *Billboard* listings. Infamously, the record reached number one in Montgomery, Alabama.

The band's live show became increasingly surreal. Russell would attempt to knock himself unconscious with a giant wooden hammer onstage, which actually happened in Texas.

Harley Feinstein: "We went in a sedan halfway across the country to a redneck nightclub in Houston called the Liberty Hall at 1619 Chenevert. It had only just opened as a venue. It was pretty much beer-drinking, gun-toting, cowboy-hatted guys – and they loathed us. It was there when Russell brought the hammer along that he bought from a local fairground, threw it up in the air and it hit him on the head."

The band, and even Russell himself, thought the incident rather humorous, but his brother did not.

Larry Dupont: "When Russ beamed himself over the head with a mallet, as soon as Ron got a chance to voice an opinion on the subject, it was one of tremendous stress and angst. It was funny no longer. We had to haul Russ out to the hospital."

In fact, the whole Houston sojourn was filled with incident, as Dupont recalls: "The drive there was horrific. We were in rental cars. One broke down in the middle of the desert. When we finally got to Texas, it was raining so hard [and there was] thunder and lightning. Lightning was literally forking over the road. Rain was coming down so hard, the only thing I could do was occasionally see a line down the middle of the highway. At one point, lightning shot over a group of trees and we went round a corner and there was this house in flames. When we got to Houston I said 'Were you guys scared?' and they said 'Well somehow we felt that you had it under control because you didn't seem scared.' I'd been absolutely scared shitless but I didn't know anything else to do but continue to drive, as insane as I thought it was. And then Russell pounded himself over the head. We were pulled over by a State Trooper at some place in Texas and I got a photograph of the entire band posing with him next to the guy's car."

Strange Texan gigs aside, building on this modest head of steam, the group returned to the studio. Their second album, *A Woofer In Tweeter's Clothing*, was stranger yet somehow more coherent than their debut and owed a great deal to the music of the Weimar Republic. Todd Rundgren would not be returning to produce it.

James Lowe: "He had another record to make [in London], *Straight Up* by Badfinger. I am sure they would have stuck with him as a producer had he been available."

Speaking in 2008, Russell was unequivocal about the debt the group owed to Rundgren. "[He] seemed like a kindred soul… Todd liked us for what we were. He thought that the uniqueness of our approach and the sound, even then, was something that he only needed to make a bit more hi-tech – less like a demo. He encouraged all of our eccentricities, like using cardboard boxes for percussion, and we give him credit for that."

James Lowe: "Todd knew I was familiar with the style and asked me if I wanted to produce it. I said yes. I liked them very much. They were completely different. What rock'n'roll should be."

Lowe and Sparks clicked. "It was like going through the war together. We set up a session at Wally Heider's Studio to record a 'demo' together and we did 'Girl From Germany'. I got to insert more 'rock' into it than the first record, so I was happy and I guess they were too because we started blocking time at ID Sound where I recorded the basic tracks."

Although his years with Dylan had taught him to not get in the way of the artistic process, Albert Grossman believed that Sparks had that extra dimension that could make them successful, even though they looked so weird. Despite Dupont's assertion that Grossman "didn't understand who they were", Lowe says that Grossman was a keen supporter: "Albert liked Sparks. He called me after the first record and since I was going to make the second, asked if I could get Russ' vocals up front more. People were having a hard time understanding [Russ]. I agreed because the lyrics were the thing with this group, but I found it was not a function of level so much as the way Russ was enunciating the words. Albert probably called me three or four times about this.

"It was an odd mix of characters but it was glued together once they sprinted into a song. It all sounded kind of strange. Like a club no one but the group belongs to. If you look at the cover of *A Woofer In Tweeter's Clothing* you can see it looks like you drew from five different groups to get these guys. One with a mullet, frizzed-out glams, and head-banging demon-seed shit. 'Oh yeah, we want to record a song in French!' Somehow it all worked... I loved the first record and you know how you hear the material for a few weeks and you start singing the songs in your sleep? This one was stronger."

Although Ron and Russell were clearly the creative directors of the project, all members of the band played a strong role: "Earle was interested in engineering so he and I would mix it up about guitar sounds," Lowe says. "He liked a gnashy sound on some things and I was always trying to bring it into focus with some clarity. It was good-natured and we both got our way. Jim was darker and more the quiet type, what a bass player should be. He was down there on the bottom with definition like in 'Nothing Is Sacred'. I really like some of the bass on that record. Harley was a good-looking guy with a different style of playing, kind of trashy but very intense. I remember him always running off to school or something. He would be taking down his drums just after the last beat to go take a test. They were easy guys to get along with. No attitudes."

In a catalogue that frequently harbours on the bizarre, *A Woofer In Tweeter's Clothing* is pretty odd. Anything was fair game, and there was a sense of magic in the air.

James Lowe: "We needed a kid's voice for 'Batteries Not Included'. Earle went out of the studio on La Brea Avenue and came back in a few minutes with a 10-year-old and his mom. The kid stepped up to the microphone and just did it. On 'Beaver O'Lindy' we decided on an accordion. I called Kip Tulin, the 14-year-old brother of Electric Prunes bass player, Mark Tulin. He came down to Hollywood and played for us. He was scared to death but did the job. So this record was made by kids, for kids..."

Lowe is not far off the mark when opining that virtually everything on the album is "cool". The opening track, 'Girl From Germany', which enjoyed a renaissance when Sparks hit big in the UK in 1974, sets out the album's intent; Ron's off-kilter love song involves a man bringing his German girlfriend home to be greeted by his parents who cannot get over the Second World War. "To my knowledge, no other bands were dealing in the same subject matter at the time," Russell wrote in the notes to *Profile*. In the main he was correct, although 10cc in the UK were ploughing a similar furrow, which had begun at the quirkier end of Sixties' British psychedelia.

The only full-group composition, 'Beaver O'Lindy', about an imaginary rock singer, is a patchwork of pipe organ, military drumming, cheerleading, varying speeds and a thrash-metal sensibility. 'Nothing Is Sacred' is notable for Earle Mankey's Zoot Horn Rollo-like guitar and marks the first appearance on record of Russell's falsetto, which was to be the centrepiece of Sparks' subsequent period at Island Records. The string quartet on 'Here Comes Bob' was possibly influenced by Larry Dupont's love of classical music, which he was always trying to get the band to listen to.*

'Moon Over Kentucky' was another example of how Sparks melded all the various facets of their tastes – the guitar of 'Lucifer Sam' by Pink Floyd with an element of the work of Bertolt Brecht and Kurt Weill. While, as already mentioned, there were few contemporary acts performing material like this, the impact of the film *Cabaret*, released in February 1972, could not have failed to have influenced Sparks. The Bob Fosse picture, based on Christopher Isherwood's play *I Am A Camera*, was set in the doomed Berlin of the Weimar Republic as the National Socialist Party's power is on the rise. A time of decadence and opulence that had to come crashing down; doomed romance; the skull beneath the skin – very Ron Mael. After all the chintz and glitter, the church organ-style coda at the end of the track could well have been played by Vincent Price in *The Abominable Doctor Phibes*.

---

* Although Russell said that it didn't sound like a real song, it was in the *Sparks Show* sets of the early 21st century.

The album contained one of the group's exceptionally rare cover versions, except it was not as obvious as 'Baby Come Back' from their old stage repertoire. 'Do-Re-Mi' from Rogers and Hammerstein's *The Sound Of Music* had been written in the late Fifties for the stage production of the film, which had gone on to be one of the world's highest-grossing movies of all time. Sparks' version – a recent live favourite in their set – was, predictably, a hoot, with Jim Mankey's heavily strummed bass in the middle section welcoming the tumult of Ron's keyboards. It was at this point on stage that Ron would throw confetti into a cooling fan in order to spread it around the crowd, but which frequently failed to disperse. It was, as Russell said, "the best live tune as it resembled something that everyone had heard".

'Angus Desire' has, in Russell's modest opinion, "one of the best titles in the history of western music." The song about drawing nude models in art class finds his singing sounding uncannily like Bryan Ferry's. While Sparks were aware of Roxy Music, it's unlikely that they would have heard them at this early juncture – ironic, considering the two bands would spend the next few years being closely compared and scrutinised.

Earle Mankey followed up 'Biology 2' with the fabulous 'Underground'. The Doors debt is again writ large with Ron's throbbing organ chug. The simplistic tale of bands trying to make it in their basements almost undermines the grandeur of the rest of the album; all the pomp had been removed for something a lot dirtier. This is only a brief interlude as 'The Louvre' follows, sung by Russell largely in French. There was a lengthy studio debate as to whether the whole song was going to be recorded in French (Ron had got his friend Josee Becker to translate) or in English. As the session dragged on, it was decided to splice both versions together.

James Lowe: "I wanted to tap into the darker side of what they were doing as it seemed slinkier to me... when you're engineering and producing a record, you are hands-on, whether you want to be or not. We had built up trust from the first recording so there were no egos or disagreements. I had been left alone with the band on the first record for a few sessions so we were not on unfamiliar ground.

The sense of play and experimentation runs riot throughout *A Woofer In Tweeter's Clothing*, the product of a band who are clearly together. Jim

Mankey enjoyed the experience: "Jim Lowe was a much more laid-back guy. Todd was always very judgmental and Jim was just a happy guy who tried to set the mood so you could play music without discomfort, whereas with Todd, the idea was instead of performance, he'd kick your ass."

After the daft 44 seconds of 'Batteries Not Included', a song that let deviant minds think was about marital aids, the album closes with 'Whippings And Apologies'. A song about domestic spankings that misled some into thinking the group were S&M freaks, it became the climax of the original band's live set. The track builds and builds for a minute before Russell crashes in with his incredibly tremulous vocal. It was, as Ron described, "recorded loud and without bass. The bottom, if one exists, is the left hand of the keyboards. Two chords always make the best chord progressions."

A Woofer In Tweeter's Clothing was released in October 1972 but went largely ignored in the rock press. The sound was, as Joseph Fleury noted, "dense and acrid", while the sleeve was another collaboration between Ron and Dupont.

Larry Dupont: "We'd been satisfied with the results for the two covers for the first album, so I photographed *A Woofer In Tweeter's Clothing*. I never had any control over the artwork, but I had a degree of influence. I didn't like the way that the band looked, so Ron and I manipulated the colours."

A Woofer In Tweeter's Clothing also marked the last time more than two members would be on the cover of a Sparks album.

When *A Woofer In Tweeter's Clothing* failed to reach a wide audience, Lowe was devastated, having invested enough of himself in the project to call himself by his full name, Thaddeus James Lowe, on the sleeve.

James Lowe: "I left the music business and went into directing and producing TV shows because I thought I had lost the ability to spot a hit after we made that record. At that time if you didn't get a hit, you didn't continue in music very long. I thought Sparks should have gotten some recognition and I promised my wife if they didn't, I would get out of that crazy business. They didn't, I did." Lowe went on to become a successful television producer, and left Sparks' world behind. "I did see some album covers in stores. They always made me smile, whether they were in kimonos or hanging off the transom of a speed boat. Clever stuff." *

Larry Dupont: "For me *A Woofer In Tweeter's Clothing* is a masterpiece. I often wonder what the [original] group would've been like if it had stayed together. The combined influence... they worked well together. Their music could have been eye-openingly brilliant. It's an early learning album. That was not a mature Sparks, that was a beginning. But you can see the things they were willing to try."

It started becoming apparent that Sparks' European sound could translate better overseas than in their native America.

Jim Mankey: "Ron and Russ had gone to Britain as backpacking tourists – they were college students at the time. They travelled to England and were obsessed by it. I loved all those bands but I didn't have their level of obsessions." Larry, Earle Mankey and his wife, Elise, had also been to London at various times.

Larry Dupont: "Roy Silver pretty well figured it's easier to break [Sparks] in England than it was to break the States. Not only is it a smaller environment but the band would have the novelty of being American. That would pay dividends as they were so unknown in the US, they could come back as an English band."

Silver's technique of getting the group to the UK had been to go into Bearsville every day and continually ask about when Sparks were going to England.

Larry Dupont: "He'd ask when the tickets were coming through and talk as though it was already happening, taking the view that sooner or later, something would happen."

England with its fog, beefeaters, B & B's, twitching curtains, hypocrisy and pride would provide the perfect backdrop for Sparks to feel at home.

---

* At around the same time as Lowe's retirement from the music industry, rock scribe Lenny Kaye, the compiler of *Nuggets: Original Artyfacts From The First Psychedelic Era 1965–1968*, placed 'I Had Too Much To Dream Last Night' by The Electric Prunes as the opening track of this influential collection of lost Sixties American garage and psychedelic groups. The album was to be the first step in the continuing interest in Lowe's former band, eventually resulting in a Prunes reunion in 2001.

Chapter Three

A Cross Between Bobby Vee And The Mothers Of Invention Or Marlene Dietrich And The Stooges Or Frank Zappa Meets The Monkees

"People mostly thought that they were a bunch of shit."
John Hewlett, 2009

In the first week of October 1972, Sparks made their New York debut at Max's Kansas City, the legendary Warhol hangout. A review from the *Village Voice* edition dated October 5 suggested that "Sparks is a rock novelty act with a humorous approach". Joseph Fleury wrote three years later, "The audience in New York was appreciative, but a bit strange. It consisted of a handful of hardcore fans, a few critics who felt they'd discovered their own personal little cult band, and a bunch of Manhattan pseudo-decos."

This was all very well but their debut album had sold next to nothing, and hopes for their forthcoming release, *A Woofer In Tweeter's Clothing*, were not high. Larry Dupont sensed there was stress between the Maels and their record company. Steeped in art, "Ron and Russ had a strong sense of how performers should behave. They could be very surly with people."

Dupont had struck up a good working relationship with the team at Bearsville from the secretaries up to Roy Silver himself. "When we got to New York, I'd had prior meetings with Bearsville before the band got to them. Even though they didn't know exactly how to deal with the band in terms of promoting them, the people there were looking forward very enthusiastically to pursuing them."

The goodwill dissipated very quickly as Dupont remembers: "They [Mael brothers] showed up with so much added attitude and anger, full of 'Why aren't you doing more for us?' They figured you could go in there like drill sergeants. In 10 minutes maximum, they completely undermined months of work. It was very exasperating to watch."

However, enough goodwill and cordiality remained for the record company to be in favour (after a fashion) of Sparks' visit to Europe. Plans for the visit had been hatched that summer when Silver suggested to Bearsville's UK press director, Derek Taylor, that the band would be best suited to UK audiences. Taylor, the effete, much-loved former Apple Records' press officer, was a personal friend of the Silvers, and was staying with his family at Silver's mansion up in the Hollywood Hills.

Taylor, full of resolutely old-world charm, was immediately struck by the Maels when they came to Silver's house, and was delighted by the gift of bobbing head Beatles dolls they brought him – another from their stockpile of novelties and ephemera.*

Silver had been able to extract from Bearsville a sum in the region of $10,000 to take the band to the UK, though no one knew exactly how this budget would be managed.

James Lowe was not surprised that Sparks decided to decamp to England: "I had played over there and knew the audiences were much more ready for the odd spice of this concept. Americans needed someone to tell them it was cool first. I thought it was a good move on their part."

---

* Taylor later wrote how thoughtful the brothers were in his 1983 autobiography, *50 Years Adrift (In An Open Necked Shirt)*.

Nor was future Sparks producer Tony Visconti: "The UK was always open to eccentric people. I think of Sparks as a British group. Before they came over to Britain they probably heard that sound in their head and they realised where they had to go to get it."

Sparks, with Larry Dupont now playing the role of *de facto* tour manager, set off for London and took up residency at the South Kensington Hotel, near South Kensington tube station. Taylor and the UK wing of Bearsville, part of the enormous Warner-Elektra-Asylum empire, would look after the band while they were in Europe.

Taylor's reputation and suitably lavish business approach meant that the group was going to be well cared for.

Harley Feinstein: "Derek Taylor pretty much assumed responsibility for us; he showed us around, took care of us, and compared us with The Beatles. One word from Derek and things would happen."

One thing Taylor couldn't influence, however, was the weather. "When we went to England for the first time, it snowed," Jim Mankey recalled. "I'd never seen the stuff before." Taylor was able to help them stay warm, as he recounted in his memoir *50 Years Adrift*. "Roy had told me that even in California, Ron and Russell slept in pyjamas and I realised that winter in England would seem to them especially cruel. When they arrived, therefore, I pushed for the company to buy them all leather overcoats and my wish was granted, though not without demur."

While no dates had actually been booked for Sparks, there was a belief that something would turn up.

Larry Dupont: "We were set up in the hotel, and the band wanted to imitate real bands and so we had numerous headaches I had to deal with in the hotel and various other places," says Dupont. "Somebody thought it would be fun to play with a fire extinguisher. Ron and Russ developed a certain level of mischief. They thought it was cool."

Realising that the band needed somebody with experience to guide them in London, Roy Silver informed the band that they would be greeted by John Hewlett, whom Silver had met when he visited Apple Records back in 1968. Silver had called Hewlett and asked him if he would manage Sparks' affairs in the UK.

John Hewlett: "It wasn't like I had notice to do it – it was a case of 'They're coming over, can you get some things going in a short space of time?' It wasn't a matter of panicking, it was a case of doing what you had to do. It was fun."

Born in Surrey, Hewlett was encouraged into music by his parents. Leaving Carshalton Technical College where he'd been studying history and English, he became the bass player in John's Children, a free-wheeling, Surrey-based art-pop-mod combo. Originally known as The Silence, the group also featured vocalist Andy Ellison, drummer Chris Townson and guitarist Geoff McClelland, who was replaced by Marc Bolan.

Bolan stayed in the group for around four months, starting in March 1967, and it was during this time that they released his composition (and John's Children's third single) 'Desdemona', which was banned by the BBC for Bolan's simultaneously saucy and mystical lyric, "lift up your skirt and fly". Hewlett, who would be the first to admit that he wasn't the world's greatest bass player, became something of a protégé of the group's manager, Simon Napier-Bell.

Napier-Bell was the epitome of a UK music-biz hustler. Larger-than-life, openly homosexual and encouraged into management by his friend, *Ready Steady Go!* editor Vicki Wickham (with whom he co-wrote Dusty Springfield's 1966 hit, 'You Don't Have To Say You Love Me'), Napier-Bell managed The Yardbirds for a brief period that same year (which included the release of Sparks' favourite 'Happenings Ten Years Time Ago'). According to Napier Bell's recollections, after being approached by The Silence, he renamed them John's Children after Hewlett, the weakest musical link in the band, so that the others wouldn't sack him.

After John's Children imploded, Hewlett got a job at Apple Publishing through Napier-Bell's friend Terry Doran. While at Apple, he'd signed Scottish songwriters Graham Lyle and Benny Gallagher and also worked closely with Paul McCartney. Hewlett recalls with a mixture of horror and amusement sitting in John Lennon's office while a stark naked Yoko Ono was having a dress fitting, without Lennon batting an eyelid. He can also clearly be seen in the *Let It Be* film watching The Beatles play their final gig on Apple's Savile Row rooftop on January 30, 1969.

Hewlett, who made his first forays into management looking after McGuinness Flint, met Roy Silver at Apple when Silver and his partner, Artie Mogul, had come to discuss the US distribution of Lennon and Ono's *Two Virgins*.

"I enjoyed Roy Silver's company," Hewlett says. "He was the typical Jewish entrepreneur in LA. Coming from Surrey, I hadn't met many of those before. He was a huckster, full of the chat without a great deal of substance. He ran a Chinese restaurant as well. Roy was a character. He had a huge office, but when you looked further there was no secretarial support."

Silver appointed Hewlett to run the UK wing of Tetragrammaton. After the label collapsed, Hewlett went to Feldman's publishers, where he met Albert Grossman and Bob Dylan. While at Feldman's he also met Ian Kimmett, who formed a group, Jook, with mutual Surrey music friends, ex-John's Children drummer Chris Townson, Trevor White (guitar), and Scottish bass player Ian Hampton, with Hewlett managing them. Hewlett was a methodical, straightforward but pleasant hustler and his vision would become central to Sparks' success.

The Maels loved the fact that their new British manager had been part of the harder 'mod' sound from mid-Sixties London. John's Children's maverick (if amateurish) approach to performing was very much up their street. "Ron and Russ were aware of every detail of John and John's Children," Jim Mankey confirmed.* As they were that Hewlett had worked with Marc Bolan, who, in 1972, was enjoying his final year of superstardom in Britain and Europe.

Hewlett was impressed if somewhat bewildered by what he saw. "My perception of LA music was Linda Ronstadt and Crosby, Stills and Nash. So when I heard Sparks it really appealed to me. They were cool. They were professional, interesting and definitely had potential. I liked them all. They were young people my age and had their act together, but it was obvious it wasn't going to work because they were

---

* John's Children's few recordings were released on the Los Angeles-based White Whale label and their first single, 'Smashed! Blocked!' (re-titled to the less controversial 'The Love I Thought I'd Found' in the UK), received much airplay on local LA stations in late 1966.

an 'act' rather than a band. It was somewhat contrived, intentionally so. The heart of it really worked, but there were elements that you thought just weren't sensational. Ron and Russell were really good at their parts."

Warners had an unusual and somewhat schizophrenic approach to their new act: if it involved taking the band out for a lavish meal where the executives could join in, that was fine; if it meant buying new equipment, this was not so fine. It all seemed rather calamitous.

Larry Dupont: "The record company people eventually showed up but that was very informal. By that point we were playing a shell game with them. The [American record company] had pulled the wool over their eyes. They had funding to get us there but we didn't know what it was. Roy would occasionally be in touch, but it was my job to relate with the record company. Roy used to con people right, left and centre. He knew that nobody knew what to do with [Sparks] in the States and the reason nobody knew what to do with them was that nobody understood who the hell they were…"

The band was still waiting for an itinerary. At this juncture, not knowing a definite schedule of exactly how long they'd be in the country was all part of the adventure.

Larry Dupont: "Mandy Newell was Derek Taylor's secretary and she was most involved with following what was going on. I started to get the feeling that Mandy was starting to question where the hell the money was."

Sparks finally found a place to begin their UK gigs – the reopening, after renovation, of The Pheasantry, on King's Road, Chelsea. The Pheasantry was a historic Georgian building, originally used to raise pheasants for the royal household. Princess Astafieva opened her Russian Dancing Academy on the first floor in 1916. The princess' most famous pupil was the young Peggy Hookham, who later became Dame Margot Fonteyn.

By the mid Sixties, the Pheasantry had become an artists' colony that had a club in the basement. Oz artist Martin Sharp roomed there with his friend Eric Clapton (Sharp designed the sleeves for Cream's *Disraeli Gears* and *Wheels Of Fire*) and Germaine Greer wrote *The Female Eunuch* within its walls. The Pheasantry hosted gigs by Queen, Lou Reed and was also the venue where Andrew Lloyd Webber and

Tim Rice first discovered Yvonne Elliman for their rock opera *Jesus Christ Superstar.*

It seemed a fitting location for Sparks to make their UK debut. However, Chris O'Donnell, one half of the Morrison-O'Donnell management partnership, doesn't have quite such fond memories of The Pheasantry. "It was where you played if you couldn't get any gigs anywhere else. It never really cut it as a venue."

Hewlett, too, took a negative view of the venue. "It was a naff place to play. It was the sort of place you played if you couldn't get the Marquee. It wasn't the greatest of gigs, but then they weren't the greatest of bands and it *was* a gig. The main thing was them playing *anywhere*. At that point they were West Coast-looking, playing this off-the-wall music. I think people mostly thought that they were a bunch of shit."

Harley Feinstein: "[The Pheasantry] was still in a state of construction. They put up a huge picture of us in the doorway and I was handed the authority to sign the tab for the band. I was pretty much in heaven." The bartender took a shine to the handsome Californian and made sure the band were supplied with champagne.

The King's Road suited Jim Mankey: "We walked into the vicinity looking at the stores and marvelling at those wonderful English suits. A small guy like me could look good in a suit if you bought it off the rack in London. The suits are cut nice there for someone of my size. I don't know why that is. People in England aren't tiny, are they?"

Hewlett invited Jook down to Chelsea to see his new charges, as guitarist Trevor White recalls. "I really liked it. The music was a bit strange but I was knocked out by the visual thing. Mainly Ronnie – you couldn't ignore that, really. He had the long hair and the eye make-up, it was really something. I ended up not listening, just looking at him."

Without a definite touring schedule the band would be ready at the drop of a hat to go wherever the work took them, such as Harrogate, North Yorkshire.

Harley Feinstein: "A roadie would drive us up the M1 and we would play there, and then we'd go down to Bournemouth to open for The

Kinks, and then we'd go and do a radio interview in Holland or some TV in Switzerland. It was a random kind of thing – we would get gigs, but then we'd sit around."

Larry Dupont: "It was just very poorly put together from the point of view of what the promoter did. Not so much the promoter, but the venue. Things were just not working right."

An occasional upbeat presence was Roy Silver, who lifted the mood after a double-page review slated the band.

Larry Dupont: "The band was furious, despondent. Roy said 'No, no, no, you just got two pages. You should be ecstatic'. That, I think, pretty much speaks the differences in their inability to understand what was going on. All Sparks wanted to do was music. What they wanted to do was perform, what they wanted was to have people screaming and shouting and waving and saying 'They're wonderful' and being appreciated."

Through the promo team at WEA, Hewlett was able to get Sparks on to the UK's leading (and, in fact, only) grown-up rock TV showcase, *The Old Grey Whistle Test*. Broadcast late on unfashionable Tuesday night on BBC2, the programme had first appeared in 1971 fronted by *Melody Maker* rock journalist (and soon-to-be Island Records Head Of A&R) Richard Williams. With its distinctive Area Code 615 theme tune, 'Stone Fox Chase', the *Whistle Test* became the must-watch programme for serious music heads. When DJ Bob Harris took over presenting in 1972, the template was struck for the rest of the decade. Harris' laid-back mumble and air of authority gave a voice to a generation of AOR connoisseurs, and the programme was responsible for breaking acts such as Bruce Springsteen and Lynyrd Skynyrd in the UK.

Record companies would clamour to get their artists on to the programme as everyone in the business would be watching. The pressure to get turns on there would often result in some disparate bills. For example, on the same edition that Sparks appeared, Neil Sedaka was hitting the promotional treadmill for his *Solitaire* album, soul man Bill Withers performed 'Use Me' and 'Ain't No Sunshine', while prog giants Wishbone Ash were captured on film performing their *Argus* epic 'Blowin' Free' at the Cambridge Corn Exchange. "Nice..." as 'Whispering' Bob was wont to comment.

44

In a country with only (then) three television channels, people sat and watched each week mainly because there was little else to do on a dull Tuesday in early Seventies Britain. "That one show did wonders for us," Russell said. "There was a bit of excitement and that's what ultimately generated the interest that led us to Island Records."

Sparks pre-recorded 'Wonder Girl' and '(No More) Mr Nice Guys' for the show transmitted on November 21. Feinstein recalls the group watching it at the hotel they had moved to, the Snows Hotel on Cromwell Road.

"There was a television room where all the residents would watch the telly. There was one guy who'd be there every night, a drunk, wild-man character. He was hilarious – always yelling at the screen, shouting hostile remarks at us. We were scared to death of him. While we were trying to watch our performance, he was bellowing 'You look like Hitler!' at Ron."

As the group put up with this tirade, they struggled to hear what fellow guest Neil Sedaka was saying. "He'd already gotten old and fat," Feinstein continues. "He was being interviewed by Bob Harris, and Sedaka said he didn't like us – he said 'That group that was just on' was representative of a type of group that he really didn't like. Harris sort of agreed with him."

Although hazy on exactly what was said, John Hewlett, who was with the band at the BBC studio, is definite in his remembrance of Harris' distaste. "Bob Harris really hated them. He was a bit of a musical snob. He didn't like them, but that didn't matter. I'd never liked his show, but we were on it and we got the exposure."

Depending on which report you read, Harris called Sparks either 'a cross between Bobby Vee and The Mothers of Invention' or 'Marlene Dietrich and The Stooges' or 'Frank Zappa and The Monkees'.*

Later in the decade, being disliked by Bob Harris became a badge of honour for punk bands.

---

* Harris didn't call Sparks "mock rock", though – that was a put-down reserved for The New York Dolls the following year.

To coincide with the TV performance, Warners finally put out some Sparks product in the UK, a single of the two tracks the band performed on *OGWT*.*

The band's small screen appearance had a positive effect as, overnight, bookings began to roll in: new dates took in the Growling Budgie Club in Ilford on Wednesday 6 December (30p a pop) and, more importantly, two gigs at the legendary Marquee Club on December 14 and 21. To Anglophiles stranded in LA, playing The Marquee was as exotic as it could be.

No matter how small the venue, or the crowd, it was clear that Sparks "really appreciated being appreciated," says Dupont, "even if it was by a small number of people. They were good. They were so much more original than some of the other people. Not just original, they were more creative. They were not on drugs, which meant that their minds were with them." Although Hewlett was firmly on the scene, it was Dupont who was doing the considerable amount of legwork to get everything accomplished.

Another new band playing in London at that time would ultimately eclipse Sparks in the UK. Queen were on a similar circuit to Sparks, having played The Pheasantry on November 6, and with the group now close to signing a contract with EMI, they had all the elements of their unmistakable act already in place. (A live bootleg exists from their Marquee show featuring Queen playing such songs as 'Ogre Battle' and 'Hangman'.) Sparks, in the main, were not that interested.

Harley Feinstein: "I remember they were on. We all stayed in the dressing room and we didn't go out to watch the band. I remember Jim going out to watch a bit and coming back, saying, 'That guy is really weird. He's acting very gay'."

---

* The *Sparks* (aka *Halfnelson*) album was never officially released on its own in the UK. To capitalise on Sparks' success on rival label Island, Warners re-released *Sparks* and *A Woofer In Tweeter's Clothing* as part of their double *2Originals Of* series in 1975. A beautifully packaged album, it came with a 16-page booklet containing a fascinating 'early days' biography by Joseph Fleury. There were also full lyrics and commentary from Ron and Russell. Although not a huge seller, it was a perfect introduction to that tricky early Sparks era.

As '72 bowed out, the band, living so closely together, were all up for the adventure.

Jim Mankey: "We seemed to like each other a lot. We got along fine and having worked in other groups since I can see that we did get along quite well compared with other bands."

Like most rock bass players, Jim was a law unto himself as Larry Dupont describes: "Jim was extremely quiet and he ultimately ended up locking himself in the hotel room and was never seen except to perform. You knew that there was just so much going on between those ears and it was really frustrating because everybody was extremely talkative and then there was Jim. Jim was the silent one and if he would speak, everybody would hush up and listen to whatever half a dozen words he was saying. Whatever he said was always thought of as brilliant. Then he would shut up again."

Feinstein, on the other hand, led the most rock'n'roll lifestyle of the band at the time: "My window overlooked the front door of our hotel," Dupont recalls. "Somebody was throwing stuff against my window because it was so late, the door had been locked. I look and it's Harley outside with two girls. You know, one on each arm. That was *so* Harley. He was a kid enjoying an experience that was a fantasy for someone of his age."

Just prior to Christmas, the band took an ill-advised detour to Zermatt at the foot of the Matterhorn in Switzerland.

Larry Dupont: "It was very frustrating as they were about to hit it big, and this trip was like the derailing of the train. They had five gigs in a row set up in London. Each successive one was getting a bigger crowd. The first one was good, then Russell got sick and the second one was cancelled; the trip to Zermatt came in there."

Sparks returned in time for the Warner Brothers Christmas party, yet Dupont was concerned that the lack of funds would soon be found out. The brothers' demanding attitude was not winning them fans in certain quarters.

Larry Dupont: "When we went to London, one of my jobs was to keep them out of the office. They went in and demanded to know why they weren't getting work. I was there and my skin was crawling during the meeting, because they had no sense of what was going on. They had no idea that there was this game going on and all they could think of was, 'We want more from you' and you could just imagine the company saying 'Well, let's see the books.'"

If the books had been produced, Sparks would have undoubtedly been thrown out at the end of the meeting. Although, overall, Dupont recalls the period with great fondness, he remains less than enamoured with the Mael' behaviour towards those working behind them. "They really didn't have any sense of how to treat people, the kind of respect you need to give them in order to get them to perform for you. The [brothers] never really had an appreciation for the role of the people who were going to make or break their careers."

Although Sparks had been generally lauded and loved, Bearsville simply ran out of money, and the group's European adventure was over. Despite an unpromising start, the trip on the whole had been successful and Hewlett was convinced that he could work with the Maels. By the same token, Hewlett had created a good impression on the whole band. "We all got along really well with John," Feinstein recalls. "He was a good-looking guy; he and I would hang out at The Pheasantry. We'd compete for the 'scrubbers', as he referred to them then. It was the first time I'd ever heard that term. He was a funny, regular guy."

Within six months, Hewlett would be putting a new band together with Ron and Russell.

Sparks returned to the US, and a period of relative inertia followed. They went up to Bearsville's studio in upstate New York to record what became a one-off single, a version of their stage favourite 'I Like Girls'. There had initially been talk of the recording sessions turning into those for their next album.

Although James Lowe didn't produce these sessions, his evocative description of Bearsville sets the scene: "Out in the middle of the forest you came upon this complex. It was big and well equipped. There were always people waiting to get in and record and most groups had made a commitment since they were in a small town with little to do. Foghat would be recording and Maria Muldaur would be sitting in the lobby at midnight waiting to record vocals. And The Band had a permanent set-up in the main room that had signs saying "Don't touch". I didn't."

"he UK was always open to the eccentric people." – Tony Visconti. Sparks hit West London, November 1972. From back: Earle Mankey, Ron Mael, Harley Feinstein, Jim Mankey, Russell Mael. (LARRY DUPONT)

"They really appreciated being appreciated. Even if it was by a small number of people." – Larry Dupon
Onstage at the Marquee, December 1972. L to R: Ron Mael, Jim Mankey, Russell Mael, Harley Feinstein
(TOM HANLEY/REDFERNS)

More from the Marquee, complete with Earle Mankey (far right) attempting to be, in Joseph Fleury's word
"everyone's favourite English poof guitarist." (TOM HANLEY/REDFERNS)

Russell on *American Bandstand* performing 'Wonder Girl', summer 1972. (LARRY DUPONT)

Ron on *American Bandstand* performing 'Wonder Girl', summer 1972. (LARRY DUPONT)

Ron Mael on the BIG MONSTER THEATER ORGAN (Larry Dupont) at ID Sound Studios, \, recording 'Moon Over Kentucky' for *A Woofer In Tweeter's Clothing*. "It all sounded kind of ˈange. Like a club no one but the group belongs to." – James Lowe. (LARRY DUPONT)

Joseph Fleury. Sparks press contact, management assistant and finally manager 1978 – 1991. "He loved the stuff I hated; the press, promo. I couldn't stand it as I like to get on quietly. The combination was really good. Joseph was wonderful." – John Hewlett. (JENNY LENS)

The calm before the storm. Russell stands outside the Liberty Hall in Houston, where later that same evening he would lamp himself with a large mallet. (LARRY DUPONT)

"We were pulled over by a State Trooper some place in Texas and I got a photograph of the entire band posing next to the guy's car." – Larry Dupont.

ID Studios, 1972: James Lowe in discussion about the string arrangement for 'Here Comes Bob'.
(LARRY DUPONT)

James Lowe recording *A Woofer In Tweeter's Clothing*. "I thought Sparks should have gotten some recognition and promised my wife if they didn't, I would get out of that crazy business." Lowe became a TV producer. (LARRY DUPONT)

The *papier mache* 'Slowboat' that was the centrepiece of the band's earliest performances, taken outside the Doggie Bed Factory and lit by Larry Dupont. (LARRY DUPONT)

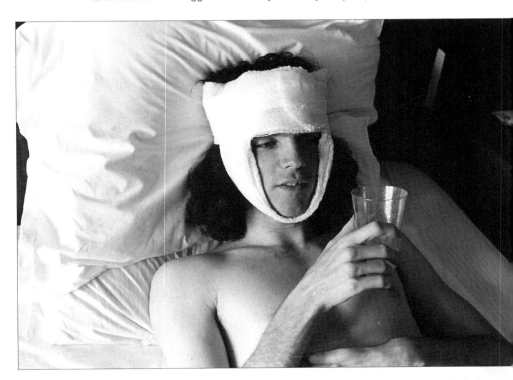

Russell in his hotel room, Houston, Texas 1972 after hitting himself on the head with a sledgehamme on stage. "Initially all the rest of the band and I thought it was rather funny." – Larry Dupont. (LARRY DUPO

iving in the UK, November 1972. "Ron and Russ had a strong sense of how performers should behave."
– Larry Dupont. (TOM HANLEY/REDFERNS)

Primed and loaded for action with a pistol, the group's ever-present prop of 1974.
L to R: Martin Gordon, Russell Mael, Ron Mael, Dinky Diamond, Adrian Fisher. (BARRY PLUMMER)

Musicians' Union

General Secretary: **JOHN MORTON**

National Office: 29 CATHERINE PLACE, BUCKINGHAM GATE, LONDON, S.W.1

Telephone: 01-834 1348

Telegrams: "Amuse London S.W.1"

PLEASE REPLY TO

Bernard F. Parris,
Central London Branch Secretary,
1 Noel Road,
London, N1 8HQ
Telephone: 01-226 9643

BP/JT

Mr. John Hewlett,
73, Northwood Avenue,
Purley,
Surrey.

17th December, 1973.

Dear Mr. Hewlett,

re: Ron and Russell Mael.

Thank you for your letter dated 4th December 1973 regarding the applications of Messrs. Ron and Russell Mael for Union membership and I regret to say that these were again rejected by the Committee.

I am sure you will appreciate that in London the problem of foreign musicians is a very real one and the Committee feel that they are serving the best interests of the members by seeking to restrict the influx of foreign musicians as far as possible. The case of the Mael brothers is somewhat unusual but after considering all the points made in your letter the Committee did not agree to reverse their previous decision as they would still be opposed to their working here as musicians.

It was noted that they are qualified in other directions and, of course, if they were able to obtain authorised employment for the required period it would eventually be possible for them to apply to the Home Office for all working restrictions to be removed, and at that stage they might then apply for Union membership.

Yours sincerely,

Bernard Parris

Bernard Parris,
Central London Branch Secretary.

Letter from the Musicians' Union, December 1973

Someone who did touch was Feinstein as Jim Mankey recalls: "The Band was set up for recording between their sessions and they said 'You can work in the studio but don't touch anything, especially these drums'. 'Don't touch the drums!' They were set up just the way [Band drummer, Levon Helm] wanted them. Anyway, Harley went over and jabbed a bunch of sticks through all the skins, kicked over the stuff. I guess he was just being a rebel… or an arsehole. Not particularly malicious, but it sure was destructive."

"We vandalised Bearsville Studios rather mercilessly," Jim adds with a huge ladle of irony. "Russ smeared a stick of butter all over the windows. They were willing to cut off their feet to make a colourful statement."

Produced by house producer and sometime Foghat member Nick Jameson, the Bearsville version of 'I Like Girls' is pared down compared with the big-band glam of the later *Big Beat* version. It certainly sounded like a single, although it was never released at the time. Other curios from this time are the jingles that the band recorded for fellow Bearsville acts. In 2009, current Sparks guitarist Jim Wilson found some material on a tape given to him by Ron that was to jog memories. "There's a minute-long commercial for the new Fanny and Bobby Charles albums – it's Sparks doing little jingles. When I played it to them, Ron was laughing so hard. It's some unheard Sparks thing that just came out. Ron was like 'Wow – thanks for finding that'."

On January 29 and 30, 1973, billed as being 'From London', Sparks played the Whisky A Go Go on Sunset Boulevard. The gigs were not especially well attended, but showed the creativity and craftsmanship of the group at a peak, having been honed in front of European audiences. Ronna Frank, who had by now moved to England and was writing, recalled: "I flew back for a visit to LA and saw them performing on Sunset Strip as Sparks. Ron was dressed as Bela Lugosi – very weird looking but fun to watch."

"We supported groups like Little Feat," Ron told the author in 2003. "The girls working at the Whisky and the groupie scene really loved us but, apart from that, no one liked us at all. It even got to the point where they wouldn't allow us to play any more and that was because mainly we were really, really loud. There was such an LA style at the time, so we thought we were an English band; we kind of pretended we *were* an English band. That alone offended most of the audience!"

"The billings we were forced to play at that time were always really incompatible," Russell concurred. "There was never a niche for us comfortably to rest in. We eventually created our own and everybody else came to it."

It was testament to the Maels' self-belief in just how well they would eventually succeed: "You know, you really had to have a thick skin to keep going back to the Whisky, playing to what was a relatively empty house, doing the things they did," Dupont states in admiration. "Pushing that boat out on stage…"

By the time of the belated UK release of *A Woofer In Tweeter's Clothing* in April, there wasn't really much left of Sparks to promote it.

Larry Dupont: "It was the closest I ever saw Ron and Russell come to quitting after the band had come back from the England trip. Roy Silver had nothing left up his sleeve for them. They were signed to Roy and they were going no place. It was the only time I ever recall seeing a sense of true hopelessness in Ron's eyes. Harley, Earle, Jim and I were moving on with life, but with them, Ron and Russ, I don't think there was any sense of moving on."

Earle would have wanted to proceed, but it wasn't his life's work as the group was to be for the brothers. Jim and Feinstein had always been, to a certain extent, along for the ride. "There was one occasion," Dupont continues. "We were heading towards the Coliseum to see a UCLA football game. We were outside the stadium some distance away when there was a very substantial roar from the crowd inside this arena and Russell said something to the effect of 'Wouldn't it be really nice if that was for us', and I realised that this really was something that was uppermost in his mind all the time."

A prospective tour of the States supporting Todd Rundgren came to nothing. Ron and Russell contacted John Hewlett. They wanted to come to England to work with him again. They initially considered taking the whole band with them, but the work permit situation disallowed this – or provided the Maels with a decent excuse to start all over again.

Harley Feinstein: "There was no other activity going on. We sort of stopped functioning as a band. I was in a period where I was really into skiing. Russ called me up out of the blue and asked if I wanted to go to England."

Feinstein was given some time to think about it, but his sense of relief at being back in LA was strong, something he feels the Maels picked up on. He called back and said he would like to return with them but heard nothing. Harley was surprised when the husband of his then girlfriend's sister saw the Maels having a garage sale. "Your buddies in the band say they're selling everything and moving over to England," he was told.

Harley Feinstein: "I later heard they tried to put a deal together that would involve us, but it didn't happen. I was never very sure about what had happened. James Lowe was rummaging through his possessions a few years ago when he came across a postcard from England from Ron, on which he said they really tried hard to get the whole band over – but ultimately just the two of them went."

"The worst time was definitely when Ron called me up one day and said 'We're leaving. Goodbye'. He was nice about it but I was upset," Jim Mankey says ruefully. "I was pretty broken up about it but now I see that's just the way things work. That was not fun. It was as simple as that, a phone call and goodbye. Pull off the Band-Aid quickly, I guess, was Ron's approach. I think I would've had something to offer to them but it didn't work out that way."

"In a way we were screwing the band, but there was nothing going on here," Ron told *Trouser Press* in 1982. "We weren't in a position to say, 'If so-and-so can't go with us then we're not gonna go.' We had two albums out that probably sold a combined 2,000 or 3,000 copies, so we packed up and went to England."

Russell was more up front in a 1993 Q interview with John Aizlewood: "We had to decide whether to save the relationship with our college buddies or cause a lot of resentment. We said fuck 'em and jumped on the first plane."

Jim Mankey is ultimately sanguine about the split. "It makes you reconsider your goals in life and to approach something else, so I went back to school and that was a good thing. I majored in electronics engineering." Although he got on well with the brothers, Jim could never quite figure them out. "They didn't really get very personal and divulge their innermost secrets but that's OK, it suited me just fine. I was

51

quite like that myself. I never expected them to be my pals, although they were my pals. They were good friends. They took their persona from here and there. There's no telling what kind of people they really are underneath all their arty trappings."

Jim could also see that England was imperative if the brothers were to achieve their desired level of success: "There was nothing in this country even similar to what they were trying to do. Anything away from the norm was unacceptable."

John Hewlett: "The [Maels] got in touch and said to me that the band had broken up and that they were on their own and asked if I was still interested in managing them. I went away and looked into it."

The first edition of Sparks ultimately hadn't worked out. Larry Dupont is still saddened that it didn't necessarily achieve its potential. "I think the band was way too sophisticated for its audiences. Certainly too sophisticated for the people managing them. They had so many ideas in their heads and so many things they were trying and most of the time they were playing over the heads of the people who heard them."

Dupont admired John Hewlett, and once he knew Hewlett would be involved going forward, he could see the potential. "I think what John did was help bring them down to earth. They really worked well together. Once they were the group that John helped put together, it was always Ron and Russ' group and only Ron and Russ' group. Before that, everybody had an input and Earle's input was certainly as strong as Ron and Russ'. Even though Ron and Russ really did the songwriting, Earle insisted on tossing in his two cents' worth. There was a real sense of cooperation in the community."

After his exhausting spell in London, his 3am lights out and 7am starts, Dupont was glad of the break and joined Feinstein on the ski-slopes. Larry had played a key role in getting Sparks to this point and had done so on love and very little money. Roy Silver had agreed with Dupont that his 24-hour days should be rewarded with a percentage, but as always it was the usual case of finding the money.

Larry Dupont: "I don't think Ron and Russ really ever understood how much of a role I actually played. I know Roy did and John did as he asked me but you know… that's life. People view things differently from their own perspective."

Dupont is anxious, however, that after all these years, his hand is not overplayed: "I'm overstated in some areas for what I did and understated in other areas. One thing is for sure, I was not in any way the sixth Spark!"

Dupont went on to be a photographer and designer, Jim Mankey went into bands and had great success with Concrete Blonde; Harley Feinstein became an attorney-at-law. It is only Earle Mankey, the Maels' right-hand man for the first three years, who continued to work intermittently with Sparks. He became a renowned producer/engineer and worked for The Beach Boys' Brother Studios.

There were two final factors in Sparks' relocation to the UK: family and Vietnam. Amazingly, Miriam and Rogie were now living near Clapham Junction in South London, having relocated the previous year. Also, the spectre of the Asian war still played a part. Although conscription ended in December 1972, as Dupont noted, "These were very strange times because, although the war was scaling down, a whole bunch of us in the back of our minds were still thinking 'We don't want to serve in Vietnam'."

Everything was about to change and, stylistically at least, everything was in place. Writing in 1975, Joseph Fleury said that Sparks' early work "represented the beginnings of a musical concept that is still 'basically the same'. In 1972, Sparks weren't a country band, or a soul act, who got the whiff of a new trend and jumped aboard the bandwagon. No, Sparks have certainly progressed, but they haven't really changed at all."

Chapter Four

Island Life

"It was like a recipe; with Ron and Russell you had the major ingredients, but you can't make a great cake without the egg."

John Hewlett, 2009

Ron and Russell Mael had made the decision that they were going to come to England to make their name. Sparks' strange, extended promotional tour of late 1972 had demonstrated that no matter how tiny, there was far more of an appetite in the UK for their music and off-the-wall style than there was in Los Angeles. After all, not only was this the land that had produced The Beatles, The Kinks and The Who, it was where glam rock had now taken over and had made lots of former struggling Sixties musicians who previously hadn't quite fitted, including David Bowie, Slade, and, of course, Marc Bolan, into stars. British comedy, too, at this point seemed to share a lot of Ron's lyrical subject matter. It was either repressed or innuendo-laden regarding men old enough to know better, continually on a bird-hunt (the tail end of the *Carry On* film cycle, *On The Buses*), or deconstructive and arty (*Monty Python's Flying Circus*). And the UK was so near continental Europe where all of Ron and Russell's film heroes resided. Aesthetically, every box was being ticked for their emigration.

On top of that, art and pop had melded perfectly with Roxy Music, who had emerged in 1972, initially championed by *Melody Maker* writer Richard Williams. Roxy Music was the first post-modern pop group. Although everything they did was presented knowingly and with considerable irony, Bryan Ferry sang, in that strange, otherworldly manner of his, love songs of great sincerity, whether it was to women, motorbikes, motorcars or blow-up dolls. And they had a strange personage poking away at a keyboard behind him. Surely there would be room for something similar with an exotic, American twist.

John Hewlett knew there was one company that would suit Sparks down to the ground: Island Records. Island had been a relatively small independent label started by its founder, Chris Blackwell, in Jamaica in 1959. It moved through licensing Jamaican tracks to UK audiences to licensing its artists to other labels, to, in 1967, establishing its legendary 'pink' Island logo.

Soon, Island had a reputation second-to-none for a variety of left-field artists, drawing mainly from Blackwell's love of Jamaican music, but also tapping fully and earnestly into the folk/hippie movement. "The label was enjoying its success," former head of A&R Richard Williams says. "The sales and marketing people were music enthusiasts, who gave the place – apologies for period slang – a real family vibe. At that time everybody was working towards the same objective. The tone was set by the number of off-duty musicians hanging around."

The year 1972 was probably the peak of Island's album success – 20 albums, covering a broad range of music, were in the Top 50. The roster included John Martyn, Nick Drake, Fairport Convention, Bob Marley and the Wailers, Jimmy Cliff, Cat Stevens and Vinegar Joe to name but a few. It also licensed the work of Chrysalis, which meant Jethro Tull were on the label, co-owned Manticore with Emerson, Lake and Palmer and, from an art-pop perspective, the EG management stable.

That same year, the label had released Roxy Music's debut album through EG. Their bright, ironic, cinematically informed work displayed a clear precedent for Sparks to find a perfect home at Island. The label also had a small, committed team headed by Blackwell, operating out of St Peter's Square in Hammersmith and Basing Street Studios in Notting Hill, both in west London. Blackwell had already begun to step back from the running of the business as he was taking care of the acts in which he had a personal stake. "At that point I had been with Traffic and they were touring a lot in America," Blackwell recalls. "1973 was, of course, when Bob Marley started coming on the scene and I started getting involved with that. It was a period when I was mostly travelling and in the studio."

In his absence, Island was run by David Betteridge, who headed up the day-to-day affairs with his team of Tim Clark as Director of Marketing, Richard Williams, Head of A&R, and former Spencer Davis Group bassist, Mervyn 'Muff' Winwood, as the Head of A&R at Basing Street studios.

"I'd joined Island in September 1962. I'd worked with Chris when he was with Leslie Kong," David Betteridge recalls. "We'd built a solid base when we had the West Indian label, and by the early Seventies we were cooking with gas."

By 1973, there were two distinct camps within Island – Blackwell and his people in one and Betteridge, Winwood and Clark occupying the other. Betteridge, whose forte was marketing and promoting, had his own A&R team and an unwavering belief in what he was selling. John Hewlett struck up an excellent relationship with Betteridge and, on hearing of Ron and Russell's intentions, Hewlett got an initial handshake deal to bring them over.

Although nothing formal was yet in place, Betteridge had heard of Sparks. The approval of Winwood would seal the deal and Hewlett played him the Bearsville albums. Like Hewlett, Muff had been a bass player in a Sixties four-piece and, also like Hewlett, he was arguably the least musical of his group. Winwood's first major signing to Island had been his younger brother Steve's progressive act, Traffic.

Muff Winwood: "I was aware of John when I worked in A&R at Island. He asked if he could come and see me because he'd got this record from America and he wanted to bring the band to England. This was the time when rock was just exploding with the big heavy guitar bands really starting to make their name. Suddenly, I hear music that is so weird but still incredibly rhythmical."

Tentatively impressed by what he heard, he asked to see a picture of the band. If he thought the music sounded weird, he was now staring at a picture of Ron Mael. "That did the trick," Winwood exclaims. "They looked so bizarre; you just had to give it a go."

Hewlett got the air fares arranged, and secured a provisional deal. "I could get into companies because I knew people in the industry," says Hewlett. "David gave me money and I was able to do what I did to bring them in."

Muff Winwood: "I met them and that was enough really. It was obvious to me that they were so different from anything else that was happening. I knew that somewhere down the line they would strike a chord and John Hewlett seemed like the kind of guy who would make things happen."

Although verbally committed to the principle, Betteridge and Winwood still needed the decision rubber-stamped by Chris Blackwell.

"At that time, Island was one of the first places for an act to try and sign," says Blackwell. "As I was on the road a lot, they'd come and see David, Muff or Tim. Tim had signed Roxy Music and Muff brought me Sparks." To say Blackwell was initially cool towards the band is an understatement. Many recall his view to be similar to his attitude when first encountering Roxy Music – ice cold.

"Sparks was not Chris' sort of music," Tim Clark recalls. "It showed in what he signed and liked – look at Steve Winwood, Robert Palmer and Bob Marley and you get an idea of the outstanding singers that he went for. He was ambivalent; he certainly wasn't very involved."

John Hewlett: "Chris didn't like Sparks; I mean *really* didn't like them."

However, Blackwell believed in the people around him, and soon warmed to the idea of having these American brothers on the label. "I thought it was totally different to anything I had heard before," Blackwell states. "They were and are totally unique – there's nothing like them. I've always been attracted to something that is really different, so although it wasn't immediate for me, I got there. Their whole thing, their graphic sense, their sense of show business, it was to become so much more than just regular records. There was something about them – they had a style all of their own."

John Hewlett: "Ron and Russell were under contract to Bearsville and Roy Silver. As along as the contractual situation was sorted, I said that I would be happy to bring them over. That was that."

Although Roy Silver had a great deal of confused affection for his group, he realised that the game was over. Bearsville released Sparks from their contract in summer 1973 with not a jot of protest.

Larry Dupont: "When they left Roy in the dust, I felt really bad for him. He had given many months of his life to try and break them."

Silver continued with his stable of artists, eventually making Bill Cosby one of the highest-grossing television stars the US had seen.

Ron and Russell arrived in London in the early summer, initially staying with Hewlett at his house at Northwood Avenue, Purley, south London, while visiting their mother and stepfather up in Clapham at weekends. They came armed with, according to Nick Kent in his 1974 *NME* interview with the brothers, an album's worth of demotapes – crammed with tunes like 'Marry Me', 'When I Take The Field Friday', 'Green Thumb', 'I'm About To Burst', 'Alabamee Ride' (*sic*), a paean to the supermarkets of America, and 'My Brains And Her Looks' – that might never make it to record. It was now a case of turning these demos and their undoubted potential into something that would be commercially viable.

With his experience at Apple, Tetragrammaton and Feldman's, Hewlett negotiated a competitive publishing deal for Ron and Russell with Lionel Conway at Island Music as well as part of the package, with rights reversion to them after 30 years. The final signing of the recording contract would take a little longer to complete.

Winwood loved the material he heard and the initial demos, but thought them too weedy and that they needed the raunch of a conventional group behind them. Along with Muff, Clark and Betteridge were very much Sparks champions at Island, impressed by the low-key yet charismatic approach of Hewlett. Hewlett, of course, had worked with Bolan first hand and seen his old John's Children cohort go on to be the biggest thing in British pop. It was wholly possible Hewlett's association could do the same for Ron and Russell.

Tim Clark had achieved much recent success with Roxy Music. "Roxy influenced our whole thinking with Sparks," he admits. "As I had been working closely with [Roxy co-manager] David Enthoven, we saw [Sparks] as a new, very glammy Roxy Music. We weren't trying to slavishly copy them, but we knew we wanted that same sort of glossiness. The very name Sparks meant to us that the music would lend itself to a very glossy and arty feel."

Not all saw the similarity, however. "There was something more different and complex about Sparks with their stops and starts and tangents," Chris Blackwell opines. Richard Williams, too, was not so sure. "I wasn't so keen on them, actually, but I didn't bother voicing the opinion inside the company because it wouldn't have been helpful. I hadn't signed them and they didn't need my assistance. I certainly didn't think they'd do the label any harm. I didn't think we had the 'new Roxy', although I'm sure others did. But apart from the fact that I was indifferent to their music, I didn't think they had the capacity to propel cultural change in the way Roxy had done."

While Winwood set about finding a suitable candidate as producer, Hewlett put an advert in *Melody Maker* in July 1973 looking for musicians. One of the first applicants was a young, classically trained bass player, Martin Gordon, who was working as a technical author for a shipping company. He had taken the job for the simple reason he could sit by a telephone and try for better things.

"Oh yes, I was *desperately* in love with maritime engineering and oil tankers," Gordon laughs. "My parents were technophobes and they had no telephone. The only way I could see of getting into the world of professional music was via the back of the *Melody Maker* and you'd need a phone for that. There you'd see that King Crimson needed a lead vocalist or Supertramp needed a bass player. I saw that Sparks and Roxy Music needed bassists and I figured out that as this thing was all done over the telephone, the only way to do it was to look for a local job that would give me a desk with a fixed phone line. The only thing I could find was this maritime engineering company and I bluffed my way in at the age of 18."

Ipswich-born Gordon had been in his job for about nine months when he saw the advert for Sparks. "I rang the ad because I remembered that Bob Harris was extremely snotty about them on *The Old Grey Whistle Test*. There must've been something in it. I wasn't particularly impressed with the singer but I went to the local record store and listened to some tunes – *I didn't buy them, I stress* – but I listened to them and then when I saw the ad in the paper I thought, I don't mind if that pans out."

Gordon had little grasp of popular music, and had seen and heard only glimpses. "There were no radios tuned to pop music stations in my house and I didn't see it on TV. If it wasn't written down in the *Daily Telegraph*, where was I going to see it?"

In August, Gordon went to audition at Hewlett's house in Purley for the Maels, with his friend, drummer Bob Sturt. The duo made the tortuous pre-M25 journey from Hitchin, Hertfordshire in the drummer's battered Jaguar. Gordon's first impressions of the Mael brothers were clear. "I can only talk about it from my perspective of today – I didn't have the tools and vocabulary in those days. I see now that they were extremely introverted and probably very uncomfortable for whatever reason. I always felt that it was pretty much impossible to make any personal connection."

Although it was clear that Sturt was not what they were looking for, they chatted with Gordon. At this meeting, the kernel of an idea was placed in the bass player's head, that of being a collaborator with Russell and Ron. "John asked me what I wanted from being in a group," Gordon explains. "I replied being able to contribute ideas. I asked Ron what he was looking for from the person who was to join his band, and he replied 'A Lennon for my McCartney'. It sounded kind of OK. It certainly gave me the impression that this was a cooperative venture, at least to some extent, which suited me fine."

Hewlett says that initially, he saw it as "there was always an opening for other people to write, but it always had to be acceptable to Ron and Russell. At that early stage it wasn't acceptable, but later on it could have been like George Harrison in The Beatles. He didn't write early on but later wrote some fantastic stuff; even Ringo did." Although the audition had gone cordially, Gordon returned to Hitchin and heard nothing.

Hewlett eventually called Gordon again, and invited him for another audition at the Friern Barnet Cricket Club, equidistant between Hitchin and Croydon. Gordon played this time with Jook guitarist Trevor White and drummer Chris Townson. "Chris used to live in Friern Barnet and the cricket club was at the bottom of his garden," Gordon recalls. "That's where he used to practise.

"In the intervening time, I had all my hair cut. Previously I'd had traditional college student, shoulder-length hair when I'd been down to Purley to meet them. I'd thought 'Sod it, this isn't going to happen' and suddenly went and got all my hair cut off. They took this to be an enormous improvement."

Liking what they saw, the players rehearsed their way through old Sparks favourites, the 'girl' trilogy 'Wonder Girl', 'I Like Girls' and 'Girl From Germany'.

Martin Gordon: "Then Ron gave me £10, which was a huge amount of money then and he said, 'This is for you and this is going to cover your expenses next time you come down.' From that, I understood that I was in the band and I thought that maybe you could make a living being a musician."

Gordon was the first member of the new Sparks; White and Townson were too involved with Jook at this juncture to make any permanent commitment to Hewlett's new charges. Gordon was recalled to Basing Street studios in Notting Hill for a further run through of some new material. Original demos were made with sometime Roxy Music bassist John Porter, who would have made the connection between the two groups even more implicit, and also ex-Pink Fairies guitarist Paul Rudolph.

Throughout October, the group auditioned again. Witty adverts were placed in the wanted section of *Melody Maker* – "drummer – must be an exciting, inventive drummer with a really good face that isn't covered with a beard". Lead guitarist – "must be incredible looking and an exciting, accomplished guitarist". And so, an exciting, inventive drummer and an incredible-looking guitarist were eventually located.

The first recruit was the self-taught Norman 'Dinky' Diamond on drums. Almost as much of a selling point in the UK line-up as the Maels, Aldershot-born Diamond had been playing in local bands while working in electrical distribution, influenced by then-recently deceased UK jazz drummer Phil Seaman. His mixture of aggression and finesse produced, as Trevor White was later to describe, a player who was a cross between Keith Moon and Ringo Starr.

Guitarist Adrian Fisher was the last to join. He had the most experience of the new players, having been in ex-Free bassist Andy Fraser's short-lived Toby, and had played with the young Gary Moore in Skid Row.

With his music-business knowledge, he was not willing to sign anything until his lawyer had been consulted.

Fisher added a considerable amount of grit to proceedings; as he said, his ambition for the band was to "butch things up a bit and get a blues lick in everything".

John Hewlett: "Adrian slayed them all. He was the best. He was the business. He was one of the greatest guitarists that I've ever heard, a fucking brilliant player. The band was definitely Ron and Russell's choice, and they were good choices. It was a real rock band."

It has long been reported that there was talk of Roy Wood, formerly of The Move and ELO and then enjoying chart success with Wizzard, producing Sparks for their Island debut. However, Muff Winwood suggests that it was actually Wood's former Move and ELO cohort, Jeff Lynne, that the group wanted.

Muff Winwood: "I had this brilliant idea that Jeff would be the perfect producer. Because of his strong musical thing and the fact he'd been in bands that had very weird ways about them and he was a very strong musician. I thought he'd be ideal. I remember taking it to him and he loved it, but ultimately he turned it down and my whole brilliant idea of how this was going to work fell to the ground."

Lynne at this point was intent on breaking ELO in the US market, something that he, along with manager Don Arden, set about doing with élan in the mid Seventies.

Winwood decided to keep rehearsing Sparks until they were ready for a name producer to come in and be impressed enough to work with the band on the spot. It was during this further period of making demos that the perfect choice was staring them in the face. "We were at the rehearsal studios and I set about doing things with the band," Winwood laughs, "and I was kind of directing them in many ways and Hewlett said to me, 'Why don't you do it?' and it hadn't really crossed my mind so I said 'I'll go in and we'll do a couple of tracks and see how it goes'."

Although Winwood had produced several acts, such as Patto, the thought hadn't occurred to him as he had been spending so much time overseeing Island's Basing Street division.

From a modern vantage point, Hewlett thinks Winwood is being a tad disingenuous: "When Muff came to rehearsal, you could see his jaw drop. Maybe he didn't want to produce it, but I don't believe a word of that! It worked very well, as he was the in-house A&R guy for Island. Muff wanted to produce it the moment he saw it. He walked in the rehearsal room, and how could you not want to produce it? It was a great band with Martin in it; you could see it was going to work."

As the band rehearsed in Clapham, there was a feeling of optimism, as Gordon confirms: "There was certainly the feeling in rehearsal that this was amazing. We would play something to the point where things were all prepared and the thing would kind of manifest itself in the room. I had no idea whether it was going to be a hit or not, but how we sounded was enough of a result. Anything further would be icing on the cake."

As a band the early Sparks were simply sensational. The song 'Barbecutie' was one of the first things that they played, and there was talk about it being Sparks' debut British single. Listening to the track now, it demonstrates just why Gordon was invited to join the group, with his aggressive bass playing well up in the mix. As the album took shape, 'Barbecutie' was considered out-of-step and was left off the running order to be issued as the B-side to the first single.

Hewlett observed how the three new players really unlocked the Maels' writing and performing. What before had been over-mannered and gimmicky now began to rock. It was like some good old British power pop and hard rock had slipped into the mix, ratcheting up Ron's writing and Russell's performance. "I loved that full in-your-face stuff," Hewlett says, "but you have to have melody; songs are the root of it all." And Ron was certainly bringing songs to the table.

Studio time was booked at The Who's south London facility, Ramport, in Battersea.

Muff Winwood: "It was reasonably cheap in there so we went in and we planned to cut this record. I tried to keep the band good and rocky, some good hard guitar parts in it to try and anchor down the very high-pitched Ron and Russell stuff. That was the basic idea and it seemed to work really well."

Although, thanks to constant rehearsals, the band was very tight by this point, Sparks would never be a 'group'. It was always the Maels and the three other players. "I don't think they ever really clicked," Winwood continues. "They were John's mates really and Ron and Russell accepted them early on because they didn't know anybody better. There was never a close relationship really. It was very much a put together kind of a group but it worked well live. Everything got them to the position that when the records eventually happened, they were ready for the off."

Gordon remembered Hewlett and Mael's "Lennon to my McCartney" discussion, but was content to sit tight at this juncture.

Martin Gordon: "The album took quite some time to prepare. We began in late summer and it was finished in January. It took a big chunk of time and I wasn't so bold as to immediately charge in and say 'OK, well I've got 15 songs, why don't we rehearse them?' But I was quite happy to do my arranging and collaborative thing on a secondary level."

Through Gordon's classical background and also his time in the National Jazz Youth Orchestra, he was able to assist with the arrangements, and he acknowledges that there was a fruitful period of cooperation. Fisher and Gordon became close: "I related to Adrian because he had something to say for himself. I got the impression that Dinky's main goal was to have a job. I don't know if he was particularly interested in music; he may have been, but we didn't communicate on that level."

Muff Winwood was the glue to the recordings, shaping the sound, working closely with engineers Richard Digby-Smith and Tony Platt.

Martin Gordon: "Muff was a hands-on producer in the old school sense. He isn't an engineer/producer. He was very good at looking at the bigger picture: he suggested, and I knew that I would never have thought of it, the coda in 'Hasta Mañana, Monsieur', where it stops and comes back in again. He'd come up with great ideas – such as making things a little faster. He was very good at 'big picture' ideas but the extremely competent engineers looked after the minutiae."

One person who definitely wasn't contributing musical advice was Hewlett, as Gordon says good-naturedly. "John Hewlett is completely and utterly clueless as a musician, so he was looking after managerial things and not musical things."

One track kept resurfacing during the sessions called 'This Town Ain't Big Enough For Both Of Us'. Originally titled 'Too Hot To Handle', it had been written by Ron on a piano at his parents' house in Clapham.

It was a grand cinematic subversion on the classic love song, based on Ron trying to master Bach's etudes. As his practising became more frenzied, the song started to take shape and as he started to put a lyric to it, the idea hung around the ultimate movie showdown, the challenge from one gunfighter to another. In his excitement to finish, Ron hadn't realised he'd written it in a key higher than the one in which Russell usually sang.

Muff Winwood: "I can remember cutting 'This Town Ain't Big Enough For Both of Us' and engineer Richard Digby-Smith coming up with the wacky idea of putting gunshots on it. I often get credited with that idea. It was his. We'd cut the track and then had a lunch break. When Ron and I and a couple of the others got back, Richard said, 'Here, listen to this.' He'd found a BBC *Sound Effects* record in the studio with the gunshots on it. He played the track with the effects over and that was it. It just sounded fantastic. At least the rest of us were smart enough to realise it was good."

David Betteridge kept an eye on proceedings in the studio: "I was hands-on in the sense I made the decision how much money was going to be spent. I'd drop into the studio out of courtesy, but not to get involved. Muff was a very competent head of A&R. Artists liked him because he'd been an artist himself, he was a calm sort of character, good with money and good to talk to. I totally supported what he wanted. I thought Sparks were great; they were very poppy for Island Records. They were considered an oddity but you have to remember that at the time Roxy Music, now everyone's seminal band, were seen as very poppy."

The Island boss was conspicuous by his absence. "He never appeared," says Gordon. "I understood that Chris Blackwell disapproved of us highly, which you can imagine as it's not really Blackwell's sort of thing. He left it all to Muff. David Betteridge was very personable but it was hard to tell whether anybody actually thought it was any good or not."

The contract between Sparks and Island Records was signed by Betteridge, the Maels, Diamond, Fisher and Gordon on November 22, 1973. The deal was for four long-playing albums.

Martin Gordon: "With it being my first band, I took John Hewlett's advice at face value. Here was somebody who had been doing it for donkey's years, at least as far as I was concerned. I didn't know the

66

first thing about PRS or anything at all and if he said in his infinite wisdom, 'This is how it works', then I had no information to contradict it. Adrian got a very good deal because he had obviously been in other bands. I remember at the time we were rehearsing in Clapham and the Island deal was ready to be signed. Adrian held the whole proceedings up because he kept saying 'No no, I've still got to talk to my lawyers about this and there are some things which we have to work out', and of course the entire band and John Hewlett were mad about this, myself included, because I felt he was jeopardising the whole thing when in fact he was just being very sensible."

Hewlett also had the not inconsiderable matter of getting the Mael brothers into the British Musician's Union. Hewlett sent a letter to the organisation on December 4, pleading with the Union to accept the brothers. On December 17, they were again rejected. Bernard Parris, the Central London Branch Secretary, replied, "I am sure you will appreciate that in London the problem of foreign musicians is a very real one and the Committee feel that they are serving the best interests of members by seeking to restrict the influx of foreign musicians as far as possible."

This red tape was to prove a considerable stumbling block the following year.

Chapter Five

"Christ! There's Hitler On The Telly"

"SHEESH! One way or another, 1974's turning out to be quite a year for rock 'n' roll."

Ian Macdonald, *NME*, May 1974.

"It's got the musical extravagance of Wizzard, the sophisticated feel of Roxy and the menacing power of the Third Reich."

Sounds, 1974

David Bowie and Roxy Music had made it clear that there was room in the mixed up, disposable teeny world for literate, considered, ironic pop. By 1974 these characters had finished their first cycle at the summit and the pop world was ready for fresh blood: Cockney Rebel were evidently the new Bowie; Sparks were to become, initially, the new Roxy Music. Mixed with vaudeville. And a moustache.

After stints at Ramport, AIR and Wessex studios, the final stage of recording the album – now titled *Kimono My House*, a pun on the

Rosemary Clooney hit 'Come On-A My House'* – took place at Island's Basing Street studio. The sound the group made was dizzying, intense; a rush of ornate glam, hard mod and power pop, topped off with Russell's striking delivery. Winwood and Hewlett were exhilarated.

It was during these final sessions that two points of disagreement developed with Martin Gordon: "I still thought my ideas were welcome, but we – the English lot – were excluded from the entire mixing process. We were summoned after the mixes were done. There was one thing which I thought was really wrong, a break in 'Falling In Love With Myself Again' where the guitar was clearly inaudible. I remember pointing this out. It was a 'pin-drop' moment."

When the mixing was nearly complete, the Maels and Winwood were having issues with the sound of Gordon's bass on 'Amateur Hour'. "They asked me to replace the bass part playing Ian Hampton's Fender instead of my Rickenbacker, which was my signature sound," Gordon continues. "I was extremely uncooperative and did it with as much bad grace as I could muster. You could see the secretaries in the office through this glass door from the studio at Basing Street. I turned my back on the band and played the entire thing looking out and waving to them to make the point that I wasn't amused. That probably, more than comments about inaudible details, sealed my fate."

It was only afterwards that Gordon twigged how Hampton's bass kept popping up everywhere – at the rehearsal rooms, in the studio. At the time, "because he was in Jook and also managed by John, they were all basically around and we used to cross over at rehearsals. I should've thought, when his bass was about, that there was more going on than met the eye but I didn't."

Once the album was completed, Hewlett immediately got the band in to rehearse for live performances. Sensing that he might just have a phenomenon on his hands, Hewlett booked the cinema on Fulham Road that Emerson, Lake and Palmer had turned into Manticore Studios, part-owned by Chris Blackwell. To flesh out the live sound, a second keyboard player was required, and so another specific advert was

---

* 'Kimono My House' had also been an episode of the Sixties Marlo Thomas and Ted Bessell US TV comedy series, *That Girl*.

placed in *Melody Maker*: "Organist required by major label recording band – image extremely important (no beards or bulges)."

Peter Oxendale answered the ad and an audition took place on February 16 at The Furniture Cave at 533 King's Road. Oxendale's tenure was brief, but long enough for him to be immortalised in Joseph Fleury's *Sparks Flashes* magazine, which came out just ahead of the release of *Kimono My House*. Being frightfully well bred, unlike the rest of the band, he was quickly anointed 'Sir' by Adrian Fisher. Years later, Oxendale went on to be a music litigation specialist after working for Chris de Burgh for many years. "Peter Oxendale should never have been in there," Hewlett says, laughing. "But he could play. He delves into piracy these days. He was very, very good at what he did. God knows why he was there."

Sparks rehearsed for about a week at Manticore with Oxendale on organ. Rehearsals continued through to March, by which time the band heard the early radio plays of LP taster single 'This Town Ain't Big Enough For Both Of Us'. It was during these rehearsals that the resentments between the Maels and Gordon reached a pitch.

Martin Gordon: "One day, I made the enormous, grievous mistake of suggesting that I had a song which I felt was appropriate for what we were doing. I think you could've heard another pin drop. This was not me even suggesting a song to record, we were just looking for material for live dates. That was the moment probably when the red flag went up. I would've played it on a cassette or something but we didn't get that far." The song, 'Cover Girl', became one of the staples of Gordon's subsequent act, Jet.

Hampton's Fender bass reappeared and Gordon was again asked to play it. "It was weird to me as it wasn't the bass itself. It can be a very defining instrument but actually it's based on what it plays rather than the *sound* of what it plays. What I was doing in musical terms was completely acceptable in terms of notation, if you consider they were objecting to the bass rather than just me. It was a very strange idea to think that if you change the sound of the bass then everything would be OK."

This all seemed to mask that Ron and Russell were not happy with Gordon. "John later said to me that they were, in his words 'frightened by me and the angle I was taking', so it's the whole thing I guess. I wanted to keep the bass as a very dominating instrument."

71

Music aside, the band was simply not gelling as a solid unit: "There were a few social occasions and they were really excruciating," Gordon says with a grimace. "We went to the Hard Rock Cafe in Green Park once and the tension didn't come from previous arguments or disagreements, it was just there. The two Americans were not the kind of people with whom I, at any rate, could strike up any kind of meaningful relationship for whatever reason."

There was something Gordon *did* admire that Ron wrote for *Sparks Flashes*. "It was kind of a list of 'things to do' musically – how to make things better'. It was very tongue-in-cheek musicality done in a popular manner. I remember being quite impressed by that, even though I've not followed any single one of those recommendations!"

Entitled 'Jam Proof Your Composition (It's The Same Old Song, But Only Shorter)', the list was hilarious, giving 10 bullet points to achieve well-written songs, although to be honest, it was akin to Brian Eno and Peter Schmidt's *Oblique Strategies* cards, which appeared a year later. The Mael checklist included: 'Avoid the key of E. Avoid the key of A'; 'Never use A major or minor, when an augmented or diminished will do just as well'; 'A good rule of thumb is 'when a solo soon will grate, modulate"; and two that Sparks have continued to follow – 'Save your cleverest lyrics for those long passages in one chord' and 'Whenever possible, all solos should be restricted to the final passage of a song where they can be quickly and cleanly faded.'

'This Town Ain't Big Enough For Both Of Us' was released as a single on March 22. It was a bold choice at the time. "It was so wacky," says Winwood. "We knew there was something about this, but although on the one hand it seemed obvious, on the other I wondered if it could possibly be a hit. It was so different from anything else that there was in the charts."

The song received its first play on Nicky Horne's Capital Radio show on March 11 and it soon won Capital Radio's People Choice slot, comfortably beating new releases from Martha Reeves ('Power Of Love'), Harry Chapin ('WOLD') and Charlie Rich ('Behind Closed Doors'). At the BBC, John Peel supported it on his popular, taste-making Radio 1 show, as he had done with some of Sparks' previous Bearsville sides. Of Peel's fellow DJs at the Beeb, Anne Nightingale championed the single on Radio 1, while on Emperor Rosko's *Roundtable*, Elton John dubbed it "a smash". Fellow guest and co-writer Bernie Taupin mentioned that he had seen Sparks at the Whisky in LA the previous year (so it was *he* alongside those waitresses). However, the single did not immediately explode commercially. Thanks to Tim Clark and the Island marketing team keeping the pressure on, however, by the start of May it had started to climb the charts.

The world of The Rubettes, Ray Stevens and Abba, the Swedish winners of the Eurovision Song Contest, was the musical milieu into which Sparks were launched in the UK. The sleeve notes for the 1990 Island Records CD *Mael Intuition*, by Gummo Mael (a nom de plume for writer Paul Morley) aptly describes 'This Town Ain't Big Enough For Both Of Us' as "a startled, shiny/matt, smooth/rough, opaque/translucent, thick/thin collision and bruise song, a crammed scam through the imagined Mael world of inzany pressure and emotional crack. It was a bit of heart beating shock to a tamed pop system, and shot them into the charts, just like that."

'This Town...' was one of *those* records. As Richard Williams describes in the Island 50 celebratory volume, *Keep On Running*, it was "wonderfully camp and melodramatically multi-faceted". Chris Blackwell put aside his previous reservations and learned to love it: "It had this syncopation. It wasn't like a regular song that would have a beginning, middle and end, it just had all these complex arrangements and different sounds."

'This Town Ain't Big Enough For Both Of Us' created a huge splurge. From its initial piano fade-in of advancing menace, it is one of the strongest, most striking singles of the Seventies, or any decade for that matter. As Joseph Fleury wrote in *Sparks Flashes*, "if only ONE John Wayne movie was one tenth as exciting as this track, we could forgive him his expanding paunch. Powerful stuff."

One of the great tales propagated by the Maels was that Elton John bet against the record being a hit. Although Winwood had ultimately plumped for it as the leading single, he had expressed his doubts as to its commerciality to Elton who, being a neighbour, used to pop round to Winwood's house in Pinner to play table football.

Muff Winwood: "I knew Elton and Bernie Taupin very well. One night they were over and I played it to them. Elton thought it was fantastic. It was the other way around [to what the Mael brothers claimed]. Elton said to me, 'Listen, I'll bet you a hundred quid that that makes the Top 3'." Winwood's wife agreed that it would be a smash, and Sparks' producer's doubts were assuaged.*

"I know that it didn't take us very long to realise that we had a huge hit on our hands," Tim Clark says. And he was spot on. The single's momentum arrived as Britain was recovering from the three day week, and had three television channels featuring precious little pop music. There were occasional pop guest turns on *The Des O'Connor Show*, slots on *The Golden Shot*, *The Mike and Bernie Winters Show*, *Presenting Nana Mouskouri* and magician David Nixon's show, but all eyes were on the weekly Thursday-night pop fix, *Top Of The Pops* on BBC1.

Sparks should have first appeared on the show on May 2. However, the Musician's Union dispute from the end of the previous year reared its head again.

Martin Gordon: "I was quite excited. I realised that *Top Of The Pops* was kind of defining the real market by that point and I thought 'Ah ha, OK, I'm going to make it.' We went to the studios and we got kicked out. We weren't allowed to 'perform' because they had no work visas and Hewlett, in his managerial efficiency, hadn't realised that because they were Americans, they needed a work visa to do *Top Of The Pops*. The producer, Robin Nash, said 'Come back next week'." Martin Gordon turned 20 the following day and did not achieve his dream of being on the show as a teenager.

Sparks were replaced by The Rubettes, whose single 'Sugar Baby Love' had been stuck at number 51, as their guitarist Tony J Thorpe commented. "We were very lucky to get on *Top Of The Pops*; the work permits for Sparks fell through at the last minute and we got on in their place. Our hats became bigger than the band."

Sparks got their chance again a week later. On the day that the Watergate hearings began in Washington and a New Jersey singer-songwriter played a concert in Cambridge, Massachusetts, that made

---

* It is unreported whether Winwood and John ever settled up their account.

rock critic Jon Landau write, "I saw rock and roll's future and its name is Bruce Springsteen," the band appeared on a *Top Of The Pops* bill that included UK talent show *Opportunity Knocks* winners Paper Lace singing their future US chart-topper 'The Night Chicago Died'. Overnight, Sparks became a huge talking point.

"It was one of those songs that one had to have immediately," future Duran Duran bassist John Taylor, then a 13-year-old in Birmingham, says. "It's a great song, it's a great production. Every Friday morning you were talking about somebody – I remember seeing Cockney Rebel for the first time; David Bowie for the first time. Queen had their *TOTP* moment with 'Seven Seas Of Rhye'. For some artists it was just the beginning but with Sparks that song is still the one."

Another viewer was Taylor's future Duran Duran bandmate Nick Rhodes. "That period in pop was one of the most golden. Every week on *Top Of The Pops* there was a new treasure unveiled and Sparks were right in the middle of that with 'This Town Ain't Big Enough For Both Of Us'. I saw the Mael brothers and thought that I'd never seen anything like this in my life. You instantly knew that there was something about them that was very different. I was immediately fascinated with that song. The arrangement is pretty extraordinary, the lyric surreal – unlike anything else out there at that time. The physical sound of it and the use of the gunshot, the guitar break, that voice!"

This *TOTP* performance was to become the stuff of legend. It was a striking, stunning performance. Arriving for most people out of the blue with no recourse to the band's history, it seemed so assured, as if (which was indeed true) the viewer had arrived in the middle of something that had already been in place for a considerable period.

There the Maels were in all their glory, with the act honed from the 'Doggie Bed Factory', through Max's, The Marquee and The Pheasantry, played out on prime-time TV. Ron remembers the performance with tremendous affection: "That level of notoriety was something – all of a sudden you've gone from playing to six people at the Whisky to being on *Top Of The Pops* – where 25% of the country saw you!"

The image was something that struck future punk chronicler Jon Savage: "[Sparks] certainly enlivened *Top Of The Pops*, with their great brother double act. Russell wearing women's jackets was a big thing with the padded shoulders. It was a bit androgynous as well, which is a good thing. Then there was Ron Mael's look, capturing the mood of austerity with the sort of tie that Vivienne Westwood and Malcolm McLaren were selling in their shop, Let It Rock."

John Hewlett: "I was sick of blue jeans and rock'n'roll dress. I was all for the mod-eqsue sharpness, a bit cleaner." There was certainly a link between the look and sound of Hewlett's former group, John's Children, and Sparks – an incredible edge to their look and an economy in their grooves. As well as the Sixties, the Thirties had become fashionable again with films such as *The Great Gatsby* and *Cabaret* presenting definite looks of the decade that were distinct from the war and the depression. Art deco had become a popular collectors' item and flea markets were popular. "There was really the idea of a kind of 'pop culture/retro' going on," Savage continues. "And a looking back to the Sixties with the compilations *Hard Up Heroes* and *Nuggets*, which were available on import. I was the only person at university who had the original singles."

Savage, who would buy his singles on London's Golborne Road, points out that a lot of the people who were involved in pop in 1974 had been involved on the fringes of the Sixties beat scene. "You had this link between that weird psycho hard mod of 1966 and suddenly it cropped up in 1974. Sparks are not mellow in any way. They were an important preparation for punk." Looking and sounding like nothing else around at that point, Sparks became a national pop talking point.

A seldom-seen promotional film, directed by Rosie Samwell-Smith, then wife of former Yardbirds man Paul Samwell-Smith, was shot for 'This Town…' at Lord Montague's Car Museum in Beaulieu in the New Forest. It was never seen at the time as there were too few outlets for promo clips then. In it, Gordon shoots Russell with a double-barrelled shotgun. A prescient image …

With the release of the album due, and the single climbing the charts, John Hewlett realised he would need support. His first port of call was Larry Dupont. However, a year was a long time and Dupont had been hanging out, skiing, while putting his life back together after an intensive year with Sparks.

Larry Dupont: "John was great. He'd taken what Island wanted and produced something that was finally successful. He remembered our time together in London and he asked me to continue working with the group." However, as they spoke, Hewlett could hear how settled Larry was. "John said 'You're saying you're really happy now. What would you rather have – happiness or excitement?' It was a very eloquent way of putting it. I said 'Happiness'. John is the kind of person who would've opted for excitement." Dupont did not rejoin the operation.

Joseph Fleury, the wordsmith and Sparks fan from New York, was next on Hewlett's list for assistance. "Ron and Russell told me this guy was really a fan and really good," said Hewlett. "It was such a good move; Joseph loved the stuff I hated – the press, promo. I couldn't stand it as I like to get on quietly. The combination was really good. Joseph was wonderful."

Martin Gordon: "Joe was a lovely guy, very open and very approachable. It was actually fun to be with him. He just appeared. He'd be the guy who would make the calls and tell us when rehearsals were, so maybe he was actually kind of understudying John in a way."

With Fleury on board, the support team was completed by Lee Packham, Muff Winwood's PA at Island, who would assist with the paperwork and shipping of equipment. "It was a wonderful team," Hewlett says. "Muff, Joseph, Lee and myself, with David Betteridge at the record company, it was really cool." Adding Fred Cantrell in Island sales and Dave Domleo, the label's promotion guy, the team were ready to sell Sparks.

Having no British origins for people to relate to, Sparks could be as enigmatic as they liked, adding to their novelty as Americans in England – and the UK was receptive to something exotic and mysterious as an antidote to the grimness of Britain in 1974. With Fleury at the helm, Sparks' communications with the outside world took on a deceptive, yet hilarious sheen. In a world today inured by spin, back then it was all old-fashioned huckstering. Working with Brian Blevins in the Island press office, Fleury, with not inconsiderable help from the Maels and Hewlett, went into overdrive, planting Sparks fables in the media.

The global village in 1974 was tiny. There wasn't scope for verifying 'facts', and with the brothers' sense of the absurd, coupled with their overall drollness, an incredibly gullible audience was prepared to take these tales at face value. Why would they not be true?

The propaganda machine went into overdrive, spinning a web of elaborate exaggeration and fantasy to complement their image. In *Sparks Flashes* they were the children of Doris Day, the Kennedys had somehow been involved, they were living in David Bowie's old flat in Beckenham, and they were about to write a cookbook.

Spinning such yarns was straight out of an old-school Hollywood publicity department. "Making a cookbook was a fun idea," says Hewlett. "The Kennedy thing, the Doris Day stuff was a typical Joseph or Ron and Russell scam. Joseph loved all that. I think it was actually quite destructive over time as it is a lie: even something put out in pure fun permeates and it causes confusion. At that time it did add some mystique."

And what did they look like? With Bowie talking of his sexuality and nobody being quite sure *what* Brian Eno was, there were, of course, mutterings about Russell's androgyny and the brothers' sexuality. It was all extremely good for business. "Pop has to be an area of play," says Jon Savage. "It's not classical music. A lot of people are really afraid of playing. Just because you wear a woman's jacket, it doesn't mean you're gay, and if you are, what the hell? If you want to mince about, mince about. I don't have a problem with straight boys pretending to be gay. Gay people get terribly fundamentalist about all this stuff. It is pop; entertainment. Music in context of time and place, it was great fun."

Another story had it that the brothers found the band members in a pub playing songs from the first two Sparks albums. Gordon explodes at this: "Oh, that was just bollocks, tired, uninspired American witticisms. I was irritated by the presumption of even thinking something like that was funny. 'We were English musicians who were Sparks fans and played Sparks music in a pub?' It was kind of jaw-droppingly boring, you know? I don't think I told them that at the time though."

With the value of hindsight, it might just be possible that the Maels had sussed how the bassist would react.

Chapter Six

Hasta Mañana, Monsieur

"As an objective onlooker, I think for me the best time to leave Sparks was right then."

— Martin Gordon, 2009

In a decade in which the album cover became an art form, *Kimono My House* was one of the most striking of the Seventies. To construct the sleeve, Island was looking for Japanese women on the idea that Ron had had for *A Woofer In Tweeter's Clothing*, therefore gender high-jinks prevailed with cover stars Michi Hirota and Kuniko Okamura.

Tim Clark: "My main involvement was with the artwork and the marketing for the album. We chose Nick De Ville simply because he had been so involved with Roxy's sleeves. We wanted to achieve something of the same glamour. We weren't trying to emulate Roxy, but we definitely wanted to have that really glossy feel to the whole thing and that's why we brought him on board. Nick was the one who art directed it. I worked closely with Nick on achieving that. The sleeve itself formed the basis for all that we did graphically with marketing and advertising. It was sort of a no-brainer."

From the Maels' idea, De Ville enlisted Karl Stoecker to shoot the cover. Stoecker's pedigree for album sleeve photography was remarkable; he only shot a handful, but when that handful included the first three Roxy sleeves, Lou Reed's *Transformer* rear sleeve and Bryan Ferry's first two solo albums, it was a pretty impressive CV. Stoecker, who was principally involved in fashion, had become involved with Roxy Music through their style advisor, Anthony Price. Stoecker, speaking from his Miami base where he has become one of the world's leading fashion photographers, states he was not aware of Sparks' work. "I was into reggae at that time. I never really looked into their music, to tell you the truth. I very rarely, for any of the album covers, listened to the music."

The stunning image of two Japanese women against a green background made it one of the standout covers of the decade. For Stoecker it was, of course, just another day's work. "I was working at a studio in Paddington on St Michael's Street and I got the call. We were looking for oriental girls. We got them from a Kabuki theatre in town touring that classical Japanese Noh stuff. We got Michi and Kuniko to the studio and they arrived with everything, all their costume and make-up."

The session started with the girls striking a range of formal, studied poses with serious gestures. "Then, all of a sudden, they were just like regular girls and after a while they started laughing and then they were cracking up a bit. That entire classical thing was out."

The pictures of shock and winking were absolutely right; the series of cover out-takes are even more hilarious, with v-signs and mugging the order of the day. And no, they hadn't just been shown something. "I think that they were like that because we got them laughing," says Stoecker. "I think that they were just giggly and a little bit self-conscious and just looking at nothing. It was just me and my assistant, Perrashe, and Ron just standing there."

This was, of course, the era of finding deep meanings nestling in album sleeve images and there was a persistent rumour that the girls were actually Sparks in drag. Stoecker refutes this: "Absolutely not! Isn't it amazing how people want to make more of things as time goes on? People want to force reality. It's so strange." Collecting his £250 fee ("It took care of my needs at that time"), and having captured one of Sparks' defining images, Stoecker returned to the world of fashion photography. *Kimono My House* was the last album sleeve he worked on.

The rest of the sleeve took a more conventional route.

Martin Gordon: "The back cover, in a feeble gesture to promote band good feeling, was supposed to be pictures of the five members in the spotlight. That was overturned. The next stage was to have extremely small, black and white pictures of the players down one side and we could choose our own picture. Of course, I chose my own picture and it wasn't the one that appeared on the back of the record."

Like the first three Roxy Music albums, the original plan had been to make it a gatefold sleeve, with the small shot that appears on the inner sleeve, showing the members by huge cut-out letters spelling out the group's name, blown up across the gatefold.

Martin Gordon: "Adrian of course is the only one who has got his back turned to the camera, as Adrian was wont to do. He thought it was all total bollocks. So there wasn't a single picture of Adrian's face they could use, which I thought was very funny."

John Hewlett: "It was a concession for the group to be there with them. It was difficult because we were trying to set it up as a posy, Roxy-style cover and Adrian with his jeans and his cigarette didn't really fit that image."

As has been made clear, Martin Gordon had not exactly endeared himself to the brothers. Coming from outside the music business, he didn't fall into the role of good-natured oik like Diamond, or self-contained artisan (Fisher), nor did he have the Californian weirdness of the early Sparks. Gordon hailed from Hitchin, and could be a spiky customer.

"There were people in our surroundings I got on with," Gordon says. "John Hewlett and Joe Fleury – with these people, I made a very good, reasonable two-way connection but with the 'Moles', it was always incredibly stiff. Not unfriendly but it was kind of question-and-answer stuff."

In *Sparks Flashes* appeared a Monkees-style, skittish play called *A Bon-Bon Named Desire*. As the cast are introduced, the entire band has fairly light-hearted and jocular descriptions such as:

DINKY DIAMOND: The Funster Of The Band. Blonde and eager.
His drums are as fast as his puns.
PETER OXENDALE: New guy on the block. Keyboard ability belies
his tiny frame. Swept into the mayhem known as Sparks.

However Gordon's précis speaks volumes:

MARTIN GORDON: Tall and cool. Ex-school boy who still reads a lot. Knows his abilities and makes them clear.

The following vignettes, provided by Gordon on his website, describing the aftermath of the May 8 *Top Of The Pops* recording, illustrate how the divide between the bassist and the brothers had become unbridgeable. "After the show, I wave goodbye to the brothers as their expansive limousine glides off with a hiss into the evening drizzle, smoked windows raised against the clamouring of the hoi polloi who surround the BBC TV Centre, eager for autographs. I struggle across the road with my cumbersome bass to take the tube back to King's Cross, where I wait once more in the rain for that lonesome midnight train back to, errm, Hitchin."

The following night, Gordon was in London, watching the broadcast at 'Sir' Peter Oxendale's flat. "We had a party. I think we saw it on a small black and white portable on the other side of the room but I was probably too pissed to see it clearly. People immediately offered to shag me afterwards, which at the time I took as a joke but then I soon realised, wasn't. So I thought the least I could do was to agree."

On the Friday, Gordon socialised locally. "I went out in Hitchin with a good friend of mine and we celebrated my good fortune. After a good night out, I was awoken from a drunken state at 4 am by my friend Joseph Fleury. I think the conversation went something like 'hello Martin' and I replied 'hello' and he said 'It's Joseph. They don't want you in the group any more'. He hadn't mastered the art of preamble, but then I guess that's New Yorkers for you. I said I'd sleep on it and get back to him in the morning. It transpires that no one else in the organisation wanted to make the call to me; positioned at the bottom of the ladder, Joseph got the job."

The brothers had acted decisively; from the choice of what bass to use, to wanting to do his own material, from thinking he had ideas above his station, the plain-speaking bassist was now out. Gordon spoke to Hewlett the next morning, who confirmed it to be true and non-negotiable.

John Hewlett: "At the time I was bewildered when Martin went. I was told it was because he couldn't deliver live and couldn't play in the studio. I went to Muff and Dinky and asked their opinions. The guy had just made an album that sounded sensational and they were now telling me it had been difficult."

Hewlett tried to discuss it with Ron and Russell but they wouldn't budge. The reasons given were the reasons given. The process was alarming for Hewlett, who didn't want to let anyone down, as he had signed the whole band. "Here I am managing Martin as well, and being told that he has got to go; it was very disturbing."

John Hewlett: "I regret I wasn't strong enough to tell them to reconsider. It was a personality thing. I was being told that this successful thing that we had made was being broken up about a month before we got out there on tour. It was crazy. I asked everyone if it was for real. I still don't know why they did it. Joseph and I were shocked."

Gordon has a variable view of Hewlett: "He's a Simon Napier-Bell protégé, so there was the mould John was attempting to be in. He has offended many people in his long and illustrious career and not least me. I think personally John was a very nice guy and he was very plausible. You always had the feeling that if John was saying 'Let's come up with an idea' it would probably be quite a good one and that it wouldn't be a waste of time." However, the bassist was confused and ultimately disappointed by Hewlett's actions.

John Hewlett: "I think Martin has suffered tremendously. To be in a major band, you've just had a hit and your heart is in it, and then to be told you're out just as it's about to really take off. I think it's a travesty. I was a part of it, and apologised to Martin for my part in it, but on reflection I just don't understand it. They told me he couldn't cut it live but I think it was more of a challenge to Ron and Russell's position as leaders of their band."

And that was it. Gordon still had his bass, and only when we spoke in 2009 did he recall that he hadn't collected his amp. "Maybe I should add that to my list of gripes…" he says with a laugh. "It's worth thinking about!"

Gordon didn't hear a word from Diamond or Fisher, "Although I knew Adrian told Hewlett at the time that – this sounds very biblical –

'When my time comes, tell them to do it to my face otherwise I will kill one of them' and he probably would've done." [*]

Gordon went on to form Jet, then played in Radio Stars, the power-pop punk act that featured none other than John's Children singer Andy Ellison on lead vocals, before making a career in music as a respected producer/performer/session man. He has become Sparks' permanent outsider, a witty counterbalance to the silent ranks of ex-members.

That same month of May, *Kimono My House* was finally released. It was – and remains – one hell of a record. Although 'This Town Ain't Big Enough For Both Of Us' is unquestionably the best track, the rest of the album doesn't merely bask in its halo effect; it is simply stunning. The tautness of the production and the strength of the performances show how rehearsed the group really were. It plays to all five members' talents and underlines not only the Maels' justified self-belief but Hewlett's faith in them.

"I can't imagine *Kimono My House* being the success that it was having been made with American musicians," Ira Robbins says. "There's just something about the intensely British sound of that period. It was just amazingly distinctive."

Kimono My House has grandiose production, comedy, lyrics, puns, double entendres and Albert Einstein. 'Amateur Hour', which was to become the second single, is another lyrical milestone. It is grand, ornate even. Fleury wrote it was about "young ladies in the hinterlands turning inexperienced boys into pros. Can such things be said on a record? Methinks not. This is downright vulgar, yet Ron writes things with such charm, so what can one say? The chorus hooks you into submission and you wish there was a young lady instructing YOU on the plush green lawns. A theme song for the first X-rated quiz show. But we will not tell you which buzzer you have to press."

---

[*] In an email to Finnish Sparks fan Petteri Aro, Fisher wrote, "[I was] Shocked about Martin, but he was a threat to Ron and Russell – much better image than they had foreseen, before they knew it. Pissed me off. Felt for M.G."

'Falling In Love With Myself Again' is "a beer-drinking song for non-drinkers", beginning a career-long flirtation with narcissism in Ron's lyrics that would continue through 'I Married Myself' on *Lil' Beethoven*. 'Here In Heaven' has one of Russell's best vocals. The tale of Romeo looking down from heaven because Juliet hadn't gone through with her part of the suicide pact showcases Ron's wit and education.

Fisher's cascading guitar intro heralds 'Thank God It's Not Christmas'. In it a man is dreading the Christmas season as he will have to be at home with his family instead of hanging round bars attempting to be adulterous. At over five minutes, it's a fantastic showcase for Fisher – had his Leslie-speakered solos at the end of the choruses been on a progressive rock album, they would pop up in best lists frequently. The *NME* described it as "pure magical originality". The first side ends with Diamond crashing a gong, like the interval of a spectacular.

'Hasta Mañana Monsieur' again highlights the wall of sound created by Winwood, whose idea it was to insert the break and the run-out at the end. The song, about a man's confusion at how to communicate with his foreign lover, is possibly Ron's most hilarious lyric still. There is a serious point about language barriers being made, but once Kant, Michelin Guides and iron ore have entered the equation, it is forgotten. However there is nothing light about the arrangement – Fisher's guitar and Ron's keyboards sound incredible.

'Talent Is An Asset', a song about pushy mothers influencing even the most serious of scientists, provides the album's glam punch. "A personal favourite," Fleury beamed. "Dinky starts the tune, and we go to handclapping, Tinkertoy piano and Martin's neato bass line, A 'March Of The Wooden Soldiers' beat surrounds quaint lyrics and rather startling vocal harmony." "Even science has an air of showbiz, as long as mother is around." The irony of this song provoking stage invasions from teenage girls, many of whom had never heard of Albert Einstein, was never lost on the brothers. With its handclaps and glam stomp 'Complaints' is one of the few songs about retail, conflating working in a complaints department with the nagging of a partner. The call and response between Ron's piano and Fisher's hard rock solo is quite unSparksian.

'In My Family', a song that had been a favourite in rehearsal, was "a quick knot about Auntie Veronica's left ear-lobe and a nervous leap off cousin Teddy's dandruffed shoulder." It nods to 'Family Tree' by Jake Thackray, whom the brothers may have watched on BBC1's *That's Life!* while staying at Hewlett's house. Its tale of the suffocation of family life leading to suicide demonstrates how unsuitable a lot of this content was for an audience of teeny-boppers. It also demonstrates what a brilliant drummer Diamond was, while the backing vocals show how tight a performing unit Sparks Mk. 2 were.

The album closes with 'Equator', a tour de force on an album that had not been without incident. As Fleury suggested, it was "Charlie Parker meets Mickey Mouse and neither comes out the loser. For the first time on record, Sparks swallow the ball of pride in their throats and own up to their true influence – free-form jazz." As the record ends with Russell singing solo with a mellotron (not sax player King Boots Coltrane Jr as Fleury quipped), his vari-speeded female harmony (again not Lynsey De Paul's sister, Babette) provides an unnerving climax.

Kimono My House shows how quickly Ron and Russell had developed from *A Woofer In Tweeter's Clothing*. If they had done nothing else in their career, they would be remembered for this album. It entered the album chart on June 1 and within weeks it was number four, spending most of the rest of the year on the LP listings.

The reviews were largely favourable. In *NME* Ian Macdonald noted "SHEESH! One way or another, 1974's turning out to be quite a year for rock 'n' roll" and put the album up with that year's *Pretzel Logic* by Steely Dan and, coincidentally, Sparks' former producer Todd Rundgren's magnum opus, *Todd*, before concluding, "*Kimono My House* is the real breakthrough – I think you're gonna love it." *Sounds* said grandly yet correctly that the album had "the musical extravagance of Wizzard, the sophisticated feel of Roxy and the menacing power of the Third Reich."

"*Kimono My House* was a very desirable item," young fan John Taylor remembered. "It was just beautifully presented. I've never tired of this one. It's a classic… Every song on there is terrific."

His bandmate Nick Rhodes concurs: "At that time, along with *The Rise And Fall Of Ziggy Stardust* and Cockney Rebel's *The Psychomodo* it was really one of my favourite records. I played it to death!! There was a lot of different moods on that album. Each song had something which was really special. Even back then, a lot of records you'd find two or three songs on there which you thought, 'Those are the great standout tracks'. With *Kimono My House*, I loved every second of it and I would play it from beginning to end. You'd never find yourself skipping anything. Clearly a masterpiece."

The album united musicians who would end up at different ends of the musical spectrum. On June 14, 1974, Steven Morrissey, an avid contributor throughout his teenage years to the *NME*'s letters page, said of *Kimono My House*, "Today, I bought the album of the year. I feel I can say this expecting several letters saying I'm talking rubbish." Staff writer Charles Shaar Murray wrote in reply, "The eyes of Mr Morrissey gleam with a missionary zeal that shames into submission the cringing doubts of those yet unconvinced."

The *NME* cartoonist of the day, Tony Benyon, legendary for his Lone Groover strip, accompanied the letter with an astute drawing: his illustration of Sparks as a firework. Written on the side was an amusing swipe at the band and the Island hype machine. "Warning – this could be a damp squib – if it does not go off please approach quickly with more publicity and cash."

Jon Savage notes that "Morrissey would've liked [Sparks] because if you wanted intensity in that period, it was very hard to find. *Kimono* goes along at a hell of a lick with lots of twists and turns."

In a 2006 interview with Maels on his *Jonesey's Jukebox* radio programme, Sex Pistol Steve Jones said that he and Pistols drummer Paul Cook used to listen to *Kimono My House* (and *Propaganda*) obsessively in Cook's west London bedroom alongside Roxy Music, David Bowie and Mott The Hoople. One of the lead letters in *Sparks Flashes* was from one Simon Barker who said that "I feel Sparks are definitely the group to make it in 1974". Barker would go on to be one of the Bromley Contingent, alongside Siouxsie Sioux and Billy Idol.

It's alleged that Nirvana leader and poster boy for a generation, Kurt Cobain, nominated *Kimono My House* as one of his favourite albums of all time.

With a tour less than a month away and promotional performances needed for the chart-climbing 'This Town...' finding a replacement for

Gordon was of the utmost priority. It was also felt that a second guitarist would be viable to flesh out Fisher's tricky *Kimono My House* playing onstage. Gordon's replacement was the affable Ian Hampton, whose bass had kept appearing everywhere. Edinburgh-born Hampton had been playing music since the age of three when his parents bought him his first harmonica. He'd taken piano lessons when he was six, which put him in good stead when asking for a Hofner guitar on his 12th birthday. With his best friend from school, Ian 'Ralf' Kimmett, Hampton began playing in a series of rock'n'roll bands.

"One day, out of the blue I got a call to join a band," Hampton remembers. "Ralf got a guy up from London, Trevor White, with him. We rented the proverbial cottage in the country and we got Jook together, with the proviso that I start playing bass, which I'd never played in my life before. I got a cheap bass and we put it all together."

Jook found a style that added grit to glam and John Hewlett was involved from the off.

Ian Hampton: "[Hewlett] was a hustler, and he'd always devote his time to the major act he was working with, which is fairly typical of the age." Hewlett hooked Jook up with Mickie Most, signing a deal with RCA. "Although John really made us feel part of things, our biggest regret was that Mickie and his brother Dave didn't do any production for us," says Hampton. "It was all farmed out to other people."

Although their live reputation was immense, none of Jook's singles really connected with the UK public.

Ian Hampton: "Sweet and Slade were huge successes at this time. We were kicking against the norm because we refused to have long hair and spandex. There was an aggression in our live performance that never manifested itself on the records." A band Jook encountered was The Bay City Rollers, who were to have considerably more success with a sanitised version of the same formula. "The Bay City Rollers and Tam Paton came into our dressing room and told us we had a great image," White says. "Within a month we started to see great similarities in the band's appearance to ours."

Hampton first became aware of Sparks through Hewlett. "He started mentioning them, and I saw their first gig at The Pheasantry. Initially I was mind-boggled – nothing had been heard remotely like it before.

I saw their *Old Grey Whistle Test* appearance as well. We hung out a bit, they came to some Jook gigs – this was long before there was any conception that Trevor and I might join them. I was aware that the other guys had gone back to LA and John was looking after them, but it was never really mentioned beyond that."

With Martin Gordon out of the group, it seemed natural for Hewlett to enlist his old bass player. "It was a panic job," Hampton says, chuckling. "John told the brothers that Jook were winding down and I was available… It was straight in at the deep end, two weeks' rehearsals and then out on the road. *Kimono My House* is not the most straightforward of records to learn. It was a complete jolt to the system, completely different to the usual 12-bar rock stuff that I was used to playing, a real breath of fresh air."

Hampton seemed to suit the equilibrium just fine. Soon, Hewlett also brought Trevor White into the fray. "Jook was Ian Kimmett's chance to do it and he gave his heart to it," says Hewlett "I couldn't get Jook a record deal after RCA dropped them, and it was then they had just recorded their best stuff. It was a terrible dilemma for me. I ended up offering Trevor and Ian the gig and that shot Ian Kimmett and drummer Chris Townson in the foot as well. Ian feels aggrieved to this day that I let him down. Unlike the decision about Martin, which I had nothing to do with, I knew totally what was going on with Jook. In fairness to Ian and Trevor, I couldn't let that opportunity pass them by."

Hewlett and White had been friends for many years. White had previously been a member of Surrey group the A-Jaes and had sold Marc Bolan a Gibson SG ("He paid me money, I presume he liked it"). White was to have replaced Bolan in John's Children had they not fallen apart. White's aggressive style fitted in with Sparks' playing perfectly.

Trevor White: "I still feel strange about leaving Jook to join Sparks. At the time, I thought it was crazy but it was the only thing to do. We'd been doing Jook for three years, touring and whatever. I had a wife and family and was offered the opportunity to join a band that had just entered the charts; it was a pretty difficult one to turn down. Later on, Ian and Chris were cool, they would have done the same thing. We weren't stars. I would have loved to have carried on as we'd just made those demos and started to get really good."

Any initial reservations the auxiliary guitarist may have had about stepping on Fisher's toes were unfounded.

"Adrian was absolutely fantastic to me," White says. "I wondered when I joined whether he would feel put out as I was the rhythm guitarist – he said 'Fantastic, I've got another guitar player to talk to.' That was the way he was, just wonderful. If I didn't know something, he'd teach me to do it. He was a very generous guy."

Neither Hampton nor White knew Martin Gordon and weren't aware of the issues surrounding his departure. "I didn't know Martin," says White. "I'd seen him once or twice, but I didn't know him. Ian and I were there doing our thing. It was just a case of some guy had left and I'd joined."

The first duty was to record another *Top Of The Pops* performance, with hardly any rehearsal, for broadcast on May 24.

Ian Hampton: "We had to pre-record in those days as the Musicians' Union would be down on you like a ton of bricks if you mimed."

Because this *TOTP* performance of the single is the only one to exist in the BBC archive, aside from the rarely seen promo video, it's as if Martin Gordon never existed.

Martin Gordon: "I was sitting in Bombay when I was working with Boy George many years later and he didn't believe that I'd been in Sparks. I told him to go back and watch *Top Of The Pops*. He came back after watching a BBC compilation of the show, and sure enough it wasn't me."

In reality, all eyes were on what was happening out in front. It was all about Ron and Russell. It was such a strong, unforgettable image.

"Television had just become important and the close-up had begun to matter," Ron told *The Word* in 2006. "On TV you could make an impact with a small, subtle action that would have had no effect in concert, in a big hall. You could strike people in a big way – a raised eyebrow, a changed expression, a moustache. I'd done them live before, but nobody had noticed! Now they began to have a massive effect."

However, no matter how sizeable the effect, 'This Town...' just could not get past the number two slot. Tim Clark had been in an identical position before. "We had the same thing with Free's 'All Right Now', which was kept off the top by Mungo Jerry's 'In The Summertime'. We pulled out all the stops to get Sparks to the top... Island didn't actually get a number one until Buggles [with 'Video Killed The Radio Star'] in 1979."

Bedecked in their white berets, studio confection The Rubettes, who had benefitted from Sparks' absence from the show on May 2, were at the top with the Fifties pastiche 'Sugar Baby Love', which had taken over the top spot from Abba's 'Waterloo' on May 18, and stayed there, resolutely, for four weeks.

Sparks were now the hot ticket. Ron and Russell were invited to the premiere of George Lucas' *American Graffiti* at the Empire Leicester Square in June. The dailies clamoured to speak to them: Sparks' keyboardist told the *Daily Express* that he was in fact not related to Charlie Chaplin. Of all the articles written about the group during 1974–1975, it was said that only two failed to mention Adolf Hitler. Even Bearsville got in on the act, issuing for the first time 'Girl From Germany' B/W 'Beaver O'Lindy' to capitalise on the group's new-found success.

Sparks' first full UK tour ran between June 20 and July 7, 1974 and commenced at the Winter Gardens in Cleethorpes. This off-the-beaten track venue provided a chance to break the band in before going to the more familiar Southend Kursaals, Birmingham Top Ranks and London Rainbows that lay ahead.

Trevor White: "It was really strange. The first gig was totally ridiculous. I had no idea it would be like that at all. We'd spent ages rehearsing intensively with Sparks. It felt like we had been shot into something different. I was in a daze. I knew the songs back to front, but all these people were going absolutely crazy."

Oscar and Miriam Rogenson would periodically turn up, supporting their boys.

John Hewlett: "It was strange having the parents there. They were just fans. They were really interesting. It was cool; they were real supporters of their kids. I liked them, got on well with them. They would always be at a gig in the background out of the limelight."

Their inaugural UK tour ended at The Rainbow, formerly the old Finsbury Park Astoria. As Howard Sounes described in his book *Seventies: The Sights, Sounds And Ideas Of A Brilliant Decade,* it was "one of the largest movie theatres in the world when it was built in 1930... its escapist décor – Moorish foyer with fountain, Spanish styled auditorium lending a faux grandeur to any gig".

And faux grandeur was exactly where Sparks were at. Ira Robbins was in London to promote his newly founded magazine, *Trouser Press*. After a visit to the offices of *Zigzag* magazine, he found out that Sparks were playing in town that night. "I remember that Rainbow show very vividly because Russell was wearing a loose-fitting white linen suit and girls were throwing themselves on the stage and wrapping themselves round his ankles while he sang. I knew who they were obviously but I knew them to be an arch, iconic, ironic sort of band of thoughtful artists, and really they were being treated as I imagined The Beatles at Shea Stadium had been – just complete pandemonium. It delighted me no end. It really changed my vision of them because I had kind of taken them to be sort of Roxy Music: very stylised and sophisticated. To see they were making 10-year-old girls go absolutely crazy, I was just fascinated. It was enormous fun and was one of those pivotal events where what you think you know is completely wrong and something else replaces it in an even better way."

Robbins' description emphasised the dilemma Sparks were to face for the next 20 months, as Ron said in 2003. "The only downside was that the teenybop following alienated a section of those people who only wanted us to be an art-rock band. All of that screaming forced away a lot of the people who appreciated us musically."

"Sparks were an American band being promoted as a British band," Ira Robbins suggests. "It was a prideful thing for me; I just thought that they had gone onto the other side in the best way. In 1974, the idea of two Californians being accepted as Brit-pop superstars to me was kind of miraculous."

To capitalise on the single's success, a second track was pulled from the album, the ebullient 'Amateur Hour', backed with another non-album B-side, 'Lost And Found' ("It's not really a metaphor for anything," Russell said in 1991. "It's just about a guy finding a wallet and not wanting to give it back.") Despite a strike at the BBC that forced *Top Of The Pops* off the air, the record climbed to number seven in the UK chart.

"Singles have a lifespan of about four minutes in England," Russell said in 1991. "Thus, while 'This Town...' was losing steam, 'Amateur

Hour' was released as the follow-up. It was satisfying that a song that was so different in nature from our initial success with 'This Town…' could also be successful with the British and European public."

Although it was said that the Maels lived in a flat in Beckenham (boasting a "variety of gas and electrical heaters that the Maels hope to convert into geranium holders for the upcoming warm weather"), Ron and Russell moved out of Hewlett's Purley home and took up residence in a rented flat in Kenneth Tynan's South Kensington house. It wasn't exactly the big time, but they had come a long way in the space of a year: a hit single and album, a sell-out tour and, more to the point, a record company that liked the product and wanted more.

More interesting still for Ron and Russell, *Kimono My House* began to excite the more discerning US rock writer. The New York-based music press were especially interested as there had been a great resurgence in Sixties power pop, in places such as Max's Kansas City and the recently opened CBGBs where bands such as Television and Ramones were playing.

Ira Robbins: "It took a while to sort of get a hold of who they were and what they sounded like, but the idea that Sparks were under the care and feeding of someone who'd been in a band with Marc Bolan was kind of amazing. That kind of tied it all up in a neat bow."

Chapter Seven

Spewing Out *Propaganda*

"Sparks aren't going back to the '60s — it's to the '40s. Nazis, Jews, troops, the military, and the ever present war between men and women."

Phonograph Record, 1974

"I think mystery is a good thing."

Ron Mael, 1974

"For anyone who says 'It's lonely at the top', lemme tell you — it's great at the top"

Russell Mael, 2003

The past six months had been a whirlwind. Sparks started to make the transition from being earnestly written about in *New Musical Express* and *Melody Maker* to the covers of children's magazines *Look-In* and *Mirabelle*. Their story began to fan out across continental Europe thanks to a series of launches involving sweets and pastries orchestrated by Peter Zumsteg, Island's European press and marketing co-ordinator. His job was to keep the label's distributors in Europe — such as Ariola in Germany and Sonet in Sweden — happy. Like the media they were delighted with this interesting and exotic confection.

However, the Maels seemed threatened by the fact that the group as a whole was being accepted as a proper band, not simply the brothers and hired hands. The boys in the band occasionally run riot, of which the Maels did not approve.

Adrian Fisher: "We were in Paris for a TV show. Trev, Ian and me, after getting severely pissed in the George V, went to get some nightclub life. We found this very flash sleazy club but we didn't realise how expensive it was, and had to make good our escape from this outrageous bill. We just made it out and lost the pursuing bouncer some way up the street. More drinks, some place. It's about 5 am and we get arrested for being drunk and singing 'You Are My Sunshine' at the top of our voices. Trev and me could not talk [too pissed], Ian could [just] and told the police where we were staying, so they told us to basically 'Shut it!' and get inside as we were nearly at the hotel. We went to one of our rooms and demolished the fridge contents and passed out... Oh yes, we will always have Paris."

There was a clear divide between the boys on one side and the brothers and, at that time, their manager, on the other.

John Hewlett: "Ron and Russell and myself, we were straight. I don't think I even smoked, a joint until much later on. They didn't drink and didn't smoke, which was pretty cool. It's OK if you don't partake, but if you look down on those who do, I don't like that. To make judgments and be aloof, that to me is a negative attitude. Total respect to them for keeping their minds free, but it doesn't necessarily bring about compassion."

To capitalise on the success of the debut and mindful of the shelf-life in pop, Island demanded a follow-up album, one that would introduce Hampton and White on record. *Propaganda* was recorded at AIR Studios between August and September 1974, with Muff Winwood returning to produce. While *Kimono My House* had undergone an 18-month gestation period, *Propaganda* had about three months to be written and recorded.

"[That] album was incredibly hard because there was a lot of pressure," Ron Mael told *Trouser Press* in 1982. "*Kimono* was incredibly popular in England, and we were under the microscope. Anything we did was going to be judged. We went into the studio with a lot of songs, but a bit scared. We kept thinking about The Beatles and their constant rise. We tried to make *Propaganda* a little more complex than *Kimono My House*"

Ian Hampton: *"Propaganda* was great fun. It was a great time, best time of my life. It was a huge buzz learning the songs, fiddling around with them, changing them here and there. Muff was a great producer; he did a great job, getting that amazing rock sound out of Sparks. These are instant records. It felt very rock'n'roll. We tempered that by being sober and restrained and trying to get it all down properly. For the English guys it was a different kind of music. The brothers would come in with the songs and we'd throw it up in the air and we'd all be critical of each other's input – it was very democratic, I must say."

Like Martin Gordon's experience, Fisher was not getting along with Ron and Russell, largely due to lifestyle and musical differences. "Anything I played [that I thought] was any good ended up on the floor in my absence," the guitarist told Finnish Sparks fan Petteri Aro in 1997.

John Hewlett: "The brothers didn't like Adrian, as he represented something they were against. He played the blues, and that would piss them off. That was their petty posing. They disregarded Adrian and his brilliance."

Trevor White: "I don't think Adrian deliberately played the blues, he just played what he thought was right. I don't think he went out to antagonise anybody, he just realised during *Propaganda* that it wasn't for him."

This led to some resentment, and also some highjinks. One night, Fisher watched Russell storm out of the studio. Thinking that he was going into an adjoining office, the singer had chosen a soundproofed store room that couldn't be opened from the inside. The guitarist knew where he had gone, but neglected to mention it to anyone. An hour and a half later he was found, suitably distraught. "I think he thought it was a lift or something," White says diplomatically today.

After the album was completed, Fisher was next to go. "Adrian left before he was pushed," says White. "He didn't feel appreciated. It wasn't his sort of music, but he played it really well."

Fisher came to an agreement with Ron, Russell and Hewlett to take a fee for the album, not wanting to be involved afterwards. As a result, White played rhythm, and Fisher came in when asked to do a guitar part.

"The [Maels] blew it big-time by dumping Martin and Adrian," Hewlett reflects. "Adrian was pure rock 'n' roll. He was all the things that Ron and Russell posed to be, but Adrian was it." After the first tour and album that they had done as a six-piece, the band went down to five. Ever the diplomat, Russell told *Rock and Folk* magazine in 1974 that "Adrian Fisher was a great guitar talent and expert blues player... although his playing was perfect for our previous album, we want a different style for the following album and we needed someone who was prepared to move in the same direction as us."

Fisher went on to join Mike Patto's Boxer and played a variety of sessions before relocating to Thailand, where he died in March 2000 of a heart attack.*

Toying with a replacement, the brothers considered Ian North from Milk'n'Cookies but rejected him. Hewlett also approached Bill Nelson from Be-Bop Deluxe. At the same time, Ron and Russell had been keeping an eye on the band they had met back in 1972. By now Queen had released two well-respected albums (*Queen I* and *Queen II*) and Brian May had quickly established himself as a very competent and stylish player, with a manner that was quite unlike any other guitarist.

"John approached Brian May, which I knew was going to be a no-hoper," says White. While recording Queen's third album, *Sheer Heart Attack*, May was ill in bed when he received a call asking if he would like to join them. Contacted for this book, May confirmed: "Yes, they did offer me a job, but, although I thought Sparks were nice guys and the band was interesting, I never gave it a moment's serious consideration."

Ultimately, Trevor White continued alone. "I think it was Dinky who suggested that I could play the parts and why were we looking elsewhere."

The lead single from the album was the eco-friendly and forward-thinking 'Never Turn Your Back On Mother Earth' (with the early *Kimono My House* demo track, 'Alabamy Right', on the flip), which the band duly plugged via *Top Of The Pops* on October 24 and then again on November 7, pushing the single to number 13.

---

* Although they may not have always seen eye-to-eye during his brief tenure in the group, Ron and Russell were deeply saddened by Fisher's passing.

Ian Hampton: *"Top Of The Pops* was great – it was an honour to be on it, a privilege – as a vehicle for the Top 40 it was unassailable... There were a lot of dropped jaws. Russell carried it off and Ron just scared the hell out of everyone."

"Our new single is different from our last two," Russell said. "It's a bit slower, and it's now a rock band playing with greater use of the studio. Singles a lot of times are musically stronger than albums. There's no room for padding in a three-minute framework." It was a great single, richly autumnal and sweetly melancholic, if slightly wrong-footing their new legion of fans. The brothers' teenage hero Ray Davies reviewed it on BBC *Roundtable* and accused the group of taking a hippy earth-child approach.

On October 26, *Mirabelle* was offering an opportunity to win a date with their cover stars "Russ and Ron". While teens and pre-teens were filling in their competition forms, *Propaganda* was about to be released in time for the Christmas market. The album drew largely favourable responses and went on to reach number nine in the UK chart.

In many ways, *Propaganda* is tremendously accomplished. Not as good a record as *Kimono My House*, but pretty damn close – the sound inside the Sparks bubble, at the peak of their UK fame, and it showed how accomplished Ron Mael had become as a songwriter.

"*Propaganda* was more an evolution than a change of direction," Russell told *Record Collector* in 2008.

The opening a cappella 'Propaganda' gives continuity from the last remnants of the previous album's 'Equator' before charging into the sinister 'At Home, At Work, At Play'.

"One of the elements we thought could make it more grandiose was the singing," Ron said in 1982. "The song 'Propaganda' was originally an acoustic guitar thing; we just kept recording voices. It was a lot easier to do things with the vocals than to figure out extra guitar parts. I think that vocal style was really influential to some big English bands that have since done pretentious albums." *

★ Ron is undoubtedly referring to Queen. On October 24, the two bands' paths crossed again at *Top Of The Pops*. Sparks were plugging 'Never Turn Your Back On Mother Earth' while Queen were singing their number two record 'Killer Queen'.

'Reinforcements' was either another example of the brothers' Weimar Germany fixation or an offcut from *The Producers*. 'B.C.', about a man dumped by his wife and child, is perhaps a little too clever for its own good, while 'Thanks But No Thanks' takes a child's eye view of parental authority. 'Don't Leave Me Alone With Her' was one of Russell's favourite tracks on the album.

"I try to avoid clichés musically, or to use clichés in ways that haven't been used before, which makes things more interesting," he told Martin Aston in 2005. "It's the same with romantic situations. Love songs are generally either happy or sad, but there are so many ways to talk about relationships and put them in a new context. 'Don't Leave Me Alone With Her' takes the opposite tack to most guy's wishes."

'Something For The Girl With Everything', another blaster in the mode of 'This Town Ain't Big Enough For Both Of Us', sounds as if it starts during its middle. 'Achoo' is probably the only song ever to feature a sneezing solo, which replaced a removed Adrian Fisher guitar solo – too bluesy, perhaps.

The grinding propulsive guitar at the close of 'Who Don't Like Kids', played by White and Fisher, recalls what Gordon had done with 'Barbecutie' earlier in the year, creating a noise that sounded exactly like punk some 18 months ahead of time. The album closes with 'Bon Voyage', which is reminiscent of 'Slowboat' from *Sparks*. There is simplicity to a great deal of Winwood's arrangements on *Propaganda*, and his work on this track, along with Fisher's lead playing, makes it one of the most satisfying run-outs in Sparks' career, perilously close to a wig-out.

"The sound of Sparks is… intriguing and imaginative," *Melody Maker* wrote. "They blend early production techniques and tricks that worked well to make the records of the '50s and '60s so successful. The band rely on dynamics and rhythmic changes to carry their tunes rather than depend on one basic melody line."

Phonograph Record said that "Sparks aren't going back to the '60's – it's to the 40's. Nazis, Jews, troops, the military, and the ever present war between men and women." *Rolling Stone* was undecided. "In some ways Sparks seems one of the most fascinating bands of the '70's," wrote Ken Barnes, "in other ways they're a difficult listening experience… it's likely that some listeners will love them, some will hate them and large numbers will remain ambivalent."

Martin Gordon subscribed to at least one of those categories. "If one listens to the next record [*Propaganda*], I find all the things that began to irritate me. I can't hear unanimity. I can hear people doing what they're told."

Although an unsurprising viewpoint from the ousted bassist, there is a kernel of truth in his comments. Apart from 'Something For The Girl With Everything', 'Bon Voyage' and 'Never Turn Your Back On Mother Earth' the album lacks the sonic blast of *Kimono My House*, though the writing is just as strong. Whatever, it made a worthy successor to its predecessor and ensured that Sparks retained their presence in the UK albums chart over the Christmas period. To support the album's release, the brothers were interviewed on Sally James' *Saturday Superstore*, where they summed up their success: "We came to your country. It sold. That's the history of Sparks."

Carrying on the bold statement made on *Kimono My House,* the cover concept for *Propaganda,* devised by Ron and photographer Monty Coles, was striking. This time Ron and Russell were on the front of the sleeve, with the rest of the band relegated to the back. However, this wasn't to be a cheesecake pose – the brothers were bound and gagged on the back of a speedboat. A sticker in the top right corner identified it as the new Sparks album and not one of the real-life crime journals that were so popular back then.

The back cover found the pair tied up in the back of a car, with the band, sans Fisher, standing outside, looking very much as if they were going to take the pair away for a little roughing up. Sparks' road manager, Richard Coble, can be seen under the bonnet of the Humber dressed as a garage forecourt attendant. The sleeve was perhaps in grim taste as kidnappings, like hijackings, had become dismally fashionable by the mid Seventies, with arguably the highest profile incident happening earlier that year when newspaper heiress Patty Hearst was snatched by the Symbionese Liberation Army

The sleeve locations were taken on the same day at Littlehampton, Sussex and a petrol station near Island Records in Westbourne Grove, west London.

Ian Hampton: "The front cover wasn't so much fun as it was a really stormy day. The terror on the guy's faces was genuine. We all went on the boat for a while, but that was the picture that stuck."

Trevor White: "We spent the whole day on a beach in a gale-force wind being blasted by sand as we'd been waiting for Ron and Russell who'd been out on the boat. We were hanging around. The original idea was to have a picnic on the beach but the weather was so horrendous."

John Hewlett: "I loved it. Freezing cold, good idea, good concept. The band was a little bit abandoned, but it worked. It was all good."

It provided another iconic image for Sparks. "The artwork for *Propaganda* provides another twist, creating these weird personas," Jon Savage comments. "You've got this kind of bondage thing going on and when you look at it, you are immediately drawn to the story: how did they get there? Who are these people? It's a terrific image: they're both really skinny, they are both wearing really weird clothes; Ron's got these flared trousers, pullover and great sunglasses and Russell's got this weird kind of allure. And that's before we get to the back! Something is clearly wrong; the rather hard-looking band, the Humber car, the clothes, the concept; absolutely unbelievable."*

Ira Robbins, founder of *Trouser Press*, was one of Sparks' long-time American supporters: "They just struck me as a band that had all the right attributes for making great music and the fact that they went to England and became British pop stars was just a little extra icing for my taste."

Trouser Press was extremely supportive of British acts and owed a great deal to *Melody Maker*. "We used to read *Melody Maker* all the time," says Robbins, "and yeah, Sparks and T-Rex and Slade and Mud were all we cared about. That was our emerging culture, because there was nothing in America that really did anything for us so we were very aware of Sparks' success."

In the autumn the band returned to America for a great deal of promo. On October 8, they taped a showcase on the ABC TV special

---

* Ironically, the number plate of the Humber had the initials 'MU' on it – the abbreviation for the Musicians' Union, which had blocked what would have been Sparks' debut *Top Of The Pops* performance earlier that year, giving The Rubettes a leg up to number one.

Wide World In Concert (broadcast a month later), introduced by two of Ron and Russell's heroes, Keith Moon and Ringo Starr. In New York, Sparks' US launch occurred the following year at Burger King on 58th Street in Manhattan.

Ira Robbins: "It was the kind of exotic, over-the-top record company party of which there are no more. We were given free rein of the place. It was just a remarkable idea. We would go up to the counter and demand more cheeseburgers and more milkshakes and more fries and it seems incredibly bizarre, although now that I recount it, it sounds pathetically normal. At the time it was a big deal. It was a very big event in New York circles. There was a theme in New York that Sparks fitted comfortably into, which The New York Dolls had started.

"From [the American] experience, it's a little hard to characterise because the glam-rock era in Britain seems, at least from this remove, to have been a very consistent and well developed phenomenon. In the States, it arrived as a very odd bunch of radar blips. You know Roxy Music and Slade and a few other acts, they were all kind of separate in America; they weren't on the charts so they weren't on television every day and they weren't on the cover of all the papers, so it was a very different phenomenon. But Sparks were welcomed by the same club of 200–300 people in New York that liked the Dolls and that liked Bowie and Lou Reed.

"They were kind of building their own sort of cultural lifestyle out of artists that made sense then. Sparks walked right into the middle of that, even though they were from California, which was a large and very suspicious place for New Yorkers. Yet they just seemed smarter and funnier, sharper and more sardonic than anybody else around and so we pretty much welcomed them with open arms.

"They were really interesting guys," Robbins assesses. "They were absolutely delightful and exactly what you'd imagine them to be – smart, funny, charming, clever and self-aware. It was really reassuring to know that."

Unlike their UK counterparts, American audiences saw that this was tricky, intelligent and grown-up music, which, although using the pop form, wasn't a million miles away ideologically from Zappa or Beefheart.

Trevor White: "It was very different. We went from teenybop mania to respectful silence and we were quite disturbed. When we finished there was loads of applause. It was such a novelty for people – it went down really well."

In Los Angeles, writer Harvey Kubernik caught up with the brothers at the Continental Hyatt House where the group pondered on their past and present. Ron also gave an insight into his songwriting techniques. "Rock is always bravado. I like using the little guy approach… I like to go at it in a half-serious way to bring out the point sometimes. I don't write funny songs, I like things where it's really blurred, and you can't tell if it's funny or not funny. I think mystery is a good thing."

The persistence with the US paid off, and *Propaganda* became the group's greatest success there to date, peaking at number 63 in 1975 on the *Billboard* Hot 100.

Ira Robbins: "There was a brief period in the Seventies when glam rock and glitter got a look-in on American television because of the colour and the costumes and the sensationalism. There were these concert shows on American television that hadn't existed before, like *Midnight Special* and ABC's *In Concert,* which started putting on bands like Sensational Alex Harvey Band and Slade and, of course, Sparks. The bands that were coming from England that had cool clothes and great stage shows, got a look-in but it didn't necessarily translate to acceptance or record sales, but they suddenly became part of the culture. *Circus* magazine was very mainstream-oriented and eventually became very devoted to bands like Kiss. Colourfulness was in and Sparks got swept into that a bit, which was nice. It was cool to turn on the TV and see them on there."

Mainstream America, however, remained largely impervious to their charms, as Robbins confirms: "I don't think Sparks ever became competitive for the American record buyer along the lines of the BTOs and Lynyrd Skynyrds – the simple, obvious, party bands that were popular at the time."

The Maels' British success began to filter back to the original band members. "I had no way of knowing what they were up to," says Harley Feinstein. "This was before Myspace. I'd forgotten about them. One day an envelope arrived at my house – and then out pours a bunch of clippings from *Melody Maker* and it showed that they had become big stars. It was a total and utter shock to me."

★ ★ ★

The cut and thrust of Sparks' new line-up created havoc on a British tour starting at York University on November 2, closing in Dunstable on the 28th. The 20-date tour included Swansea, Stoke-on-Trent and Southport with a show at Hammersmith Odeon on November 11.

Ian Hampton:"I loved it. I didn't think the art was being compromised. There were two camps. There were the heads and the screamers; never the twain met. It was great fun. It got kind of dangerous at times, kids pulling Russell off the stage. The teenyboppers were there for all of us, but mostly for Russell."

Nick Rhodes saw them on November 27. "We were very lucky in Birmingham as the Town Hall was a great venue to see people. It was exciting, it was vibrant. There were *lots* of screaming girls. The band didn't have spectacular visuals, it was all about the songs and the delivery, but yeah the audience was pretty crazy."

A short European tour followed that saw an incredible performance at Amsterdam's Concertgebouw. *NME* witnessed the show and noted how tight the band had become: "This version of 'In My Family' dispels any crap that Sparks are a "cute" band, as Trevor's lead rips into a savage burst of feedback that sends the crowd bananas."

While on tour, the Maels shared their love of fine food and faddish diets. "It was an understatement that we ate well," Hampton recalled. "Most of the tours were planned around Egon Ronay or the *Michelin Guide*, as long as there was a decent restaurant there or on the way to the gig. As Brits we were used to the Blue Boar [a notorious rock 'n' roll greasy spoon] up the M1. The Rosette-awarded restaurants we never even knew existed – the Maels are true gourmets."

Island's laissez-faire approach was proving beneficial, having always been a nurturing presence.

"I kept an eye on their career when they were with us," says Chris Blackwell. "I can't say that I was involved in it a lot as I was really involved with Bob Marley. In the case of Sparks, they had their whole thing together in a way. With Bob I was moving him from a singles act to an album act."

However there were the first hints of dissension in the ranks from those that had originally championed Sparks at the label.

"I probably realised the law of diminishing returns after the first album," Tim Clark says. "I think the second album was a bit of a disappointment, compared with the first. *Kimono My House* was this wonderful piece of work, a real breath of fresh air. They didn't follow it up too well."

David Betteridge: "It's always a danger; artists have a short lifetime of experience that goes into this first album. It's like they've filled the glass right up to the top. They have success; and then the second album syndrome happens that so many people haven't got past. When we heard *Propaganda* we wondered where the big hit was; all artists have a crescendo."

The Island team were largely supportive of their polite, if aloof, charges.

Tim Clark: "I had dealings with Ron and Russell during sleeve shoots, saw them at gigs. 1 knew them and worked with them insofar as it pertained to what we were trying to do for them. I didn't spend huge amounts of time with them."

David Betteridge: "They were a very interesting couple. Russell and I got on well but there was a shield there; there is always a shield between record executives and artists – the record company is always looked on as a suspicious character. I liked Russell, I found him a decent guy. Ron I never got to know at all."

John Hewlett was a more reassuring and communicative presence.

David Betteridge: "John and I were good friends. I liked John a lot, I thought he was a very caring individual. In this period, we became good friends outside out of the music business. I thought ultimately he lacked the real strength and power of a lot of managers I knew. It's a very interesting talent, a good manager. A manager can damage an act far more than anyone in the record company; you can really have managers who fuck up the artists' lives and your investment. I think John cared deeply, but he lacked a certain amount of direction.

"He seemed a pretty straight fellow, he didn't even smoke. John may have got drunk with me a couple of times. He had a great deal of good qualities, but somewhere in the small print of the management manual, there was something he was missing. He was very helpful to us but he was probably too nice. The music business takes no prisoners."

Christmas 1974 provided the brothers with a chance to reflect on what had been a pretty crazy year. They had made some good friends in the business, one of whom was Island's international man, Peter Zumsteg. "We were playing darts in a pub round the corner from Island in Hammersmith," Zumsteg recalls. "Chris Blackwell wanted me to go to Jamaica with Bob Marley and then on to LA. This was the night before I went, so the Maels gave me the key to their parents' house up on the hill in Hollywood."

While on tour in Holland, Sparks outlined their hopes for their third Island album when interviewed by Max Bell for *NME*. "The next album should be recorded in America," Russell offered. "Still with Muff, though we hope to have Earle Mankey, our old lead guitarist, engineering." Mankey returning to Sparks at this point with the English band would have made an interesting proposition. "We do have the element of local-boys-made-good, and the English element as well, plus this is our best-ever combination," Ron said. "There's a lot of, I know this sounds kinda naive, *youthful* spirit. We aren't the initial thing to latch on and so we do have a reputation preceding us. It will be a shock though, going back, after the success here."

As fascinating as it sounded, the Winwood/Mankey collaboration was not to happen. 1975 began with a final piece of *Propaganda* business, the release of 'Something For The Girl With Everything', backed with 'Marry Me'. Even with its *Top Of The Pops* appearances, it continued Sparks' gentle chart decline with a number 17 placing. "Another song in the hyper-acrobatic melody style that Ron had initiated on *Kimono*," Russell said in 1991. "We were now experts on the menu choices of the BBC canteen as a result of numerous *Top Of The Pops* appearances."

Sparks returned to America at the start of 1975 for further promo on *Propaganda*, making a televised appearance on *Don Kirshner's Rock Concert*, filmed at New York's Beacon Theater, playing 'Something For the Girl With Everything', 'Talent Is An Asset', 'Hasta Mañana Monsieur', 'Thank God It's Not Christmas', 'B.C.' and 'Here In Heaven'.

Hewlett was delighted that, even with the personnel changes, the band were performing well. "Sparks were hot by that point. Just look at the Don Kirshner show. They were playing all the time. They were all good. Dinky was the machine behind it. He was a fantastic drummer."

Round the various TV studios, Sparks saw and made friends, as Trevor White says: "We were doing one TV show and I watched Abba.

107

Afterwards, the girls came up to us and asked us if we were in Sparks and they told us how much they liked our music. I thought that was something I'd keep with me forever."

With a year that concluded with three Top 20 singles and a potential foothold in the US, it was decided that the next album would really be targeted towards America. Ron and Russell took a break and considered their next move. It was now time for the brothers to show what they could *really* do.

Chapter Eight
Just Almost Overcooked: *Indiscreet*

"The versifying of Ron Mael introduced a new style of pop poetry and the scattershot pace of Russell's vocals sounded like someone running out of a burning house."

Morrissey, 2007

"Tony's really affable – the combination of Ron and Russell meeting him was when it went off the wall a bit."

Trevor White, 2009

Given that cinema had influenced Sparks' work so greatly and that the group had been creating quite a visual stir, it was altogether appropriate that the Maels should wish to make a move into film. Jacques Tati and Sparks. Art-rock meets art-house. It was a thrilling proposition that just could have happened. Tati was one of the avatars of French comic film. Born of Russian parents, the young Jacques Tatischeff impressed his friends by being an accomplished mime. After a successful feature-length debut, *Jour De Fête*, in 1949, he introduced the world to his creation, Monsieur Hulot.

Hulot was a bumbling, well-meaning everyman, respectful but not stupid, at odds with the world in which he lived. This fundamental joke was continually magnified throughout the first three Hulot films. In 1953's *Les Vacances De M. Hulot*, he is increasingly riled by a loud American, who has colonised the blissful Brittany beach at which they are both holidaying. In 1958's *Mon Oncle,* it is the modernism of life with which he comes into gentle battle.

By 1967's *Play Time*, what went on in one house in *Mon Oncle* had by now permeated an entire city; the dislocation and alienation caused by the things designed to make our lives easier is written as large as the fake skyscrapers Tati had painstakingly constructed for the film.

However, as he grew older and wearier, Tati was still developing the ultimate Hulot adventure of them all, *Confusion*. In what seemed to be a never-ending cycle of pleas for fundraising, Tati held to his vision of directing the film in which Hulot, increasingly dwarfed by his circumstance, would be written out early – possibly killed. The action would then centre on a television director and technician stringing together a series of visual puns and strange soundtracks. Tati had struggled with his masterwork since 1969, after the ambitious, widescreen *Play Time* collapsed at the French box office. Although diverted by his 1971 Netherlands-funded *Trafic, Confusion* was on the agenda when Tati encountered Sparks in 1975.

Confusion began as an idea for a television series in 1969. The project was given a further lease of life when, while Tati was touring what was to become his final film, *Parade*, in 1974, writer and broadcaster David Frost's David Paradine Productions announced it would back the film. To give it a contemporary edge, it would have cameo roles from a variety of current celebrities. James Harding, writing in *Jacques Tati: Frame By Frame*, suggested that "Tati prepared a scenario in which he made concessions to satisfy potential backers: he would have guest stars as a means of ensuring wider distribution." In early 1975 Sparks would have fitted that bill perfectly with their European sensibilities and star rating.

Ron, Russell and Tati were introduced by Peter Zumsteg, who was coordinating Island's promo and marketing activity in continental Europe. Working out of St Peter's Square and a small office in Zurich, Zumsteg was a colourful character who thought that Tati would be enchanted by

Sparks' left-of-centre approach. A meeting was set up between them at the Paris Hilton.

Peter Zumsteg: "We'd spent a lot of time together. I knew where Ron and Russell were at and what they were interested in. At the time it was very difficult to find out how you could contact people like Jacques Tati. I'd been phoning friends and friends of friends in the business. Finally, I managed to talk to his assistant, Marie-France. We managed to organise a lunch meeting. Tati walked in, just like the guy out of his movie, like he was M. Hulot."

Zumsteg "had thought there were similarities in sensibilities between Tati's world view and ours", Ron said in 2006. "We were under no illusions as to the relative genius of Tati versus Sparks, but we kept our mouths shut and a meeting was set up."

Surprisingly, the whole band were also invited. "I was familiar with Jacques Tati's films," Trevor White recalls. "Ron and Russell were ensconced with him, making plans."

The meeting was weirder still for John Hewlett – he realised he knew Tati's assistant, Marie-France Siegler, from cycling with her while in France years previously, although not making her connection with Tati.

On March 15, a press release was sent out with an accompanying photo of the French legend with Sparks and Zumsteg.

"Comic Genius Jacques Tati has joined with Sparks' creative sparkplugs Ron and Russell Mael for a major motion picture, tentatively titled *Confusion*, and planned for filming later this year, with Tati and the Maels co-starring. Oscar winner Tati has been developing the script in Paris, with continuing consultation from the Maels, and he'll also direct. Sparks likely will perform the *Confusion* title tune, to be written by Ron Mael."

A series of meetings happened throughout the year, culminating in a Swedish television show on which all three appeared. Tati explained to the brothers the scope of his idea: visual puns such as characters leaving the frame of the film mid-dialogue, colours running through the frame and out-of-context sound effects being deployed. Tati seemed obsessed with exposing the artifice of motion pictures. This had, of course, been done before, especially in 1952's *Singing In The Rain,* but this enterprise was to be more Brechtian and discomfiting.

As if to underline Sparks' desire to work with Tati, Ron Mael was quick to put a 'Confusion' theme song together, which was delivered as something of a goodwill gesture and statement of intent. However, the project simply ebbed away. As Ron stated in *The Sparks Guide Book,* "Soon our meetings with Jacques Tati occurred less and less frequently. Perhaps there were financial problems. Perhaps there were health problems. We never knew. Finally sometime late in 1975, our meetings stopped."

Sparks never did realise their dream of appearing in an art-house film. The missed opportunity is one that weighed heavy on the brothers. Ron was later to reflect, "How ironic that after 30 years as a musician, my sole regret is not being able to have appeared in a French film, a Tati film."

Tati himself continued trying to raise funding, and died in 1982 with the project still to be realised.

But were Sparks pop or were they art? This dichotomy was epitomised by the February 15, 1975 edition of UK teen mag *Jackie.* At a time when the Maels desired to work with Jacques Tati and stretch out their art, they were in the pages of the teeny press alongside David Essex and Suzi Quatro talking about Valentine's Day. "That's the most fun day of the whole school year," Russell said. "Over here, it's different, because you don't sign them," Ron added. "That's no fun – it doesn't take any courage! In America, everyone knows who's sent the card, so you're really committed."

On the artistic side, the Maels knew that they had stretched the *Kimono My House* formula as far as it could possibly go with *Propaganda* so for their next Island album they wanted to do something different and more experimental. Muff Winwood, who was very much up for a change in direction, thought his old friend Tony Visconti would be superb for the job. With Visconti sharing the characteristic of being a US exile in the UK and with their knowledge of UK pop history, Ron and Russell were eager as well. John Hewlett knew of Visconti through his work with Hewlett's former John's Children bandmate Marc Bolan and through Visconti's then-wife, Mary Hopkin, as Hewlett had dealt with her publishing during his time at Apple.

The transplanted boy from Brooklyn was one of the most fashionable producers of the early Seventies for his work with Bolan and T. Rex and had recently renewed his professional relationship with David Bowie, having just returned from Philadelphia where he had produced *Young Americans*. Visconti had also worked with acts as diverse as Gentle Giant and Wings and was later to work with Irish hard rockers Thin Lizzy.

David Betteridge: "We wanted to do the right thing for them [Sparks] and us. Tony Visconti had a great pedigree. His track record was such that if you didn't bow, you certainly nodded your head to the man."

John Hewlett: "I'd known Tony for a long time and thought he was cool. He took [Sparks] further down a road that took them away from rock. Ron and Russell thought, because he had done Bowie and Bolan, that he was going to do wonders for them."

Tony Visconti: "I remember 'This Town Ain't Big Enough For Both Of Us'. That's when I first became aware of Sparks and it had an amazing effect on me. I couldn't believe that this pop record was so well made. No one had ever done anything like that before... Muff summoned me to Island and told me that I would be a good producer for them. I think the world of Muff as a producer but he told me that he had one trick – getting a good sound on the instruments and then double-tracking everything. That's pretty much how most people made records in those days so he knew he couldn't do what they wanted. It was out of his realm. He didn't work with string players and brass players and all that. He gladly handed the baton to me. That decade of my life was just so busy. I was asked to do Hall & Oates around the same time but I just didn't have the time."

Visconti and the Maels hit it off immediately: "It was so refreshing to talk to them because they weren't like a rock'n'roll band. They were very cultured and that's pretty much the way Bowie is too. Russell and Ron were so articulate and intelligent and knew exactly what they wanted."

After *Propaganda*, *Indiscreet* was to be a remarkably complex record. "We wanted to get more outside instrumentation," Ron told *Trouser Press* in 1982. "Tony Visconti knew about scoring. We had done two albums with the band format and wanted to elaborate on that more, which isn't necessarily a good idea. We had a lot of songs, but I don't recall the recording taking that long."

On March 17, Ron and Russell began recording in Visconti's home studio in Shepherd's Bush, west London. It was one of the first domestic

113

recording facilities in the UK as Ron recalled, "Tony had a studio downstairs the size of a phone booth. There was no room for a bass amp, so bass speakers had to be built into the walls. It was incredibly tight, but it gave you the feeling you could concentrate without anyone knowing what you were doing."

The brothers were impressed by what the producer brought to the table. Things such as him playing the bass part to 'The Man Who Sold The World' just prior to recording 'Happy Hunting Ground' had the brothers in awe. There was a feeling something special was in the air and that a masterpiece was about to be created.

Tony Visconti: "That's what we set out to do. I knew it was going to be stunning in the end and I kept questioning the guys 'Are you sure you want to go *all the way* in that direction?' and they told me that it was the band that was always holding them back. They were probably quite envious of the way The Beatles and George Martin worked post-*Revolver*, where you hear all these radically different sounds on one artist's album. Russell and Ron were looking for that kind of a relationship and they couldn't get that from Muff. They told me point blank they couldn't get it from the members of their band either. They really needed a person like myself to add the things that they could hear in their heads but we were trying to make it damn good and interesting and, of course, pop art."

Visconti brought all of his production values with him. "Whenever I make an album, I'm always aware that my contribution to culture has to be a high one and has to endure. I always try to do that with every artist I work with. For me, it was so rewarding to be given permission to do that. The [Maels] didn't have an idea of how to write for strings but they knew the sound that they wanted. They would describe the sound very well to me. With 'Under The Table With Her' they said it's got to be a Mozart string arrangement. I took my cues from them."

The album, recorded at Ramport and AIR as well as Visconti's studio, had been largely demoed by Ron first, with Visconti working with fully sketched-out material. "We never took a lot of time in the studio because we always went in with the songs," Ron said. "The ones that sound complicated, like 'Get In The Swing' or 'Looks Looks Looks', were just Tony writing out charts."

114

Indiscreet was recorded at the absolute summit of Sparks' commerciality hence Island indulged the extravagant budget involved.

Tony Visconti: "We hired a lot of session musicians, which was very expensive. A majority of the tracks on the album had some extra musician from the outside; either the string section or a big band just for 'Looks Looks Looks'." Normal Seventies studio procedure would have been to maximise the use of these external players on a variety of the sessions. Not so with *Indiscreet*. Says Visconti, "You could have made an entire pop album in those days for what 'Get In The Swing' and 'Looks, Looks, Looks' cost."

It would be the final time the brothers were given *carte blanche* in the studio until they built their own in the 80s. There is a picture taken at AIR of Ron and Russell, both wearing fetching knitwear, deep in the process of recording. "I would say that Russell and Ron were enjoying themselves immensely," Visconti says. "They were smiling all the time. They were longing to make this art-pop kind of album. We would just inspire each other and often they would produce me and I would be playing recorders or the stylophone. We just had a good time. They were so happy and so thrilled to even just have someone write those notes for them.

"There was a bass line to 'Hospitality On Parade'. It started out as just the bass setting on the stylophone. We were using every trick that we could think of to make an artistically very creative, different album. There was never really a bad day."

John Hewlett was around, allowing his charges their head, keeping out of Visconti's way. Similarly, in his A&R role, and as previous producer, Muff Winwood kept a distant yet watchful eye on proceedings.

Tony Visconti: "Muff was amazingly supportive. He just stayed away and listened to [the album]. He corrected it when it was finished. We thought we went a little too far but he could see that it had a few hits."

White, Hampton and Diamond were not so sure about the prevailing mood of creativity. In a 1991 interview Russell said, "On *Indiscreet*, we wanted to allow each song's instrumentation and arrangement to be dictated by the song rather than our obligation to use a four-piece rock band just because we had a four-piece rock band."

Ian Hampton: "*Indiscreet* was a different kettle of fish from *Propaganda*. Tony's input to that was very powerful. It started to feel a bit like the brothers and the band. There were several tunes we had absolutely nothing to do with. There was just no place for bass guitar and drums. Visconti was a revelation, he was so clever. I mean, 'Looks Looks Looks', he heard it a couple of times, went off and scored all the parts overnight, got the orchestra in the next morning and bang, it was down."

Trevor White: "Tony's really affable – the combination of Ron and Russell meeting him was when it went off the wall a bit. We were no longer as necessary as we were before. It didn't really require a rock band; it could have all been done with studio musicians … I wasn't too keen on a lot of it. When you are very involved you get to like a lot of it, but I did think it was too much of a jump from *Propaganda*. A lot of *Indiscreet* was simply off the wall. It was very experimental. Tony Visconti was there to do what the [Maels] wanted and gave them a free hand. Lots of people like it – it was just a bit too quick for me."

Dinky Diamond was the most discontented: "He was a great guy but he wasn't happy," Visconti says. "He was like a straight-up rock drummer and he wanted it to be more of a rock album. 'Looks Looks Looks' was the first time he didn't play drums on an Island Sparks record. That was a real insult to him. But we needed that arrangement, so it really made sense to hire these old British jazz musicians to emulate the Count Basie style. I don't think Dinky could've pulled it off but he was not too pleased. The other two were fine with it, they just went along with the ride."

The lack of contributions from the other members has been a little overplayed. They are there, on the majority of the album, although *Indiscreet* is certainly the start of the path that ultimately led to 1977's *Introducing*, featuring just Ron and Russell and session men. What *is* missing is any conventional soloing, but a traditional rock thrust propels the majority of the album.

Tony Visconti: "It's not a straight-up rock album but when it goes rock, I made those guys shine. They really played very well."

It's been said that Dinky took it upon himself to complain to Winwood that *Indiscreet* did not sound like a Sparks album – that it was too far out, not rock'n'roll enough, something that Hampton refutes.

During the sessions, there was a lack of socialising. A lot of this was to do with Ron and Russell's eating habits – or lack of them. "You couldn't really have dinner with them," says Visconti, laughing. "They only took one meal a day and it was kind of fetish food, it had a theme. They don't eat rice, they don't eat breakfast or lunch, so a lot of time on *Indiscreet* we might get some sandwiches and Russell and Ron wouldn't have anything. I wouldn't mind having a bag of chips and a pint with the band, but you'd never see Russell and Ron do that. They'd have to have a menu out of a restaurant picked from the Egon Ronay book. It was very funny."

Visconti was impressed with Ron's ability to visualise an idea: "I think it's a shame Ron never properly studied music, because he could probably be a killer string arranger. I felt I had the kind of relationship with the [brothers] that I also established with Bowie. Bowie loves to throw anything at me and asks for the sound he hears in his head. I used to take it for granted in the Seventies that there were a lot of people like that to work with. Sadly that kind of genius, I would say *British* (and I class the Maels in that) genius, has gone. Nobody thinks at that level any more."

With the music sounding grandiose and different, the album sleeve would need to maintain the exacting standards set by *Kimono My House* and *Propaganda* and be, naturally, high concept. This would take not one, but two photographers. For the front sleeve, Richard Creamer, who had worked with Sparks on tour, realised the witty image of the brothers escaping from the wreckage of a light aircraft on a suburban street.

"There's a small airport in Burbank, Los Angeles," Russell explained in 2008, "and, at least at the time, they had an area where they stored planes that had been in mishaps, so somebody contacted them and we set up a sort of fake suburbia." (Creamer also took the inside sleeve shot.)

The back cover picture was taken by Gered Mankowitz. "I was a little upset that I didn't do the front shot and Richard Creamer was pretty pissed off he didn't get asked to do the back cover," Mankowitz says today. "I loved the idea of the front cover. Everything about it was funny; a great image for the title, and that Russell would survive an airplane crash with just a sore leg."

The son of author and screenwriter Wolf Mankowitz, by the mid-Seventies Gered was one of the most well-known names in UK rock photography. Described as "expensive and a little artsy-fartsy but he's good" by Mickie Most, he'd worked as a freelance from the mid–Sixties and his pictures of The Rolling Stones and Jimi Hendrix in his military uniform were already iconic. Mankowitz had a long association with Island Records. "I started working with Island in 1963. I did a lot of stuff for Chris Blackwell: Millie, Owen Gray, Jackie Edwards and The Spencer Davis Group. The relationship with Island was one I valued greatly."

In May 1975, Mankowitz was in LA shooting for AGI, a manufacturer of album covers. He found Sparks a barn-like studio in Hollywood in which to take stills. The background – of a swimming pool and outbuildings – was from a company that rented scenery to movie studios. The whole session took an afternoon, and Mankowitz was impressed by the band's professionalism and just how seriously the Maels treated their visual side.

Gered Mankowitz: "When you work with inspired people you suddenly realise you can go off on a tangent and people will consider it and think how it can be made to work. We really did – no pun intended – spark off each other. I loved their wit. They wanted a complementary image that featured the entire band."

In another iconic image, Russell as the country gentleman on horseback is being escorted by his servant (Ron) to a swimming pool party. Although Russell was somewhat apprehensive of being on horseback, he treated the job like the possible former child model he may have been.

Gered Mankowitz: "My assistant Frances found the horse. It was fully trained. The trainer was just off camera and his job was to make sure the horse's ears were pricked up and that it didn't look like a nag."

This wasn't the only shot Mankowitz took that day; there is an amusing out-take of the group all dressed as LAPD officers, save for Russell, who is sitting on his horse, smirking. "The police outfits were really cool. I think the police image would have ultimately been better on the back as it was more American," muses Hewlett, who'd worked with Mankowitz coincidentally while in John's Children, "and that, after all, was what we were supposed to be going for."

The sleeves for the first three Island albums are witty, stylised and suited the times perfectly. They have many admirers. "They're great album covers," says Duran Duran's Nick Rhodes. "That was the other thing that appealed to me about Sparks. They had their visuals together. A lot of things from that period have dated in a bizarre and sometimes unkind way – theirs haven't. The sleeves still look fantastic."

With the *Indiscreet* sessions completed, the album was slated for an autumn release.* Conscious that half a year had passed since the last Sparks releases (and bearing in mind that, back then, that was a lifetime in pop), Island readied the single 'Get In The Swing' for July release.

'Hospitality On Parade', a fantastic tale of American imperialism on the eve of the bicentennial, is one of the great opening songs of the Seventies. Containing a genuine swing and punch, especially when the band kicks in, Russell's vocal inflection on the word 'king' is possibly the singer's greatest moment in a career of show-stopping vocals. Even when too stylised, the album is not without charm – 'Happy Hunting Ground' marries fabulous synths with muscular rock, while on 'Without Using Hands' – a tale that brings together lecherous men, naughty school boys and terrorism, culminating in a Pythonesque joke – Visconti's unparalleled studio prowess comes to the fore.

'Pineapple' is another song that wouldn't be out of place in *Cabaret*, one of the very few that praises, um, pineapple. It is Russell's favourite self-written song. "After all these years, to my knowledge no one else has come up with a better song extolling the virtues of the tropical fruit he says." If 'It Ain't 1918' is just over the top, 'T★ts' is superb.

"We were sure the English store chain WH Smith would ban 'Tits'," Russell said. "They would ban something with the word 'drat' in the title. So we called it 'T★ts' — real hard to figure out." The tale of a man driven to drink by the fact that his wife's breasts were no longer his sole preserve demonstrates how Ron's writing was far outside the pop milieu.

---

* There was additional material recorded for the album that later turned up on the reissue of *Big Beat*. Mary Hopkin, Visconti's wife at the time, can be heard as Jacqueline Kennedy on the B-side 'The Wedding Of Jacqueline Kennedy To Russell Mael'. She also recorded a version of 'Never Turn Your Back On Mother Earth', which was finally released on her 2007 rarities collection, *Valentine*.

So for all that expensive studio time, high-class artwork, laminated gatefold sleeve and considerable press push, what is there for the listener? If it's doo-wop, brass-driven glam you're after, then you're OK. If it's something more in step with Sparks' previous releases, you're probably not. A flawed masterpiece would be the politest way to describe it. It's undeniable that the Maels and Visconti went to town with a stylistic toolbox; scooting from the chamber music of 'Under The Table With Her' to the stomp of 'How Are You Getting Home'.

Indiscreet drew decidedly mixed reviews: Chas De Whalley, writing in the *NME* (dated October 11, 1975) called it "one of the worst albums I have heard in a long, long time" and that "The Maels and their travelling circus are doing more than anyone else towards stripping rock 'n' roll of what is left of its meaning and thus turning it into an empty image of itself."

Richard Cromelin in *Phonograph Record* was more approving, suggesting that, "Thanks to a production approach which digs a wide gulf between it and previous Sparks albums, [*Indiscreet*] could well win over some new fans for the band, in that their frantic roller-coaster style has given way to a more spacious, sedate and generally palatable sound."

Jon Savage, who'd been a huge fan of the previous two albums, was not enamoured: "Maybe because they had created such a complete world that once you had a couple of doses of it that was enough."

Bob Stanley, music journalist and Saint Etienne musician, said that, "With *Indiscreet*, the wheels fell off as the Maels delved into Gilbert and Sullivan and flapper ditties a little too deeply. The kids didn't need another Hinge and Bracket."

Despite such opinions *Indiscreet* is an album that begs repeated listening, reinforcing the great ('Hospitality On Parade,' 'Get In The Swing') and making the challenging moments ('It Ain't 1918', 'Under The Table With Her') more so. With the next listen it will change again. For all its faults – and there are several – *Indiscreet* is a cornucopia of ever-giving pleasure that is one of the brothers' most grandiose statements.

But, to its detractors, it did seem that Sparks were creating a musical edifice as wafer-thin as the studio scenery they stood in front of.

One known Sparks supporter was delighted by the album however. "I worked with Morrissey in 2005 in Rome," Tony Visconti says. "We were talking about *Indiscreet*. He asked me loads of questions about it. It's one of his favourite albums and he said that he'd lost his copy years previously. I was walking through Rome next day and bought him a copy. He was almost in tears and said 'I haven't had my own copy for so long'."

Morrissey later expounded on his love for the record in the foreword to Visconti's book, *The Brooklyn Boy*.

"Either the Maels, or Tony Visconti, were asking: 'What can we show them that is new?" he wrote. "From a tipsy teatime waltz to unstoppable violins, the pace pulverised the listener, and Russell's mouth seemed unable to close. There are so many latitude and longitude instrumental textures that the masterstroke was just *almost* overcooked."

The album's rich nature would also provide a huge inspiration to future Sparks members: "I love *Indiscreet*," guitarist Jim Wilson exclaims. "As much as I love the edge of the two previous albums they just went crazy with orchestration and took the songwriting to another level. It's real inventive – 'Without Using Hands' and 'How Are You Getting Home', I've got so many different favourites. It's like The Beatles' 'White Album'."

Much later, *Mojo* magazine's website posted this assessment: "Ron Mael proves himself one of the most overlooked lyricists in rock, falling somewhere between the narrative style of Ray Davies and the mordant wit of Cole Porter; in fact... [it] could even be Noël Coward if it weren't for the bit where the hotel manager's hands are blown off in a bomb attack. In Ron's world, everyday scenarios and facets of the human condition are played out in a surreal, disturbingly comic fashion. *Indiscreet*? Perhaps. Audacious? Absolutely."

With all its fanfare, the album reached number 18 in the UK album listings and spent just four weeks on the charts. Unlike its predecessor, it failed to reach the US chart at all.

David Betteridge: "I didn't get involved – they had Muff and John there, so I stood well back. I think by that time, we'd seen there were a few problems. We'd had a couple of good albums and as Sparks weren't really an Island act in the real sense, we started to feel we may have had our run with that one. I don't think we said it out loud; they'd lost the flush of success and that was that. I thought they went off on a path that probably the punter that was buying their records couldn't see."

121

Russell's summation of the album on its 2006 reissue demonstrates how close the brothers are to their work, especially those they deem especially important: "Oddly there were one or two criticisms along the lines of 'self-indulgent'. In our world you, as an artist, indulge yourself. We would say 'Yes, it's very self-indulgent! Thank you for noticing.'"

Although Island was starting to look at the law of diminishing returns, there was another substantial tour to support the album; after a short Scandinavian jaunt, the trek began in the UK on October 15 in Newcastle, ending at Croydon's Fairfield Halls on November 9 – the last time the UK was to see this version of Sparks.

Throughout the tour the same divide was seen between the 'heads' and the 'screamers' in the audience that Ian Hampton had previously identified. "It was really weird; the disparity between the lyrics we were singing and the young girls who were throwing themselves at us," Russell said in 2003. "The lyrics of teeny bands were not usually as substantive as ours – singing about Einstein – there was a lot of stuff going on lyrically. There's a great old video shot at our gig at Croydon – the stage was inundated by girls in a rugby scrum – I'm singing something like 'Talent Is An Asset' and there's 10 girls on top of me who are not really getting what we're on about." In the film, a palpably nervous Russell's calls for calm ("OK, we'll do one more tune for you, OK, but, but... for everyone's safety I think we should have a little restraint in the hall, OK") and vocal dropouts while being attacked give the listener some idea of the chaos of a British Sparks show at this time.

Chart-wise, 'Get In the Swing' had reached 27 in the UK; the follow-up single, 'Looks, Looks, Looks', reached one place higher. Whereas the *Kimono* singles had been Top 10 and the *Propaganda* 45s Top 20, Sparks were now a Top 30 act.

Trevor White: "The singles weren't doing as well but, in a way, if you were a total singles band that would be a problem. After *Kimono My House* I think we headed towards being an albums band in the old-fashioned sense, so the charts, for us, weren't that much of a problem. A lot of other things were going well. If it was going slightly down in

122

Britain, on the continent we were growing. When we played anywhere on the continent we had a great reception."

Just before the group set off on tour, their old support act, Queen, released a single called 'Bohemian Rhapsody'. It had been written in May that year, allegedly inspired by 10cc's groundbreaking 'Une Nuit A Paris' from *The Original Soundtrack*. 'Bohemian Rhapsody' was a record that moved from heavy camp to heavy metal in little over five minutes. With its tempo shifts, strange operatics and grandeur, at one stroke, there seemed little need for Sparks in Britain any more.

Chapter Nine

Throw Her Away (And Get A New One): *Big Beat*

"When it came to piquant takes on pop music, I was not a novitiate."
Rupert Holmes, 2009

Towards the end of the 1975 UK and US tour, Ron and Russell told John Hewlett that they were breaking up the band in favour of using American musicians. Hewlett was shocked and tried to persuade the brothers otherwise. However the Maels were unshakeable in their conviction that getting an American sound would finally enable them to take on their home market. "I have a major regret that I hadn't been more forceful in telling them not to do it," Hewlett says today. With their next two albums, breaking America would become Sparks' main objective.

After the occasionally over-manicured *Indiscreet*, the Maels knew another change of direction was essential. For some reason, they turned to muscular proto-metal, a style that recalled the early Bearsville albums, only with the overt weirdness removed.

"We got sick of England," Ron Mael said in 1982. "The weather was disgusting and we tired of the provincial atmosphere. What at first is quaint later becomes really annoying. As much as we liked the music scene there, we had to move back to Los Angeles to defrost."

There was also the nagging issue of exactly who Sparks were – the Maels liked the hush and reverence of American audiences as opposed to the screaming Brit teens. "Someone like Supertramp just had the music," Ron said in 1993. "They were as ugly as sin and in the long term that's probably the best thing." In the US there was no such confusion, as outside of the cognoscenti, few were aware of Sparks.

Columbia had picked up Sparks' contract in America, so finally a stable home for the group's releases with good nationwide distribution was in place. "I think the Maels simply wanted to use their return to the US to head in a new direction for a new label," suggests Rupert Holmes, who was to play a big part in Sparks' career over the following year.

As the Maels had done three years previously when jettisoning the original American band, it was time to do the same with the English model. Hewlett broke the news to White, Hampton and Diamond while in San Francisco.

Trevor White: "It was very strange. We were told after the show in our hotel bar. When it's as stark as that you just don't take it in. We didn't see Ron and Russell at all. John's hands were tied; it was a pretty typical Ron and Russell thing to do at the time. 'Let somebody else tell them, we'll disappear'. They'd done it before." The guitarist felt saddened as he thought the unit still had a great deal of potential ahead of them. "I just thought it was really silly. They'd gotten to a point where they were well-known, wanted to do something else and thought 'We don't need these people.'"

Conversely, Ian Hampton feels it was all happily accepted and that everybody knew it had come to a natural end: "I think we knew our number was up. We were out in LA with Ron and Russell and we discussed it quite openly, they said that the time was now. I said, 'I think you're right, we all feel the same', and 'I don't really see a point in continuing as we are.'"

So that was that. The three British players returned to the UK and hung together as a unit for a short while, cutting demos at Island's Basing Street Studios. Adrian Fisher joined them and after a week's rehearsal, the quartet recorded four tracks with *Kimono My House* and *Propaganda* engineer Richard Digby Smith.*

Beyond that, Hampton became a much sought-after session player. "I worked with Elizabeth Barraclough at Bearsville [where his old Jook bandmate Ian Kimmett now worked] and toured with her, but her album never sold." Coincidentally, another player on the Barraclough session was none other than Todd Rundgren. "I'd never met Todd before. As soon as he walked in the room, we talked about Sparks and reflected on how small the world was."

In 1976 White released a solo single on Island, re-recording the Jook track 'Crazy Kids' backed with 'Movin' In The Right Direction', featuring Martin Gordon on bass and Chris Townson on drums. Two years later, they would have called it power pop. Sadly, it sank without trace.

Trevor White: "We then worked with a guy called Mac Poole, who I knew through Ian Kimmett. We cut a reggae track, 'Without Your Woman', but it didn't really agree with Mr Blackwell. His whole thing was having authentic Jamaican reggae bands on his label. He wafted in from Jamaica, listened to what was going on and didn't like it."

Within a day or so, Hewlett had more bad news for White. Although David Betteridge had liked what he heard, White's solo career at Island was not to go any further. "It should have been a longer term development situation," Hewlett says today. "[Trevor] was as interesting as Jess Roden or some of the things that did get signed to Island at that point."

White ended up in Radio Stars, the band that was increasingly becoming a convalescence home for people who'd worked with John Hewlett, having both Martin Gordon and Andy Ellison in it.

"I really enjoyed my time with Sparks," says White. "It was a blast. I enjoyed playing. To be playing 24/7, which we were, was wonderful. If you weren't in the studio, you were rehearsing, if you weren't rehearsing, you were touring. It was just a shame it stopped. Everyone could have made a lot of money".

---

* The tracks, 'I See The Light', 'Adrian's Boogie', 'If It's Love That You Want' and 'Shot From A Gun' remain unreleased after Island decided not to pursue the project.

The player who took it the hardest was Norman 'Dinky' Diamond, by now the only constant in the group since Sparks' first UK sessions in autumn 1973.

Tony Visconti: "Dinky liked the trappings of being in a band. He used to hang around the Island offices, sit behind any empty desk and pick up phones and look at the paperwork and all that. He eventually settled down with one of the secretaries there." That secretary was Lee Packham, who'd previously worked for The Spencer Davis Group and had been a constant in the Sparks circle since the brothers relocated to Britain in 1973. The couple got married, but were later to part.

Diamond, who was frequently called 'Double' Diamond, after the Ind Coope ale that was phased out in 2003, did like a drop. All the way back to *Sparks Flashes* in '74, Fleury's gossipy titbits revealed, "Dinky, a bit thrown back by his doctor's advice that too much alcohol consumption is bad for his kidney, has been seen spiking his orange juice with pineapple juice."

Trevor White: "Dinky was in a world of his own. He was one of those guys who could get a job wherever he wanted. When he got off the drink, he'd apply and get jobs; selling cars, garden logistics, sending trucks all over the world. He was a very bright guy, but something wasn't right there. His ex-partner would say the same thing; people would ask why she was with him and she'd reply it was never dull."

The drummer drifted out of music and ended up in some unusual places. "Me and my wife were taking our nephews out for the day at Thorpe Park," Muff Winwood recalled, "and we were on this paddle steamer ride. The captain bounded up to me, calling my name excitedly." It was none other than Dinky.

John Hewlett: "OK, Dinky drank, but if he was told not to, he wouldn't. Losing Dinky was such a mistake – that was like The Who losing Keith Moon. You can't really replace someone like that."

Diamond took his own life in 2005. Russell and Ron were deeply upset and sent a wreath to the funeral. Their website carried the message: "We are very saddened by the news of Dinky Diamond's death. We hold fond memories of working with Dinky and of his contribution to several of our albums during the Seventies. Our hearts go out to his family and friends."

Working with Fleury, Hewlett was ready to oversee Sparks' next stage, although he became increasingly angry at how the Maels had let key players go. He feels that they should have embraced certain idiosyncrasies and moved forward. "You can't expect all parents to love every child the same – some kids are a pain in the arse. With a band, the main thing, though, is that you stay together; you love one another because of who you are. There was a great band and it ended because Ron and Russell were not good parents."

The story of *Big Beat* starts in England, returns to LA and ends in New York. Released in October 1976, the album has always been a problematic addition to the Sparks catalogue. Its description in *The Great Rock And Roll Discography* – "an expensively disastrous attempt at sub-metal posturing" – encapsulates the populist view. Caught between pomp and hard rock, unlike its immediate predecessor, *Big Beat* travels on pretty linear tracks, given that they are ones of boundless irony and frequent sarcasm.

John Hewlett: "On paper *Big Beat* was completely on the money. Being in New York at the time of punk, it was very much Ronnie and Russell unleashed."

The original pre-production discussions had Mick Ronson to produce and play guitar on the album. "We got along with him really well," Russell said in 2006. "He actually played along on all the songs when we rehearsed it. We have some really bad quality cassette recordings of the rehearsals." Unfortunately, nothing was to come of the arrangement. Ronson, who, at that point had been working with Bob Dylan as part of the Rolling Thunder Revue, could not commit. The cassette, according to Ron, "sounds twice as good as the album – partially from [Ronson's] playing and partially just the way the album turned out."

The brothers needed both a guitarist and a producer. As a commendable alternative, the Maels hired Jeff Salen, of the band Tuff Darts, and Rupert Holmes was selected as producer.

Much has been made about the strange choice of Holmes, who on first glance appeared too much of an AOR/MOR producer to work with the Maels. "I was asked to [produce] by CBS Records," says

Holmes. "[Holmes' production partner] Jeffrey Lesser and myself were actually quite a logical choice at that point in time. We'd become *de facto* staff producers for CBS, and we were accustomed to working with idiosyncratic and 'picturesque' artists who were not mainstream rock 'n' roll. Like Sparks, we were Americans who felt at home in England – in point of fact, I had been born in England and still had family in Cheshire."

Holmes was an interesting character and a fairly unusual artist. His first album, *Widescreen*, had been selected as one of 1974's 10 best LPs by the *New York Daily News*. Holmes had no permanent band and created a different sound for each song on an album, doing his own arranging, orchestrating and conducting.

In 1975 the BBC playlisted his single 'Our National Pastime', a tale of an oafish bloke trying to pick up a girl at a baseball game, singing his seduction to the tune of 'The Star-Spangled Banner' with a reggae beat. Instead of an instrumental solo, it featured dialogue between Holmes and the woman in question. He was also known for a Beatles pastiche, 'I Don't Want To Hold Your Hand', which, Holmes claims, "George Martin had been generous enough to call better than the original."

CBS asked Holmes and Lesser to produce Orchestra Luna. "I'm not saying that Orchestra Luna was exactly like Sparks in sound," says Holmes, "and certainly they were very different lyrically; Richard Kinscherf (later Rick Berlin) wrote lyrics that were sexually ambiguous at the least, sometimes pixie-ish in nature. The songs did not have Ron Mael's fabulous irony, scathing wit, or terrific, hypnotic grooves. But had Orchestra Luna opened for Sparks on a tour of the UK or USA, no one would have found it an odd coupling."

It was around this point that the A&R teams of Columbia and Epic merged, and the latter's slightly left-of-centre artists came together with the more mainstream acts of the former. The extravagant style of *Widescreen* had impressed Jack Nitzsche (the man who might have produced Halnelson had the lights not failed) who was working as an arranger with Barbra Streisand. Streisand was impressed by Holmes' talent and, with Lesser, he arranged, conducted and co-produced her *Lazy Afternoon*.

130

Holmes and Lesser moved to London to record Dutch band Sailor, leading to the hits 'A Glass Of Champagne' (on which Holmes plays the piano solo) and 'Girls, Girls, Girls'.

Rupert Holmes: "Sailor was certainly nothing like Sparks, but I venture that the hammering rhythm and oom-pah bass of 'A Glass of Champagne' as well as the slightly-skiffled swing of 'Girls, Girls, Girls' would not have seemed at all out of place on a Sparks album of that period. You can actually imagine Russell's voice singing the opening verses of either song."

Holmes and Lesser were asked by CBS and Don Ellis (whose name appears in the 'Special Thanks' on *Big Beat*) to produce Sparks. Holmes was aware of Sparks, but only from his time in the UK. "I lived in London and Oxfordshire for extended periods of time while producing Sailor and Strawbs, and so I caught Sparks on the telly more than once. I was very much aware of their cleverly titled albums and songs, their unique look, and Ron's sublimely ironic lyrics. I was, of course, also fascinated by Ron's wonderful 'act' at the keyboard, which I came to believe was a cleverly inventive guise used to mask his innate shyness."

The first thing the new team were asked to handle was, ironically in Holmes' case, a lush production of The Beatles' 'I Want To Hold Your Hand', which Russell wanted to record as a duet with Marianne Faithfull. It was intended to be a single, released on Island in the UK and a first CBS Sparks release in the US, after which the rest of the album would be recorded.

Rupert Holmes: "My memory of who initiated the idea of this duet with this particular song is dim. I thought it was Ron and Russell, or perhaps Russell and Marianne, although it might have been someone at Island Records, or maybe even Don Ellis. I know I inherited it as *a fait accompli*. Russ and Marianne. 'I Want To Hold Your Hand.' Big orchestra. And since Sparks' were enthused about such a lavish widescreen arrangement for the duet, featuring molto strings and brass, and my ability to score and conduct such grand orchestrations, my prior Streisand credits were a further plus in terms of working with the group.

"Russell in particular said he wanted the single to be big and glossy and hyper-arranged. I recall asking him if he wanted it to be 'movie big' (as in a James Bond film) or 'Broadway big,' and I believe he leaned towards the latter. Thus, I gave the chart an opening flourish somewhat in the style of a theatrical overture."

The brothers were keen to record a whole album with Faithfull. However, the pairing was hampered with problems right from the start, with Faithfull eventually withdrawing from the project.

Rupert Holmes: "Jeffrey and I never got to meet with [Marianne] or speak with her… As I started to write the chart, it was my understanding that she was going to sing it, and I wrote it with a harmony part in mind for her. By the time I finished the chart, the word was that we should do it as a solo for Russell."*

"We met with [Marianne] over a period of months," Russell said in 1982. "She was into the idea, it was a question of finding the song. She thought it was going to be one of Ron's songs, but we thought of doing 'I Want To Hold Your Hand' as a real schmaltzy ballad with us alternating verses. Rupert loved the idea. He did a score he was really excited about, but Marianne decided she didn't want to do a Beatles song because it was too close to the era she was a part of – too many bad connotations for her. Rupert liked it so much he suggested that instead of it being a Russell Mael solo project, just call it Sparks."

Marianne's former manager and lifelong confidante, Tony Calder, recalls the week in 1975 when "Marianne came in one day and said that Sparks wanted to record her… I thought it sounded interesting, so I went along to their hotel in Kensington to meet them with her. It was all a bit strange. We had some dinner and I encouraged her to do it. They had a piano in their room; Russell started singing songs. I wasn't really into it, so I left them and Marianne to get on with it. I got that 'Darling, don't leave me' look and I told her that she'd be fine, she was a big girl.

"When I next saw her, it was one of those 'I'm waiting for them to get back to me' moments. She'd obviously got the hump and walked out!"

Despite the partnership failing to happen, Calder, who has worked with a number of industry heavyweights over the years, remembers the Maels fondly. "I was amused by them. I didn't believe they were brothers

---

* Shortly after the completion of 'I Want To Hold Your Hand', Lesser and Holmes decided to part amicably, Lesser to produce the second Sailor album and Holmes to produce Sparks, both still under the pair's "Widescreen Productions" banner.

because they were so different. Not just as people, but musically. When listening to the music, Ron kept saying that space was needed – I had great respect for him because he knew all about space. For me, American records have space whereas English records don't."

As well as Holmes supplementing Ron's piano work, session drummer Alan Schwartzberg was a noticeable presence at the session, adding a solid rock impact to the otherwise lush arrangement. Holmes also enlisted Wilbur Bascomb, a particular favourite of his, whose electric bass glides around the dreamy bridge. Vincent Bell, with a unique array of foot pedals, provided guitar, Margaret Ross was on harp, and Maretha Stewart, Vivian Cherry, Cissy Houston and Tasha Thomas added the swelling backing chorus.

With its twittering strings and swooning, soulful arrangement, 'I Want To Hold Your Hand' remains one of the great anomalies in Sparks' catalogue. However, although slated for single release, it was withdrawn in the UK almost immediately. Although the remake of 'I Like Girls' was recorded with the same line-up at the same time, the B-side of the UK release was the quirky 'England', which saw the band reunited with Earle Mankey. As dour and experimental as 'I Want To Hold Your Hand' is over-egged and velvety, in one fell swoop, it dealt with all the questions the duo faced about the country that had been their home for the past two years.

New York in the summer of 1976 was a febrile, cutting edge location. The city was going broke, people were moving out to the suburbs and new wave had broken in the Bowery. Election fever gripped the city as it looked like Americans would finally get their chance to vote against Gerald Ford, the President they had never elected, and put southern Democrat Jimmy Carter into office.

The Maels entered this atmosphere with new drummer Hilly 'Boy' Michaels and bass player Salvatore 'Sal' Maida, formerly of Fleury and Hewlett protégés Milk'n'Cookies.

John Hewlett: "Milk'n'Cookies was Joseph's suggestion. [Keyboard player] Ian North was an interesting character. [Vocalist] Justin Strauss, who later did brilliantly in New York as a DJ, was there; the elements were in place. I thought the songwriting was good, but the album [the band made for Island in 1974] didn't rock my heart, and I wasn't really 100% into it." Sal had originally auditioned for Sparks back in 1973 and had gone on to play with Roxy Music.

At Holmes' suggestion, the Maels, Maida and Michaels decamped to Studio A at New York's Mediasound Studios for several intense weeks. "Mediasound was my second home for almost five years," says Holmes. "At times, I would be there from 10am until dawn…" Jeff Salen was also kept on as the album's guitarist.

Rupert Holmes: "Jeff was sort of an artistic sidebar to the album. I don't mean that in a negative way. It was simply that you had the feeling he had his own career ahead of him, so he became a kind of resident studio musician within the group. I remember wondering if he planned to tour with the band after the album was completed, and thinking that might be unlikely."

Mediasound had originally been a church, located close to the corner of 57th and Eighth Streets, and continued as a temple to music: its doorway and gorgeously tiled entrance hall might have been the entrance to an abbey.

Rupert Holmes: "Below the street were two other smaller studios, a couple of editing rooms, a mastering room, and tape storage rooms. Studio A had rafters that betrayed the room's ecclesiastical origins and that allowed rock bands to crank their Marshalls all they wanted. We would sometimes put microphones in the rafters to capture the ceiling's ambience. A flight up from Studio A were the business offices of the staff. The mixing studio was on that level as well."

The studio rarely closed. In addition to all the rock, R&B, salsa, and pop recorded there, Mediasound was where most of the music for *Sesame Street* was recorded. For years, there was a permanent session booked at 9am, with engineer Fred Christie always behind the console. Around noon, the Muppet folks would leave and the jingle crowd would come in – often then with Luther Vandross in full effect. In the evenings, it was rock 'n' roll.

Big Beat had the cards stacked against it from the very start due to the constraints imposed by CBS. Ron once described the album as a "screwy situation".

Rupert Holmes: "I honestly don't know the context of Ron's comment. I do know one aspect of the project that was highly unusual and that made the work more difficult for all of us. When I began work on it, Columbia Records had already set a release date, and it was ridiculously close at hand. They told me that they had to print the LP jacket before I'd begun work on the album or they'd miss their release date. Insanely, this meant I had to give CBS the song titles and their sequence on the album before we recorded them!"

Holmes, quite justifiably, complained to the label. "But what if we don't like the way a song turns out, or Sparks write a new song while we're recording the album? And how can I sequence an album that I've yet to hear?" Columbia simply informed him that this was too bad, and that if he didn't commit immediately in advance of recording, he'd be killing the originally set release date and delaying the record's release for six months.

Holmes understood how anxious Sparks were about their first release on a prestigious American label like Columbia Records, and felt it wasn't his right to sabotage their timing. Any delay would have meant Sparks would not have any product out until 1977, and by that time the band might well have been forgotten. Holmes listened carefully to the songs as the group played through them, decided they were all 'recordable' and unlikely to be cut from the line-up, and tried to come up with the best sequence that he could imagine.

Rupert Holmes: "Because of the incredibly tight timing, I had no choice but to go with a minimalist approach to recording the band, which luckily was in keeping with the Maels' new style. They were certainly in a state of total readiness for the studio. Part of this was because Sparks and I were striving for an extremely spartan, minimalist sound, unlike anything they'd done before. So there was no debate about additional musical overlays. The drum sound on Hilly Michaels' kit became the centrepiece and trademark of the album and I take some credit for creating that."

Holmes was hands-on with his suggestions. "I guess the biggest contribution I made in terms of the music itself was to 'Big Boy', in terms of its backing vocals and, in particular, Jeff Salen's guitar break. We couldn't come up with a guitar break that sounded nihilistic enough for my tastes, so I recorded Jeff playing eight random guitar solos without regard to rhythm or key. I then laid all eight solos side by side, mixed this completely random octet into two stereo tracks, and cut them into and out of the rhythm track of 'Big Boy'. So you have this four-bar moment in the song where the world goes slightly mad. In the Sixties, there was a bare basics Manhattan cafeteria chain named Horn & Hardart that used to say, "If you want something nice to look at, stare at your food." My approach to *Big Beat* was, 'If you want colours and shading, pay attention to Ron's lyrics'.

"I'd build three or four-part vocal harmonies in layers, writing out the harmony as if it were to be sung by a choral group, then teach the band members by ear to sing just one part in unison... then teach them and record a second and third part the same way. The band wouldn't actually hear the final 'Mormon Tabernacle' harmony until they went into the control room and heard the full playback. This was the case with 'Big Boy', for example. You can actually hear my own voice amid the male choir of Sal, Hilly and Jeff on that cut."

One of the biggest technical challenges Holmes faced was getting the 'I Want To Hold Your Hand' version of 'I Like Girls', complete with its lavish instrumentation, to be compatible with the minimalist sound of the album. "It had a completely different rhythm section than the other cuts. Yet I don't think the final mix I did for the album seemed alien in spirit," Holmes recalls.

One evening, two policemen sauntered into the studio. Holmes asked if there was a problem. The cops replied that there had been a noise complaint. "Now keep in mind Mediasound had been in business for nearly a decade," Holmes laughs, "and some of the loudest bands in the history of rock had recorded there. This was a very surreal moment. I've always wondered if the two cops had been sniffing around for drugs, either to make a bust on the premises or [they] wanted to be included in on the fun. If so they came to the wrong session and the wrong band."

With Sparks it was work, not play and Holmes is full of praise for the brothers' working methods. Asked to describe them both, the producer replies, "Conscientious. Positive. Energised. Unaffected. Focused. Reasonable. And did I mention conscientious?" And the rest of the band? "See all the above. Hilly was the cut-up of the group, a NewYork wise guy in the best sense, whereas Ron's intellect and wit were as dry as the Sahara. Jeff was a little bit of a 'star' but no less than he deserved to be. Sal was a terrific musician and a very likeable guy. They certainly didn't act pressured or nervous during the album. They were gracious and enthused. I don't recall a single tantrum or quarrel."

The entire album was mixed in the windowless upstairs mixing room over the course of "the longest three-day weekend" of Holmes' life. "I had from a Friday afternoon to a Monday morning to mix the entire album. I had never mixed an album in three days. Sleep was not an option. In the end, I was putting instant coffee into my brewed coffee to stay awake. The talented engineer Godfrey Diamond heroically kept pace with me. What he put in his coffee I can hardly imagine. By early Monday morning we had a finished album in the sequence I'd committed to weeks earlier, and I walked the master reel to the mastering studio to put the finishing touches on it. That was a ridiculous way to complete an album, and I lost more than sleep in the process. Perhaps this is one aspect of what Ron means when he says it was a 'screwy situation'. Maybe not."

Holmes has since worked with many acts, but continues to extol the virtues of the group. "There was no pouting. No fights. No friends or managers popping in and making suggestions. No drugs of any kind, except perhaps a few beers among the sidemen in the late evening. Both fellows always dressed in impeccable taste and style, Ron usually in trademark tie, whereas Russell would sometimes arrive in the company of a breathtakingly lovely Scandinavian blonde."

Big Beat continues to split the Sparks audience. It's brash and dumb, but that's part of the fun. After the excessive conceits and trickery of *Indiscreet*, it's like a trip back to garage land – as if Sparks had denounced their own progressive form of rock by becoming punk.

Musically everything is straightforward; guitar solos are back. What particularly stands out is Ron's piano playing. "At the time I was trying to be less stylised on keyboards," he recalled in 1982. "Since then I've realised the error of my ways and have become more stylised than ever. I started playing acoustic piano thinking it was best to try and eliminate that kinkiness." Of course, being Sparks, there is still a great deal of kinkiness; it's just a lot less complex kinkiness – a whirl of searing noise and ridiculous economy.

The opening, cleansing whomp of 'Big Boy' signals a rediscovered bite after the Sparks' listener previously sailed away on the strings of *Indiscreet*. 'I Want To Be Like Everybody Else' has an infectious swing, FM radio guitar and a comment on the speed of life and the herd mentality. 'Nothing To Do', the song that so inspired Joey Ramone, with its Beatles-like build-up, demonstrates how accomplished Ron had become as a songwriter. "Joey Ramone has told us that he has wanted to do a version of this song," Russell said in 1991, "yet has never been able to convince the other Ramones. I hope he's successful one day." *

'Nothing To Do' sits amid gloriously daft (and brief) songs such as 'Fill-Er-Up', 'Throw Her Away (And Get A New One)' and 'Everybody's Stupid.'

'I Bought The Mississippi River' opens with a flourish that recalls 'High C' from the first *Halfnelson/ Sparks* LP. It's a fanciful marriage of Sparks' old style theatricality with their new rock sensibility, and a wonderful slice of Mael nonsense, inspired by the then-recent purchase of John Rennie's 1831 London Bridge by Robert McCulloch for Lake Havasu City. 'White Women' has caused controversy ever since its appearance. "I liked to be politically incorrect even before politically correct existed," Ron told *Q* in 1993.

'Confusion', the aborted title track of the Jacques Tati film, appears late on the album. Originally recorded with Tony Visconti at the *Indiscreet* sessions when known as 'Intrusion', the song doesn't fail to namecheck the French maverick. 'I Like Girls', which had been in Sparks' live act since 1972 and was first recorded at Bearsville with the original band, got dusted down for the sessions. The lyrics of the song had actually been printed in *Sparks Flashes* in 1974 ("We at the Sparks fan club call your attention to 'I Like Girls', which seems to have become the group's anthem").

---

* It was not to be, as the Ramones vocalist died in 2001.

Big Beat was released on Island in the UK and Columbia in the US in October 1976. Like the two tracks, 'Big Boy' and 'I Like Girls', that were selected for singles, the album failed to make the charts in either territory. Unlike the wit or scams of the three previous sleeves, the cover was a simple portrait of Ron and Russell, with no other member shown. The brothers had now achieved their desire of being simply a duo. With its stark simplicity, it rates as one of Sparks' strongest images – done in 15 minutes with the legendary Richard Avedon, it captures the brothers in all their black and white beauty.

Rupert Holmes: "I don't know what [the brothers'] public attitude is today towards the records we made together in 1976. I hope in the years ahead, the Maels will be proud that they went so strongly against the grain of the music scene and of their previous sound [and even of their previous single!] with *Big Beat*, and that they will view the album with the admiration I had for it when I assisted them in making it..."

Unfortunately, the brothers' comments betrayed their less than beneficent view of *Big Beat*.

"Rupert Holmes is really good for Barbra Streisand, but I don't think he's a rock'n'roll producer," said Ron. His opinion is one that has been repeatedly reinforced over the years, yet it appears increasingly flawed as time passes. While not all the tracks stand up to the *Kimono My House* acid test, there is plenty to enjoy. Funnily enough, at the time, the album was perceived as something of a breath of fresh air.

"This is Sparks with Ron Mael's keyboards submerged in the mix under the loud guitars and belching response so it doesn't sound like 'Mr Sparky's Magic Piano Screwing A Metronome' any more," Pete Makowski wrote in *Sounds*. "This is Sparks with Russell singing like his balls have dropped at last. It sounds real not like Joni Mitchell at 78rpm. And the lyrics, there are less of them. This is Sparks with less words but stronger songs." Makowski compared the brothers to the Ramones and gave the album a generous five stars. Jan Iles in *National Rockstar* opened her positive review with the statement, "Producer Rupert Holmes has managed to rekindle Sparks' creative flame with this recording."

It's only over time that the critical position reversed; *Rolling Stone* retrospectively wrote that Sparks "abandoned the speeded-up music-hall approach and opted for somewhat less outré rock. No one seems to care."

Original US Sparks' convert Ira Robbins is not a fan either: "It was just yelling. That was a bad album. It was them abandoning what they had suddenly developed as their format. *Kimono My House* and *Propaganda* are just amazingly great sounding. I would credit John Hewlett for a lot of that and Muff Winwood's production – that really chunky guitar sound and the drum beat. I think *Big Beat* felt to me, as a critic, like a concession to America. It was like they changed labels, they were suddenly on Columbia and they wanted to have mainstream American success. It felt like a mistake. I wasn't enthusiastic. That record has more in common with the Sailor album than it does with anything that was being made in America at the time."

Tony Visconti is clear why Sparks would forever battle with acceptance in their home country: "American music's always been meat and potatoes, straight-up rock. It's part of the American culture. It's like Bowie. Bowie's actually a non-rock musician, but he uses rock to express himself. He's an actor, he's a great writer – I would tend to put Russell and Ron in that category. They couldn't do what they do in America – it's just not American-style music."

"*Big Beat* was a stiff, sales-wise," Ron declared in 1982. "It shook our confidence, because we had just signed with Columbia and moved back to the States. We thought it would be the same as when we moved to England and signed with Island. When that didn't happen it was a little maddening. So much of a record has to do with the circumstances around it, and there was no atmosphere around *Big Beat*. That was a real miserable time. I don't especially like this album, but I don't know if it's for musical reasons or just because things were not particularly groovy then."

Russell's view seemed to have mellowed by the time of the *Sparks Spectacular* in 2008. "It's an unfairly slighted record, I think. There are some contentious songs. You're always trying to come up with something provocative. A song like 'White Women', obviously, it's not meant to be taken at face value. We always tried to shake people up. We never wanted to be background music."

Background music *Big Beat* certainly isn't. To these ears, it's a brave attempt to do something different, and the fact the record is so contentiously debated adds to its afterlife. Had it been a hit, it might have been a bold attempt to go back to basics, like, perhaps, The Beatles after *Sgt Pepper's Lonely Hearts Club Band.*

Rupert Holmes: "The sound and attitude of *Big Beat* was probably well ahead of its time. As we were recording it, the music scene was tilting towards really lush disco. Had our arrangement of 'I Want To Hold Your Hand' been done to a disco beat and released as a 12-inch record in the spring of 1977 instead of a year earlier, it might have been a huge club hit for the Maels. Instead, the lean, spare sound of *Big Beat* emerged in a world that was temporarily mad on sweeping strings and Salsoul brass... If *Big Beat* had been released a few years after that, as the world was retching from a surfeit of slushy disco, it might have been received not only enthusiastically but gratefully."

As Russ Regan had said about Sparks in 1970, Ron and Russell were again about two years ahead of their time. Perhaps the biggest irony of *Big Beat* was that the brothers had split up a band to hire a band that wasn't as strong as the one they already had, and in doing so removed some of Sparks' personality. While no fan of retrospective thinking, Hewlett is convinced that the '75 line-up should have been retained for longer. "We had that big focus on America. I now think in retrospect it was an error. I think we should have saved the money after the 1975 US tour. Ron and Russell should have returned to LA, written an album, come back, rehearsed and toured it with the band, and the band should have toured Europe, Japan and Australia, worked the places where we were huge and made money; then let America take care of itself."

Sparks toured the US to promote the album, providing material for the bootleg album, *Live At The Bottom Line.* While Hewlett was involved in other projects, he temporarily got ex-Doors manager Bill Siddons to look after them: "I'd met Bill and that was it. Bill's a laid-back, smoke-a-joint type of guy. *It didn't work.* He's a lovely man, but he wouldn't be on their wavelength, too relaxed. Ron and Russell are Broadway, high tempo, Paris, the Ritz, LA, Hollywood."

The Columbia Records press pack shouted that "the *Big Beat* Tour should convert many non-believers and convince all those Sparks fans they were right all along". However, Maida and Salen were not in the running – drafted in were guitarists Luke Zamperini and Jim McAllister and bass player David Swanson.

This line-up played its debut gig in Santa Barbara on November 6, soon after Jimmy Carter had been elected as President. Sal Maida was to return after a few gigs as Swanson simply wasn't cutting it. The shows, a mixture of headlining gigs and support slots for The Patti Smith Group, saw some fantastic performances from the group, with Ron incorporating a rock'n'roll, piano-stool smashing act into the set each night.

Despite all Sparks' art and film school ambitions, their film debut was anything but the work of an auteur. *Rollercoaster* rode the wave of mid-Seventies disaster movies and for many it was the thin end of the wedge. The film starred Timothy Bottoms as an unnamed young assassin, intent on planting bombs on rollercoasters. Harry Calder, played by George Segal, an amusement park technical wizard, attempts to thwart him. In a nod to the all-star casts of the era, veterans Henry Fonda and Richard Widmark were on the bill, as was, in her first screen role, the 12-year-old Helen Hunt.

The film's big selling point was Sensurround: the short-lived phenomenon developed by Universal Studios that recalled the Fifties-pure hokum to drive people back to the cinema. The public had already endured the 1974 Charlton Heston-led nonsense of *Earthquake* and the gung-ho Jap-swatting of 1976's *Battle Of Midway* in this new format. Sensurround worked on the principle of installing large low-frequency speakers beneath the screen and also in the front and back corners of the cinema.*

In many respects, *Rollercoaster* was an extended riff on the 'Circus Circus' section of Guy Hamilton's 1971 James Bond film, *Diamonds Are Forever*. We see Vietnam vets working on shooting ranges, and Segal plays the tragicomic lead that he perfected opposite Glenda Jackson in 1973's *A Touch Of Class*, clearly having picked the wrong day to give up smoking.

Originally, pansticked rockers Kiss were lined up for the film, but negotiations fell through. "We were approached to be in *Rollercoaster* –

---

* There was only to be one further film produced in Sensurround, 1978's *Battlestar Galactica*, which acted as a pilot for the television series.

the Sensurround movie – with two of the songs from *Big Beat,* 'Fill- Er-Up' and 'Big Boy'," Ron told *Trouser Press* in 1982. "That was our first big screen appearance."

At one hour and 20 minutes into the film, the touring line-up of *Big Beat* appear at the launch of the Great American Revolution Rollercoaster (the first with a 360 degree steel loop in it) at the Magic Mountain theme park in Valencia, California. Russell looks beautiful in his vest, and Sal Maida flashes his blue Rickenbacker in front of a crowd that surely Richard Linklater would later reference for his affectionate 1993-made, 1976-set stoner comedy, *Dazed And Confused.* Bouncing along, they look like an approximation of the audience the Mael brothers would have liked to attract in the US at the time.

The sequence involving Sparks lasts for 12 minutes, intercut with footage of workmen locating the bomb placed on the rollercoaster. "The earth is shaking, so am I" section of the lyric of 'Big Boy' is featured heavily. Russell gets pulled into the crowd; Ron smashes his piano stool, both features of their current set.

Rupert Holmes: "Oh I saw it, and in the full glory of Sensurround, I believe. The Sparks tunes are the highlight of the film for me. However, my favorite George Segal vehicle continues to be *King Rat.*"

Almost three decades after the film's 1977 release, Sparks regarded it as being a huge regret and "a wart on the backside". Whatever the brothers' misgivings regarding the whole enterprise were, it remains Sparks' most widely seen performance.

Hello, hello, hello. An outtake from the *Indiscreet* back sleeve, LA, May 1975.
(GERED MANKOWITZ)

Adrian Fisher (centre) intent on his rock'n'roll lifestyle, LA, 1974. L to R: Ian Hampton, Dinky Diamond, Fisher, Ron Mael, Russell Mael, Trevor White. (LAURENS VAN HOUTEN/FRANK WHITE AGENCY)

Standing not a million miles away from the Waterloo sunset that had so influenced the Maels, 1974. L to R: Russell Mael, Ron Mael, Dinky Diamond, Trevor White, Ian Hampton. (BARRY PLUMMER)

Adrian Fisher. "If I didn't know something,
e'd teach me to do it. He was a very generous
guy." – Trevor White. (PETER MAZEL/RETNA)

Dinky Diamond – "He was a clever drummer
and a clever man. He had the perfect feel
for every track." – John Hewlett. (PETER MAZEL/RETNA)

n Hampton. Admired by all, Hampton remains
e of the Mael's Brothers most vocal supporters.
(PETER MAZEL/RETNA)

Trevor White. Once sold a guitar to Marc Bolan.
Came in at the height of the Maelstrom.
(PETER MAZEL/RETNA)

Going up to Magic Mountain, 1976. L to R: Sal Maida, Jim McAllister, Ron Mael, Russell Mael, Luke Zamperini, Hilly Boy Michaels. (BRAD ELTERMAN/LFI)

T*ts, perhaps? Russell Mael reads some literature, LA, 1975. (BARRY SCHULTZ/RETNA)

on and the Great Pumpkin?' Farmers Market, LA, mid Seventies. (BRAD ELTERMAN/LFI)

Ron and Russell Mael, LA, 1975. (BRAD ELTERMAN/LFI)

At home, at work, at play. Ron and Russell taking their ease, California, 1975. (LFI)

A selection of front covers from the height of their Seventies success.

(COURTESY AUKE LENSTRA)

"The *Big Beat* Tour should convert many non-believers and convince all those Sparks fans they were right all along." – Columbia Records. Patti Smith and Russell Mael backstage, December 1976. Rodney Bingenheimer is to Russell's right. (JENNY LENS)

Shooting the 'Beat The Clock' video, London, Summer 1979. (PAUL CANTY/LFI)

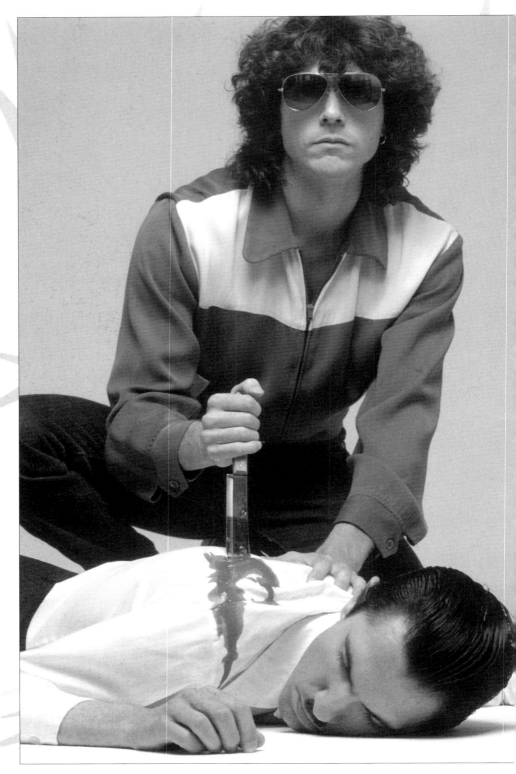

What better to promote an album than a little fratricide? From the range of photographs taken to promote Sparks' arrival at Columbia Records. (SAM EMERSON/LFI)

Chapter Ten

We Cowboys Are A Hardy Breed:
Introducing Sparks

"It felt more like an art project than a commercial project."
Thom Rotella, 2009

"These guys come in, get paid $480 for half an hour and they just assume the first take is fine cos if it is they can leave."
Russell Mael, 1982

At the end of 1976, punk rock was the new thing to hit the UK music scene. Led by the Sex Pistols, whose manager Malcolm McLaren was briefly associated with The New York Dolls, the movement was a further development from the scene that had been underground in New York for the past two years. In December, the Pistols became national *bête noires* after their appearance on ITV's *Today* programme. If ever there had been a time for Sparks to be in Britain, especially if they were aware of the respect The Sex Pistols and Siouxsie and The Banshees had for them, it was now. However the Mael brothers were back in California.

The *Big Beat* campaign ended with a New Year's Eve gig at the Santa Monica Civic Center with Sparks supported by ex-Turtles Flo and Eddie

145

and, filling in for the Ramones, a new LA band, Van Halen. It had been a strange tour; the highs had been higher and the lows considerably lower than on previous jaunts. Although there had been press interest and some remarkable shows, it hadn't been enough to gain any mass US acceptance and the album, by now a couple of months old, had disappeared from view.

John Hewlett. "We'd invested all our money in touring America. If I'd been on my game I should have told them to take a break, rehearse a new record and then tour where we were popular. I think they would have gone for that as they were so huge in Europe. I should have offered *that* carrot, rather than doing the New York thing."

With Columbia wanting to represent the group worldwide, Island offered little resistance: "I was aware when they left for Columbia," Chris Blackwell recalls. "Ultimately, we didn't do that great for them, really. The first record did well and then it slipped down a bit. We parted on good terms."

Tim Clark: "It's fair to say by the time of *Big Beat*, for us it was largely over. There wasn't great sadness when Sparks left. They weren't to be as Roxy Music in the end, with a string of really brilliant albums."

Roxy Music, the band that Sparks had been compared with in 1974, had gained the sort of commercial and critical acceptance that the Maels craved. However, although they had achieved bigger sales there, America had been as lukewarm to Roxy as it had been to Sparks. There was something about art and pop that just didn't travel well across the Atlantic. Sparks' old acquaintance at Island, Richard Williams, wrote in *Keep On Running* that "later, having acquired a fanbase that included future members of New Order, The Smiths and Depeche Mode, [Sparks] went back home to continue their unorthodox progress through the world of popular rhythm music". As a parting shot, Island put together a compilation album, *The Best Of Sparks*, released in March 1977.

By spring, the Sparks touring band had long since fallen apart. Ron and Russell were back in LA wondering where the next move would take them. Hewlett and Fleury were working with the New York new wave band Mumps, with Hewlett enjoying the novelty of being in New York. Although he had become less of a presence with Sparks, Hewlett was still overseeing negotiations for their next album.

146

The lapsing of the Island agreement was a good thing as now they would be on the same label across the world. Founded in 1888, Columbia was one of the biggest labels in the world in the mid-Seventies, boasting an enormous roster of acts of the calibre of Bob Dylan, Neil Diamond, Barbra Streisand, Pink Floyd and Billy Joel. With a big production and the cream of a backlog of songs that Ron had written since *Big Beat* in August 1976, the Maels could surely rise to the challenge of being in such prestigious company.

Bob Ezrin was the brothers' target as producer. Having made his name working with Alice Cooper, Lou Reed and Peter Gabriel (overseeing Gabriel's solo album after leaving Genesis), Ezrin's theatrical style would have suited Sparks well. However he heard Ron's new material and turned them down.

The next available option was less glamorous. Columbia A&R man Terry Powell suggested that he handle the job, assisted by the brothers. Powell's previous credit was co-producing, with Doors' associate Bruce Botnick, the debut album by Starwood, who'd had a minor FM hit with the song 'Tortuga'. After a string of name producers, for the first time Sparks worked with somebody that no one outside the industry had heard of. However that could be a good thing, as no one would pre-judge or anticipate anything from a name that would carry its own weight of expectation.

The initial trade announcements suggested that Botnick (who shared office space with Powell) would co-produce, but nothing was to come of that. The hubristic tone of these early 1977 ads, trumpeting Sparks' next work, sounds surprising: "A late summer single is planned in front of the album's release. This should be the perfect set-up for an album that is destined to become a rock classic ... the transition is complete. The challenge has begun. Ron and Russell Mael are willing to meet the cream of rock'n'roll bands on their own turf. It's an event not to be missed."

The challenge had indeed begun, but the brothers had no band. Because they had enjoyed the flexibility of working with session players on *Indiscreet,* the Maels decided to make their next record with a host of hired hands and, for the first time since *A Woofer In Tweeter's Clothing* in 1972, they would record in their home city. As *Rumours* by Fleetwood Mac became an international obsession and the disco craze reached its zenith, in summer

1977, Sparks went into the legendary Larabee Sound on Santa Monica Blvd and Larabee in Hollywood to cut their seventh album.

Introducing Sparks represents a meeting of two very different approaches – maverick outsiders and slick specialists. There were similarities – both were professional and focussed on the end result – but it was the first time that Ron and Russell had worked with players who had no emotional attachment to the final outcome. Now a long-established session player, Thom Rotella was relatively new in town when he played guitar on the album. He is one of 15 credited musicians (a whole 10 more than on *Big Beat*) that supported Sparks on the sessions, a long with future members of Toto and the backing singers from Pink Floyd's *The Wall*.

Rotella had no previous knowledge of Sparks and got the gig because he had previously worked with Al Capps, who did all the arrangements for the album. "I had the impression that they were a British group," Rotella says. "Al told me that they were a little off the wall and wanted to do something that was a bit more commercial."

New York-born Rotella had been playing in LA since 1973. He had majored in classical guitar at Ithaca and studied under Gary Burton at Berklee College of Music. The session scene was lucrative and Rotella's diary was often booked well in advance. "Back then all the producers and arrangers had their own stable of players. I'd always know about three or four of the guys that would be on any session. Al Capps was the hub if you like. All the producers had their own players, but it was all from the same 30 guys."

Capps was a veteran arranger, who'd worked with some of the greatest radio-friendly artists of popular music such as Andy Williams, Johnny Mathis, Peggy Lee and Frank Sinatra. Now here he was working with a man with a toothbrush moustache writing songs about 'goofing off' delivered by his matinee idol brother.

Thom Rotella: "Al Capps was the most conservative guy. He was quiet and mild-mannered and he was used to doing straight-up pop stuff. I remember him sitting there watching the whole thing unfold. He was amused as it was such a different trip for him."

Another day, another dollar, and Capps didn't come cheap. Spending like this, Columbia clearly had tremendous belief in the Maels. Although it was just another session for him, Rotella, who was working with his friends, drummer Ed Greene and bassist Mike Porcaro, recalls it with fondness. Sparks' freewheeling attitude came as a relief, because most of Rotello's other clients were demanding to say the least. "Ron and Russell were really fun because they just let me go. They told me to do whatever I wanted ... Everyone else wanted you to sound like Larry Carlton. I was playing a Les Paul and everybody else was playing ES-335s at that point. I was happy they didn't break my balls about not playing a 335. They just let me cut loose." Although they were very clear about how a group should look and behave, Ron and Russell must have felt adrift in a world where people would actually break a guitarist's balls if he didn't have the right guitar.

Fellow session man Lee Ritenour played most of the rhythm on the album, while Rotella added the solos. "Lenny Roberts was the engineer. He said that I was going crazy with those solos; it was one of the freest sessions I did in that time period."

The team at Larabee were a little unsure of the Maels with their strange songs and much has been made of the Maels' disgust for the session men. "Most of our songs aren't three chords," Ron said in 1982. "These session musicians who were getting a quarter of a million dollars a year bitched constantly about not being able to play in those keys and 'Wouldn't it be better to use saxophone instead of guitar?' and all that stuff. It was a joke."

The joke, however, wasn't apparent to the session players at the time as Ron and Russell kept their contempt well-hidden.

Thom Rotella: "I remember them being really cool and fun to talk with. I dealt with Russell a little more than Ron for some reason but the whole vibe was great. I remember sessions where people were assholes, but here, the mood was very open, creative and interesting. Mike Porcaro and I were talking years later and we just remembered those tunes. They were really good writers. David Paich was on it, David Foster too. These were just the everyday guys that we worked with."

Russell has been disparaging across the years: "It was pretty boring using session musicians. These guys come in, get paid $480 for half an hour and they just assume the first take is fine cos if it is they can leave."

Rotella, who, by 1977, had played on records by Bette Midler and Carole Bayer Sager, had absolutely no idea where this strange record would fit. "I loved the tongue-in-cheek thing," the guitarist says. "They were trying to take the commercial thing and do a bit of a parody on it. It felt more like an art project than a commercial project. For me, it felt like they were into their own thing and that they were doing this crossover thing in their own way – it was really cool."

And these were commercial songs that were being recorded – with a seven-piece vocal section; 'Over The Summer' sounded like The Beach Boys, 'Those Mysteries' like the ultimate show tune. "In the context of what they were doing, they took that format and did something creative and interesting with it," Rotella adds. "They could have *really* sold out and just done some vanilla stuff. They were not spitting it out – they digested it and came up with something different."

"The event not to be missed" was released in October 1977. Most people missed it. Without the fanfare that Columbia had promised at the start of the year, *Introducing Sparks* failed to anticipate the success of new wave, which Sparks had been playing since the late Sixties and which had taken Ron and Russell off into far glitzier directions. At just over 35 minutes long, its nine tracks are polished, bright and catchy yet almost entirely bereft of soul. Ron has subsequently said that the album has no sense of edge; and he's right. However, what did they expect when recording with session players in a big LA studio? The brothers have suggested that they should have taken a more stylised approach to the recording of the album, yet in some respects its straightness makes it an interesting addition to their catalogue.

About the only similarity between *Introducing Sparks* and the previous releases is that it contains the Mael brothers. For one, the sleeve dispenses with all artifice and develops further the portraiture of *Big Beat*. For this, Bob Seidemann, famous for his shots of The Grateful Dead and Janis Joplin, and who had also shot the *Blind Faith* album cover, one of Russell's personal favourites, was employed. The two lush portraits screamed there were to be no gimmicks, this was simply Sparks. Taken in a Hollywood pose, with Russell alone on the front cover and Ron on the back, we see the brothers both adopting the same posture, with one hand raised to camera. Dressed identically in red, with what looks like a fraternity ring on both their little fingers, it emphasises the brothers as twins. Their open-necked shirts suggest an easy formality. Russell's direct stare suggested that he wants to be looked at, while Ron's gaze is more distant, looking *at* the viewer. Russell's hand is more open as if he is about to comment. The inner bag put the two together. The brothers are laying themselves open to their audience, like any new act that needs introducing. It looks like a picture you would see in a Vegas lobby advertising the evening's entertainment.

So what lurks under the glossy cover? Some well-written tunes for sure, which, for the first time in their career, were co-written by Ron and Russell. The difference kicks in 28 seconds into *Introducing Sparks* with the vocal chorus of opener 'A Big Surprise'. This is proper, grown-up harmonising recalling The Beach Boys. When Rotella's guitar solo plays over the MOR horn section, it's hard to believe that this is the same group whose previous opening tracks, from 'Wonder Girl' to 'Big Boy', had been among their boldest and most aggressive.

'Occupation' has witty lyrics, cataloguing a range of professions. The backing singers seem to be having a whale of a time as they reel off a list of jobs from sailors to undertakers – and Russell's introductions to each profession as the song progresses is a touch that gives the album some character. 'I'm Not' strays into string-driven mid-period Beatles and is not a million miles away from what ELO were up to at that time. With all guns blazing and a mixed-down solo from Rotella, it attempts to add grit. 'Forever Young' clearly acknowledges punk, complete with Russell's vocal tribute to Johnny Rotten's 'Anarchy In The UK' yelp at the start. It's one of the Maels' best songs, yet the lack of bite in the arrangement lets it down. 'Goofing Off' is an expertly constructed song, based on a Russian folk dance. The cod-*Zorba The Greek/Fiddler On The Roof*-isms of this track are especially effective. Brilliantly written and played, it is a precursor to 2006's 'Dick Around'. "We thought we'd do something that would fit in with their corporate ideas," Russell said. "But as you can tell from songs like 'Goofing Off', it's still a Sparks album."

The album's obligatory girl-related songs are the two that work least. For 'Ladies', Russell sings through a list of famous ladies, while 'Girls On The Brain' is a tale of a man unable to do anything as his skirt obsession is so all-consuming. 'Over The Summer', a tale of the duckling growing into a swan over the summer break, is the album's most explicit tribute to the Wilson brothers and as a pastiche, featuring seven session vocalists singing their hearts out, it works perfectly.

"On songs like 'Over The Summer' we used session back-up singers who had done all the commercials that were supposed to sound like The Beach Boys," Ron recalled. "Our ode to summer romance," Russell added, "whereby a guy's girlfriend goes through a radical transformation over the three-month period. The demo has a naïve charm that we never could recreate using the high-priced session backing vocalists. There's a lesson to be learned."

The album closes with 'Those Mysteries', which is the Sparks song most in need of Broadway. Through a child's eyes Russell wonders about the big questions that surround him. With its well-arranged strings (the demo version shows how accomplished the song was before getting to the studio), Russell plays every possible musical lead.

Introducing Sparks was supported with a brief tour and a set of promotional pictures. Ron and Russell's zaniness was again paraded for their new army of fans to devour, as the brothers appeared in a variety of poses – in gorilla suits; Russell pretending to have stabbed Ron; Russell under the legs of a model in a bikini…

'A Big Surprise' was released as a single in the UK and 'Over The Summer' in the US but neither charted. Sparks seemed out of step with what was happening in the contemporary music scene on either side of the Atlantic. If reviewed at all, the notices were not especially favourable: *Rolling Stone* commented on the duo starting from scratch, but "old fans have disappeared and new ones are few and far between".

Hewlett was not pleased with the new direction; he didn't like the pretentiousness of the cover image or the fact that the brothers were supported by anonymous session players.

John Hewlett: "We did radio shows and some lip-syncs with it, but it was hardly rock'n'roll. I'd come from a band. They'd been a band threatening to be big and then we were doing *this*. The [Maels] don't care if others like it or not. To them it's another album. It was another lame step after *Big Beat*; trying to make a silk purse out of a sow's ear."

The recording of a European TV appearance encapsulated the gulf between the brothers and the audience. Playing with a large orchestra, the pair performs 'A Big Surprise'. Russell leaps around while Ron sits at the piano, until the end, when he runs into the crowd and smashes his chair (the 'big surprise' of the title, naturally). The audience sit motionless. This was the era of big surprises coming in the form of Donna Summer erotically intoning 'I Feel Love' or The Sex Pistols singing about abortions or putting 'bollocks' in their album title. Not a deadpan, Chaplin-esque pianist smashing his stool at the climax of an unremarkable song.

Like *Big Beat* before it, *Introducing Sparks* simply disappeared, as did Columbia's interest. As 1977 became 1978, the band seemed woefully out of step with the times. It was either the brothers' headstrong nature or simply receiving bad advice that had got them to this position. Four years before, they had created a landmark sound with a landmark album. Now they were out of contract again, unloved and on the way to being forgotten.

One of the reasons *Introducing Sparks* didn't work was that it mostly seemed to recreate the sound of fellow Californians The Beach Boys.* One of the key problems was that The Beach Boys themselves were a huge commercial proposition again, thanks to the unexpected success of the 1974 *Endless Summer* compilation. In 1976, *15 Big Ones* had been the band's biggest new album for some time, and '77's *Love You*, although not as big, had certainly kept them in the public's consciousness.

When asked in 1995 to name the worst record that they had ever made, Russell plumbed for *Introducing Sparks*. While frequently regarded as an embarrassment, it could not be further from the truth. Over three decades after its release, *Introducing Sparks* would prove to be one of the highlights of the brothers' 21 Nights series of shows, which saw their back catalogue being played chronologically in its entirety. "When you go back, you realise it was brilliant," says Sparks' current manager, Sue Harris. "There are just some great songs on there. That was one of the joys of the 21 Nights, to stand on the stage and listen to the quality of the words and music – it's an amazing record."

Ron seemed finally to warm to the album when playing it again, telling *Keyboard Player* magazine that it was "as strong as the albums of ours which were better known because of more commercial success." The album

---

★ The Maels might have been able to achieve this at less expense if they'd spoken to Earle Mankey who was, by now, engineer at Brother Studios for The Beach Boys.

was finally issued on CD at the end of 2007 and, at last, it got some attention in the music press that had so sorely neglected it 30 years earlier. *Mojo* identified "slick tracks whose humour failed to tickle the American psyche and whose smoother patina didn't connect with their UK fans". *Record Collector* said that "nothing by Sparks can be a total failure and this has its gems". *Classic Rock,* however, was not so kind; "Kimono My Arse" it said, rather snottily. Toby Manning went to town in *The Word* writing that Sparks, even on an album as variable as *Introducing Sparks,* were "a vital antidote to all that is po-faced, self-important and depressingly ordinary in rock, they are also proof that humour and music can not only co-exist but bond, mate and give birth to something between cartoon superhero and freak – monstrous yet muscular, gruesome yet gorgeous".

John Hewlett, who had moved from his humble offices in Purley to Westmount Drive, West Hollywood, finally laid his cards on the table. "It was in Munich in 1978," Hewlett told *Sausade* magazine in 1990. "We were in a hotel and Ronnie broke down and cried and said I didn't care any more, that I didn't care for his music, which of course I did."

"Ronnie is a sensitive man and Russell as well, we all are," Hewlett counters from a 2009 perspective. If you put effort into a work and your manager is critical or you can see they don't like it, it is devastating. That's why I could never really engage with *Introducing* and *Big Beat.* I was still recovering from this great band and hearing supposedly quality musicians playing. *Introducing Sparks* doesn't sound like something I would buy. I'm sorry I upset him. I'd give him a big hug now, but I could only be honest at the time."

In October 1977, Hewlett had seen The Dickies, a crazed, hyped-up LA punk band, who reminded him very much of the exuberance and energy created not only by Sparks in rehearsal for *Kimono My House,* but also of John's Children. "The Dickies just blew my mind," said Hewlett. "In their initial line-up, I would put them on a par with the Stones." This exuberance was something Hewlett hadn't been feeling his principal act had generated since *Propaganda.* With his antipathy to their recent material and his enthusiasm for this new act, Ron and Russell sensed that their managers' loyalties were elsewhere.

Chapter Eleven

Tiny Actors In The Oldest Play Or Disco

"Guitarists are jokes. They're just so old-fashioned and passé that any band that has got a guitarist is just a joke."
Russell Mael, *Melody Maker*, 1979

"I wouldn't be caught dead in a disco!"
Russell Mael, *Melody Maker*, 1979

To provide a story-so-far moment: Sparks had not always been a duo, they had not always made electronic music, but the Giorgio Moroder-produced edition of Ron and Russell's masterplan from 1979 seemed to change the Sparks dynamic forever. It focused on the small rather than the grandiose in terms of manpower and approach, and created a sound that was, at times, rather enormous. It was also to provide a template that enabled later double-acts, from Soft Cell to Blancmange to Pet Shop Boys, to shuffle the deck of irony and have their turn to sing in front of the machines that go ping.

Although highly unfashionable in rock circles, the Italian-born Moroder was possibly the hottest thing in popular music in 1978 when he received an approach from the Maels to work with them. Recording in Germany, he had begun his production work in the late Sixties and truly found his stride with the 1972 Chicory Tip hit 'Son Of My Father' ('Tu Sei Mio Padre'), propelled along by primitive synthesisers. However, the working partnership that was to define his career was struck in 1974 when he started recording with an American expat also living in Germany. Donna Summer had achieved great success in the German stage version of *Hair!*, so she stayed on in the country to capitalise on this. Moroder and his engineer, Pete Bellotte, were so impressed with her full-throated, gospel-trained voice that they began to combine her soulful authenticity with their studio mastery – and, as digital technology became readily available, their increasing use of the synthesiser.

The first single to attract attention was 'Love To Love You Baby', released in 1975 and a slow-burning hit around the globe throughout 1976. Sultry, late night and dreamy, its infamy was guaranteed by Summer's prolonged simulation of orgasm during the record's climax. Chiming with the post-*Emmanuelle*, pre-AIDS world this seemed as modern as one could possibly get. However, it was their 1977 collaboration that sealed their reputation and partnership. Heard today, 'I Feel Love' still sounds as revolutionary as it did then. Its use of sequencer was practically unheard of and its grinding, synthetic repetition, combined with Summer's strange, space-like vocal and robotic movements, was at once of the time and entirely ahead of it.

Introducing Sparks had taught Ron and Russell a valuable lesson: things had to change. The rock format as they knew it was, for the moment, finished. Working with session players, too, was not viable. Two records they'd heard while making *Introducing Sparks* made them stop and think: one was a cover of Harold Melvin and The Bluenotes' 'Don't Leave Me This Way' by Thelma Houston. The other was 'I Feel Love'. "It was now time to approach it in a completely different way," Ron said. "We heard 'I Feel Love' and we thought that there must be a way to apply that sort of sound and thinking to what we were doing."

"It was a real 'What do we do now?' moment," Russell told the author in 2003. "We had nostalgia for England and Europe, again America was not for us. So we went to Germany. We just said 'Screw it, we're tired of what we're doing and we're tired of the area we're boxed into'. What if we apply the strengths that we have – the songwriting, the lyrical slant and the singing style – and apply it in a different framework? We contacted Giorgio Moroder."

The story has often been told that while being interviewed by a German journalist in LA, Ron and Russell had discussed working with Moroder. The reporter happened to be friends with the producer and made known their desire. That may have indeed happened, but the reality was somewhat more prosaic.

In one of his final acts as Sparks' manager, John Hewlett made all the arrangements – and he was instrumental in the new direction. "I recall being bowled over with electronic sounds at that time, especially *The Man Machine* by Kraftwerk," Hewlett says. "I recall encouraging Ron to embrace synths and electronic sounds in general, and the Moroder idea was a natural part of our conversation at that time. I would not claim it was my idea or indeed Ron or Russell's, although I do know I made contact via his office and arranged the initial meeting between Moroder and the Maels."

Moroder was aware of Sparks: "I'd seen Sparks for the first time on a TV show in England," he said in 2007. "I was immediately interested and intrigued with the way Russell was singing and the way that the group was performing, with Russell being the outspoken guy and Ron playing the more austere guy who doesn't smile." The meeting occurred and the brothers and Moroder gelled immediately. Moroder offered to sign them to a production deal.

"Giorgio was interested in working with us," said Russell, "because at that time he had never worked with a band – he'd only really worked with solo diva-esque singers. None of us knew where the thing was going to go and we didn't know about electronics at the time and Giorgio did. Sometimes you have to put yourself into situations where you are not comfortable and you're not sure what the end result is going to be – then you arrive at your most interesting stuff."

Shortly after the producer's introduction, and after nearly six years as Sparks' manager, John Hewlett was dismissed in a Beverly Hills hotel lobby by Moroder himself. Typically, Ron and Russell said little.

John Hewlett: "They had obviously met and [the brothers] had made their decision. I got them involved with [Moroder] and then I was ousted. Giorgio Moroder told me that they didn't want to work with me any more. They were there, sitting very sheepishly in the background. I was really upset. He saw the potential and went for it. He wanted me out and him in. Before the record was cut, he took over."

Although he had not been happy with their last two Sparks albums, Hewlett was still a friend – and a fan. "Business-wise, I'd set them up properly, helped them buy their properties. I got them good publishing contracts with rights reversion. We saw their lawyer and drew up an agreement. I was now involved with the hot band in town, which I thought could only add to the credibility of the management."

That hot band was The Dickies. In March 1978, Hewlett was instrumental in getting them signed to A&M. He'd arranged for Derek Green, the man who had signed and then dumped The Sex Pistols from the label the previous year, to take Jerry Moss to see them, and they were snapped up on the spot. Hewlett called Earle Mankey and the two of them produced the band's debut album, *The Incredible Shrinking Dickies*, at Brother Studios. "The Dickies just blew my mind," Hewlett says. "Their live performances were something else. That's why it was easier parting from Sparks. I wasn't going to stand in Ron and Russell's way."

Hewlett became A&R man for A&M in the early Eighties, where he oversaw Captain Sensible's 1982 number one, 'Happy Talk', and attempted to sign Sade. A path of spirituality and a return to further education was to follow.* With Hewlett now gone, Joseph Fleury was promoted to the role of Sparks' *de facto* manager, a role he'd been rehearsing for all this time.

It wasn't that the Maels had a grand disco masterplan. "We didn't have a list of other ideas," said Ron. "That was the only idea we had. A lot of people thought it was a step backwards, that we were entering this disco world. Our sensibility kept it so it was a funny mixture of elements. We were in that area and outside of it at the same time – the lyrics and Russell's singing kept it separate from the wider world of disco. So much

---

* Hewlett is currently writing and recording, and remains close friends with Trevor White.

of that music was done by legitimate singers – Donna was amazing. Giorgio was uncomfortable with Russell's singing at the start. It was a combination of things that kept it from being as slick and processed as some of the other people who were working in that area at the time."

Moroder needed to have complete control of the recording. First and foremost, this meant song selection. "He's part German and part Italian and he can bring out the national characteristics of either, depending on the circumstances," Ron said. "He's very definite about what he wants. I'd be bringing songs to him and half the time he'd just reject them out of hand, which was kind of galling. Even worse, I usually had to admit he was right."

Four of the six on *No. 1 In Heaven* were Mael-Mael-Moroder co-writes – the only time that the group have shared a credit with any individual outside the band. As Ron said to *Mojo* in 2006, "Anytime we were stuck he would say, 'Boys, let me go away for 15 minutes.' And he'd go over to an acoustic piano and 15 minutes later he'd have come up with something. Even 'The Number One Song In Heaven' took him just 15 minutes at the piano."

Only two songs out of the batch Ron had written passed Moroder's quality threshold, which meant there was a pretty clean sheet to work from. That freshness and spontaneity was a direct contrast to *Introducing Sparks*. "*No. 1 in Heaven* was pretty exciting to make because there were no preconceptions of how a disco producer working with an eccentric rock band would turn out," Ron told *Trouser Press* in 1982. "This was the only album we've ever gone into with almost no material; only 'Beat The Clock' and 'Academy Award Performance' were written beforehand. Giorgio wrote the music for at least half the other songs. We tried to get as much of us as we could on *No. 1*, but at the same time we wanted an outside influence; obviously, we got it."

Recording in Munich, Westlake and Sound Arts in LA, the Maels and Moroder worked with British-born drummer and Moroder cohort Keith Forsey on live drums. It was Forsey's sound as much as anything that made *No. 1 In Heaven* so special. "There wasn't a choice actually," Ron said in 2003. "Keith was skilled at playing the kick drum for 15 minutes at a time. We were purists for live drums. When making *No. 1 In Heaven*, you could use electronic effects that would give it a rhythmic feel but as far as solid rhythms, it always had to be played. It gave it something different."

The Maels were now so comfortable with reinvention that they would spend every new release concocting something different. *No. 1 In Heaven* was nothing short of a glittering comeback. From the 45-second lazy syndrum introduction to the frantic pace-gathering on opening track 'Tryouts For The Human Race', this was clearly a very different group from the one whose last offering was the overproduced *Introducing Sparks*. If an album needed to be called *Re-Introducing Sparks,* it was this one.

In true Ron Mael style, the first song to reach the ears of more people than at any time since *Propaganda* was about sperm. That's right, spermatozoon, with Keith Forsey's live drums and the chorus vocals of Dennis Young, Chris Bennett and Jack Moran creating a very un-Beach Boys-like series of harmonies. With this opening six minutes, the Maels, with Moroder, wiped their slate clean and started over.

'Academy Award Performance' sounds very much a product of its era, 'La Dolce Vita' is upbeat with a fantastic breakdown in its fourth minute, while 'Beat The Clock' gave the group their first UK Top 10 placing since 'Amateur Hour' in 1974. A sprightly, hilarious Mael-tael about the speed of modern living, it showed Ron was writing better than ever. "'Beat The Clock' was like a Velvet Underground song when I wrote it at the piano," Ron said in 2002 to *Mojo Collections,* "and if you listen to it with that in mind, you can kind of tell. But what Giorgio did with it was amazing."

'My Other Voice' completely leaves the orbit of previous Sparks songs; while the other tracks on the album resembled, albeit in a new-fangled form, something that previous versions of the group could have played, 'My Other Voice', with its reversed computer hi-hats, was stripped of any semblance of structure. It could be called, for want of a better term, ambient house. Sparks, never a band to play to the mellow, had inadvertently created a chill-out masterpiece.

This mellow mood was continued by the closing 'The Number One Song In Heaven', the highpoint of the writing collaboration between the Maels and Moroder. The first three-and-a-half minutes is swooning, woozy electronica and then, as if a reminder of how remarkable a group Sparks could be, the final pay-off is one of the best pop songs ever to grace a Sparks album. Its speedy, breezy rush marries the old and the new – like a punk version of 'I Feel Love'. Of course, being from the pen of Ron Mael, there would be an edge somewhere, with a sly jibe at the lack of depth in disco's lyrics – it was all about the music. 'The Number One Song In Heaven' is little short of rapturous. It was this closing section that was chosen to be the first single from the album.

Sparks now needed another label – their fourth of the decade. Virgin Records seemed a perfect resting place for the group, as quirky and pioneering as Island had been half a decade earlier. Owned by the entrepreneurial Richard Branson, the Virgin label had hit paydirt from its debut release, *Tubular Bells*, by the 19-year-old reclusive prodigy, Mike Oldfield. By 1977, Oldfield was known as Mike Oldfart, and his money had gone to funding tens of critically lauded, commercially collapsed acts such as Henry Cow, Faust and Hatfield and the North.

However, Branson's acute ability to tap into the zeitgeist was vindicated when the label signed The Sex Pistols who were on the rebound from both EMI and A&M. Their album *Never Mind The Bollocks, Here's The Sex Pistols*, was released in October to a barrage of controversy and huge sales, reaching number one on the UK chart.

The negotiations for Sparks to be on Virgin were swift. Branson remembered their success of 1974 (Virgin had been distributed by Island at that point) and welcomed them on board. Although a recognisable figurehead, Branson was a very different chairman from Chris Blackwell.

"Branson and Blackwell are a million miles apart," says David Betteridge, who by now was working for RCA and would soon steer Adam Ant to superstardom before working with Branson at Virgin. "Richard, and he will be the first to say this, is not a music man and never has been. Simon Draper was his music man. When I was there I reported to Simon. Richard could get people together, if he wanted someone he would go after them. He's a putter-togetherer."

Draper engineered the deal and it was decided that a great deal of promotional clout be put behind the duo.* A lot had changed in the UK

---

* Mael studio activity for the Virgin label during this time was producing the skittish Adrian Munsey 12", 'C'est Sheep' – a parody of Chic's 'Le Freak' – and on a more serious note, French chanteuse Noel on the album *Is There More To Life Than Dancing?*

music industry since 1975. It was the beginning of a phase in marketing when the music alone was simply not enough. In the era of wacky merchandising, Virgin embraced the contemporary wave of gimmicks and pressed *No. 1 In Heaven* and its singles in coloured vinyl.

The album was trailed by the March 1979 release of the title track, issued in a 7" and, for the first time for a Sparks release, a 12" single version. The album followed in the UK the following month and, for the first time since *Kimono My House*, Ron and Russell did not appear on the cover, opting instead for fashion models. Its stark white and light blue sleeve, shot by Moshe Brakha, who went on to become an extremely influential fashion photographer, has the air of a slightly funky clinical trial. Designer Steven Bartel worked with the brothers to come up with the idea of putting a laboratory assistant on the sleeve, looking as if they'd just been knocked backwards against the wall from a possible blast. The microscope in the models' hands reflects how this work was a scientific experiment; the fluorescent strip light above their heads underlines the modernity of the moment. The spark plug logo suggests sparks of creativity, of making something new. The picture is replicated on the rear cover, referencing the twinning of *Introducing Sparks*, with a darker-skinned model.

No one quite knew what to make of the album. *Sounds* said, "I don't think *No. 1 In Heaven* will go down in history as one of the all-time hot 100 albums, but it's icy sharp and fresh," while Tony Ryans in *Melody Maker* despised the record, calling it, "pathetic…obsolete poses, clapped-out fantasies, undirected satire, tired routines".

Friends and associates of Sparks were surprised at this new direction: "I wasn't totally in love with the electronic direction but it was logical," Tony Visconti says. "I think they had to do it."

"It was a jaw-dropping moment when they reappeared with Giorgio Moroder," former bassist Ian Hampton said. "I was really surprised to see them, but then I thought good luck to them, they're branching out again, but then using Giorgio, I did think they were stepping on the bandwagon of the era."

Session drummer David Humphrey: "I'd say they went very sort of pop commercial instead of disco. It seemed to click OK. I don't know what arrangement they had with Virgin but I presume they did very well out of it."

What Sparks had achieved was to become noteworthy again. After two albums where they were simply ignored, with *No. 1 In Heaven*, Sparks became the first 'rock' band to go fully fledged 'disco'. Since The Bee Gees had reinvented themselves as southern American R&B gentlemen in the middle of the decade and gone interstellar by soundtracking *Saturday Night Fever*, many other rock artists had been adding touches of disco to their work or releasing one-off singles – examples being The Rolling Stones' 'Miss You', Kiss' 'I Was Made For Loving You', Rod Stewart's 'Do Ya Think I'm Sexy?' and Mike Oldfield recording 'Guilty' in New York at a time when that city was ruled by the wonderful Chic.

From a modern perspective it can be seen how different these artists can be and how far removed *No. 1 In Heaven* is from 'Stayin' Alive', but at the time it was all seen as the same. And in the UK, it was viewed, at best, with deep suspicion.

In a *Melody Maker* interview with Harry Doherty, Ron revealed that this suspicion surprised him: "It seems like everybody is thinking more of the motive than of the music, which is ridiculous. All parties came into this album not really having a clue how it was going to end up. When we'd finished it, none of us had a clue what the category of the thing was."

Russell's comments in the interview were prescient. "We're really resentful of how our other sound has been emulated about a hundred times since *Kimono My House*. Just wait six months from now and watch all of the new-wave, synthesiser, disco bands which will be popping up, and disco music becoming very respectable in hip circles. And then somebody else will capitalise on what we've done. The same feller that reviewed our album will be raving about disco synthesiser albums by some band that spits on stage."

Indeed, within six months many synth acts, who had been underground, became popular. Gary Numan was just about to break through with Tubeway Army and, for a brief period in 1979, The Human League were the hippest band in the known universe. Whereas Sparks were viewed as chancers.

"It wasn't the pejorative 'disco music' – call it 'dance music' today and it's cool again!" Russell said in 1983. "England really picked up on that album. In an interview recently, The Human League cited that record as the thing that got them excited and focused on what they were doing, showed the possibilities. We've achieved enough success now that people can come out of the woodwork and say, 'Sparks? Yeah, I always liked them'."

As the sprightly, uptempo zing of the seven inch edit of 'The Number One Song In Heaven' started its slow ascent up the charts, on May 10, five years and a day after 'This Town Ain't Big Enough For Both Of Us' made its debut on the programme, the band were back on *Top Of The Pops*. This time there were no Wombles surrounding them but The Damned singing 'Love Song' and The Monks performing 'Nice Legs Shame About The Face'. For everyone who remembered Sparks' dramatic appearance in 1974, it was delightful to have them back.

Like many sleeve-reading teenagers of the time, the author automatically assumed that the drummer appearing with the brothers was Keith Forsey. However, Forsey was too busy in the studio to honour promotional commitments and after their initial appearances a regular session player, David Humphrey, was hired. Humphrey was quite unique in the annals of Virgin Records as he was possibly the only person to work with the stylistically opposed Mike Oldfield (as a *Top Of The Pops* studio drummer on his disco record, 'Guilty') and Johnny Rotten.

David Humphrey: "I was actually working with Public Image Limited and I was in the middle of the *Metal Box* album. I worked on 'Albatross' and 'Swan Lake', which was to become 'Death Disco'."

Humphrey got the gig in P.i.L. when original drummer, Jim Walker, left because the manager of Humphrey's jazz-rock outfit was friendly with P.i.L guitarist Keith Levene. After recording with the group (and being replaced by Richard Dudanski), Humphrey became a regular around Virgin's Vernon Yard head office, which is where he was asked to play with Sparks.

David Humphrey: "When I was growing up in my teens, I would listen to 'This Town Ain't Big Enough For Both of Us'. They were very well known from that era to me but to actually work with them as well five years later was surreal. It's quite weird, as you can imagine."

For the next six months, Humphrey became part of the UK promotion for the *No. 1 In Heaven* album.

David Humphrey: "They made me really welcome and part of the team. I thought that Russell would be probably quite chatty and Ron would be subdued but it was the other way around. I found that Ron had a very dry sense of humour but both were really likeable guys. Russell was very quiet and I think that was just him but I got on really well with them."

'The Number One Song In Heaven' reached number 14 in the UK charts and remained on the listings for 12 weeks. It was a good start for the campaign, seeing Sparks return to the Top 20 for the first time in five years. The next release would see them climb even higher into the Top 10. 'Beat The Clock', one of the two songs that passed Moroder's A&R policy for the album, was chosen as the next single and given a lavish push.

As it crawled up the charts, the Maels and Humphrey toured the TV studios. The drummer also got the opportunity to appear on the re-recordings that the Musicians' Union demanded of all groups appearing on *Top Of The Pops*. "I was given the single to go over and learn the actual drum part. That had to be recorded so that it could be played and mimed to, so I actually was on a Sparks recording."

A third single from the album, 'Tryouts For The Human Race', was released in November, completing Sparks' busiest year since 1975.* The brothers and Humphrey mimed the single on children's TV show *Crackerjack*, possibly not the most appropriate place to hear its subject matter. November 1 marked what was to be their final *Top Of The Pops* appearance. Also on the show were The Jam with 'Eton Rifles', Thin Lizzy performing 'Sarah', Legs And Co dancing to Earth, Wind & Fire and Lena Martell singing the then current number one, 'One Day At A Time'.

A starstruck Humphrey was amazed at the people who either knew the Maels or passed through to pay their respects in the BBC canteen. "It was somewhat surreal – The Jam and Phil Lynott sat down at our

---

* A video for the single was filmed at Shepperton Studios where the brothers were transformed into werewolves.

table and started talking. These were the guys I'd been listening to for a few years and the next thing you know you're sitting next to them. I'm so glad that I was given the opportunity to do it."

Sparks brought in fellow Virgin artist Clive (or Peter Cook as he was better known) to do some amusing PR puff on the run-out grooves of the 'Beat The Clock' and 'Tryouts For The Human Race' 12" singles.

Despite all this sterling promo, 'Tryouts…' climbed no higher than 45. It would be the last Sparks single in the UK charts until 1994. The album only reached number 73 in the UK album chart – hardly the Top 10 escapades of 1974, but the biggest ripple since *Indiscreet*.* Ultimately perhaps the album's disco element was to its detriment as disco was a dirty word in certain circles. In America, this reached its apogee with the Disco Demolition Derby of July 12, 1979, where, at Chicago's Comiskey Park, the crowd, egged on by local DJ Steve Dahl, blew up 12" vinyl disco records. It was probably for the best, then, that *No. 1 In Heaven* was never released in the States.

Working with Giorgio Moroder had liberated Sparks. They had seen the future. At this moment, *they* were the future. In the *Melody Maker* interview with Harry Doherty the brothers underlined their modernity, while taking a swipe at those players that they clearly felt had held them back over the years: "Guitarists are jokes," Russell said. "They're just so old-fashioned and passé that any band that has got a guitarist is just a *joke*. We've found a way to work that's kind of sprung us from the guitarist mentality – which is a pretty low mentality. The weakest part of Sparks has always been the guitar-playing, because it was imposed on what we were doing." If Earle Mankey, Adrian Fisher or Trevor White were in any doubt about their old employers' feelings, now they knew.

"Now we're finally a more pure version of what we've always been. We want to completely strip away the whole idea of bands and the hipness of rock music, because that area is now just like a caricature of

---

* Island took the opportunity to toast the boys' success – 1977's *The Best Of Sparks* was repromoted, alongside a reissue of 'This Town Ain't Big Enough For Both Of Us' in September 1979.

itself. *Every* rock band is a cartoon now, with a guitarist and drummer and bass player and marijuana smoke and that sort of thing. Every single band is a variation of somebody else's, and, to me, no band is any better than any other band. They're all *bands*."

Sparks even seemed more ahead of their closest 1974 rivals, Roxy Music and David Bowie. That year, Roxy had reformed and made the pleasant, easy-listening album *Manifesto*, a UK-centric take on New York disco, with only the title track pointing towards their experimental edge. Bowie had just released *Lodger*, an oblique album of songs of alienation and travel that was not as progressive as his preceding works, *Low* and *"Heroes"*.

The model of the synth duo so appropriated in Britain at the start of the Eighties can certainly be traced in part back to *No. 1 In Heaven*. Aside from the four-piece Kraftwerk, who at that precise moment were seen as a novelty, the only other precedent was the New York-based synth duo Suicide. Within two years, thanks largely to the advent of cheap technology, synthesisers and synthesiser duos seemed to be everywhere. Sparks also went on to influence a whole wave of future bands, showing them the possibilities that electronic music could offer to people who'd previously only thought in terms of guitar, bass and drums.

Having been formed in 1978 by John Taylor and Nick Rhodes, the nascent Duran Duran were certainly big fans of *No. 1 In Heaven* – Taylor calling it "the most important album of Sparks for me… Duran Duran nicked quite a bit from that album's aesthetic. Keith Forsey's live drums really stick out for me. It was the first time I'd heard the Moroder sound with live drums. Moroder created this world and we all just went in – [it had an] emotionally dry, St Tropez nightclub, cocaine/nostalgic type feeling about it.

"Looking back, [the album] was such an incredibly successful concept. It was marketed very strongly," Taylor continues. "The picture disc middle singles; there was this vaguely sexy packaging – the cover reminds me of those nurse paintings by Richard Prince. After having defined themselves with the super-tricky rock-pop of *Kimono My House*, Sparks had to get that sound with the notes that all have to be programmed. But it does sound like a Sparks album, it's got everything that they had before in terms of quirkiness and cleverness and mood – it's just a little less obvious.

"It had a massive influence on us. We were listening to things like [Moroder's soundtrack to] *Midnight Express* so when Sparks came out with that sound, it was a real humdinger. It wouldn't have mattered who it was, it was such a great sound. Having said that, had it not been Sparks I probably wouldn't have heard it. They had the promotion behind them; you didn't have to go to a club to hear them. It was a marketing campaign you couldn't ignore."

Nick Rhodes: "*No. 1 In Heaven* was a revelation. There were a lot of people incorporating disco into their material but Sparks actually just went out there and made a whole album of it. *No. 1 In Heaven* was a very brave record to make to just try something completely different. It's their adaptability that I've always admired. I was hugely into the Moroder sound, as well. And this fitted into his canon just after Donna Summer and *Midnight Express.*"

No. 1 In Heaven was a pleasant and ultimately highly influential surprise, and remains so many years later. A six-track album at a time when that length was merely reserved for either prog rock or disco delicacy was really something else. The UK, with warm memories of the Sparks of five years earlier still very much in the collective psyche, welcomed the brothers back and lapped up this change of direction. Well, those who were not horrified at the proposition of a white rock act turning 'disco'.

"I like the album a lot," Ron said. "I think it has an atmosphere that isn't in any of our other albums, and isn't in anybody else's albums. It was a one-of-a-kind situation: people from different areas not having a clue how it was going to turn out ... I think it's influenced people in terms of the way of working – how a band could be a project in a certain kind of way."

"Not only was it redefining our sound, we were redefining what a band could be. Ten years later, every duo or electronic band worked like that," Russell added. "The odd thing is we get accused of stealing from people that came after us – which is a little irksome."

Chapter Twelve
Noisy Boys Are Happy Boys?
Terminal Jive

"I just wanted to get through it. The recording process was so distant from me."
Ron Mael, 2003

By the start of 1980, Sparks were an important pop force again – in the UK, at least. They had appeared alongside Blondie, David Bowie and Frank Zappa in Paula Yates' comic, controversial coffee-table book, *Rock Stars In Their Underpants*, and featured in a new teen-pop weekly magazine, *Smash Hits*, written by people who had been Sparks fans first time round. To underline how deep they ran in the psyche, Paul McCartney affectionately acknowledged Sparks in the video that accompanied his latest single, 'Coming Up'. Thanks to the video techniques of the day, McCartney played a variety of characters from pop's past as his backing band, The Plastic Macs. Among others, he dressed as Hank Marvin, Ginger Baker, Ritchie Blackmore and himself as a young mop-topped Beatle. And, dressed in a white shirt with black tie, McCartney stood behind an electric piano as Seventies pop culture icon Ron Mael. A frequent shot was 'Ron' glowering while 'Beatle Paul' shook his mane and did a trademark 'ooooh'.

"That was really strange for me," Ron later told Sparks guitarist Jim Wilson on Wilson's *Mother Superior* website. "The oddest thing was going into a dry-cleaner the day after they showed the 'Coming Up' video on *Saturday Night Live* and the guy who was working there said, 'Hey, I saw you on television last night' and I was like, 'Oh, yeah'. It was really flattering because it was McCartney and also because of the other people who he had chosen to pay homage to in the video. It was pretty amazing."

"To have a Beatle acknowledging your existence," Russell said in 1995 to *Happening* magazine, "is the goal of any musician."

Given the coverage their comeback had enjoyed, Sparks' next release was as important as *Propaganda* had been in following up *Kimono My House*. Initial meetings for what was to become *Terminal Jive* took place in summer 1979 in LA before Ron and Russell started recording. Given his rush to produce them and the subsequent ousting of John Hewlett, Giorgio Moroder appeared to have lost interest in working directly with Sparks, as he brought in one of his production team, Harold Faltermeyer, to co-produce the album. The Munich-born, classically trained pianist had first worked with Moroder on the ground-breaking *Midnight Express* soundtrack and, like Moroder, had strong musical views that often sidelined the Maels.

As had happened with *No. 1 In Heaven*, virtually all of Ron's songs were rejected by Moroder and, as a result, only one of the album's tracks, 'When I'm With You', was written beforehand. If Moroder had largely removed himself from the proceedings, unfortunately he'd largely removed Sparks as well. They became like session players on their own record.

"[*Terminal Jive*] was a lot less fun to record," Ron told the author in 2003. "Even though Giorgio was overseeing it, he didn't produce it. The special fun had gone. It was like the electro version of *Introducing Sparks*, more distant from us and more processed…"

Being micromanaged did not suit Ron and Russell, but that didn't stop them coming up with hook-laden pop songs that seemed perfect for the current market. However the market had shifted in the space of the nine months separating *No. 1 In Heaven* and *Terminal Jive*. In the US, disco had now fallen out of favour and only a handful of acts that rode its wave of popularity would see their sales continue. In Britain, the new electronica that Sparks had presaged in 1979 had a new figurehead in Gary Numan, and the 2-Tone craze and mod revival seemed to be every teenage boy's obsession. What was so in step last year now seemed frankly dated. As a consequence, *Terminal Jive* sank without trace.

Terminal Jive has little in the way of personality; a robust album of bargain basement disco. Whereas 'I Feel Love', Kraftwerk's *The Man Machine* and *No. 1 In Heaven* had located the soul of the genre, *Terminal Jive* is a case of disco for disco's sake and, ultimately, a missed opportunity. Its eight tracks are all pleasing, well-written and commercial, they're just not right. Somehow working with Moroder had made Sparks lose their sense of flair and lyrical exploration. It is hard to believe that these are the same people who wrote *Indiscreet*. Repetition has always been the backbone of the group, but outside a couple of the songs, every track builds to multiple repeats of the song's title.

Ron has said of *Terminal Jive* that "everything was sucked out of it", all except one thing, the majesty of its lead single, 'When I'm With You', one of the best things that Sparks have ever recorded. Both Ron's music and Ron and Russell's lyrics are simply touching. It's one of the few direct love songs in Sparks' catalogue – a lush, warm, emotional record amid all the synthetics. The reference to the "pressure being on" to "say something special" was possibly a reference to the fact that Moroder had made Ron rewrite the middle eight.

The *Sounds* review of *Terminal Jive* noted the importance of this track to the album. "'When I'm With You' is the major work. It possesses a hookline reminiscent of an airline jingle with swooshing synth to match; the instrumental, though, is sublime. Multi-layered, perfectly constructed, with the ever present thumping drums."

The rest of the album struggles to recover from the greatness of 'When I'm With You', especially as an instrumental reprise of it closes the first side, as if to reinforce its importance. The amusing 'Rock'n'Roll People In A Disco World' is the closest they get to finding their funny bone, as they put into song Russell's sentiment from the previous year's *Melody Maker* interview about rock bands. It also has an ironic bent, as the brothers were fully aware of their own position in all this.

Despite Russell's recent comments in interviews, guitars *were* back on a Sparks record. LA session man 'Snuffy' Walden, who had recently worked with the band Brooklyn Dreams, provided the power chords that so defined the album's second side. Walden's grinding rock guitar chords on 'Just Because You Love Me' predict the entire Eighties sound. 'Noisy Boys' and 'The Greatest Show On Earth' have a decent choppy swagger, while 'Stereo' sounds like something from the fourth side of Donna Summer's *Bad Girls* album.

'Young Girls' can be argued as putting Nabokov's *Lolita* in song, and lusting after teenage girls is nothing new in pop music. However, its explicit nature here makes it awkward listening, and distasteful to the modern ear. Russell wrote in his sleeve notes for *The Heaven Collection*, "Yes your honour, it is a song about being a dirty old man." It is nothing to be proud of, however ironic the song may purport to be.

The sleeve was rather odd as well. Although a successful attempt at Eighties modernism by recently reacquainted friend and photographer Gered Mankowitz, it didn't scream "this is a new Sparks album".

Gered Mankowitz: "During the second half of 1979, I'd met them again and we had dinner a couple of times and hung out the teeniest bit, but they were always working. I asked if they would like to do a photo session for syndication, which we did that August. We got some nice press pictures. They came to my studio in Great Windmill Street and we did four or five different set-ups. They responded very well – I had the idea of them holding flash guns and illuminating each other. They *really* liked that idea."

The brothers were taken back to their roots as fans of rock'n'roll and at break times asked Mankowitz to reminisce: "My association with the Stones and Hendrix in the Sixties is always a major topic when people find out about it. Because I had a foot in the door, they were eager for tales and stories with a cup of tea."

The cover shots for *Terminal Jive* were taken in two sessions, on October 22 and December 6, at locations across west London. For a photographer so associated with well-prepared studio shots, Mankowitz's sleeve was what might now be described as 'guerrilla photography'.

Gered Mankowitz: "I was first choice for *Terminal Jive* by them and art director Pearce Marchbank. Pearce is an extraordinarily creative art director. Not only does he have a vision, but he can get the most out of you. He is infuriating, incredibly demanding, but he gets the best out of you. It's fulfilling and demanding, even if it's exhausting."

Together Mankowitz, Marchbank and the Maels came up with a concept in the documentary/reportage style of New York crime and street scene photographer Arthur Felig, known to the world as Weegee. The four took to the streets.

Gered Mankowitz: "We wanted to be lean and mobile. Pearce freed me up a lot by saying he wasn't worried about the reflections of the flash or technical error. When you are relieved of that sort of concern, you can be a lot looser. I did it on my Hasselblad as I wanted to get the quality."

The team moved between Victoria mainline and underground stations and the Safeway supermarket on Chelsea's King's Road. "Ron was up for anything," said Mankowitz, "he just relished the grotesquery and Russell loved this style. They worked beautifully together – they were so visual, such fun, so inspiring."

It was literally shoot and run: "We got thrown out of everywhere; in those days it took people a lot longer to suss out what was going on," Mankowitz continues. "By the time they'd cottoned on to us, I'd taken a couple of rolls of film; they'd established we didn't have any permits, but we were gone. We had fun in Harrods with Ron coming out of the lift; there's one in the piano department and a strange one in the book department where Ron was about to devour a little old lady before we got turfed out on our ear."

Possibly the most memorable shots were at Victoria station. "Ron didn't mind what he did. He lay down on the platform; the famous one of him in the terminus with an old tramp pointing at him. The tramp is basically saying that [Ron's] laying down in his spot. None of the crowd quite knew what was going on; some of them may have known who the guys were, but it was guerrilla photography."

The cover is strange and unsettling. Standing on the pavement outside the supermarket window, Ron dressed in his black suit and black loafers with white socks, his hands over his ears and his face contorted as if hearing a loud noise. Russell, inside the store, looks out at Ron, concerned. Perhaps he had heard the album.

Released in January 1980, *Terminal Jive* received a mixed press. *Melody Maker* loved it: "Still obsessed with adolescence, Ron and Russell emerge with a series of memorable pop tunes, any of which would make fine singles," while Betty Page in *Sounds* saw through it. Awarding two stars out of five, she concluded. "Oh, for the wit and sparkle of the classic 'This Town Ain't Big Enough For 'The Both Of Us', or even the genuine experimentation apparent on *No 1 In Heaven*. Four good tracks doth not a good album make." *The Rock Year Book* for 1981 described it as "cartoon pop with the tap your feet dance beat. Even if it goes in one ear and out the other, you can't fail to enjoy it. A commercial flop of some note, it also highlights the Mael Brothers' dilemma of now being 'Rock'n'Roll People In A Disco World'."

The album did nothing chart-wise in the UK, neither did its two singles, 'When I'm With You' and 'Young Girls'. Just a year after *No. 1 In Heaven* Sparks had been abandoned by the UK. Again.

The album didn't even receive a release in the US. The disco backlash certainly had something to do with it. Perhaps it would have been better if they had made the same record twice; but that wasn't Sparks.

"Compared to *No. 1 in Heaven,* this is less spacey and more down-to-earth – without much character at all," Russell said.

Ron has never disguised his contempt for *Terminal Jive*: "It was the only album where I wasn't allowed to play keyboards," he told *Mixmag* in 1995, "and as I've always seen myself as the keyboard player in Sparks, it was a little rough."

The real irony is that *Terminal Jive* is possibly Sparks' most prescient album. By the mid Eighties, due in part to Keith Forsey's drum sound and Harold Faltermeyer's production work for other artists and how it was subsequently emulated, most pop records actually sounded like it.

As before, Sparks headed to where the work was and the critical glare shone brightest. 'When I'm With You' gained a life of its own in France and Ron and Russell relocated there for the rest of 1980. "The video [for the single] was shown to death in France," Russell later said. "As a result, we could walk into virtually any couscous restaurant in Paris and get the best table in the house."

The witty clip depicted Russell as Ron's ventriloquist puppet – a wry joke given that Ron wrote around 95% of what his younger brother sang. The single went to the top of the French charts, going on to sell around 700,000 units. As a result, further singles, 'Young Girls' and 'Rock'n'Roll People In A Disco World', were subsequent chart hits there.

During their prolonged stay in France, offers were put together for Sparks to play live. The simple problem was that they hadn't toured since 1976, and they didn't have a band. "We had seen a band in Los Angeles called Bates Motel that we thought would be compatible with us," Russell said in 1982. "They were all really good musicians and we thought it would be ideal to take the whole band intact and have them be Sparks' band."

Taking their name from the notorious motel in Hitchcock's *Psycho*, Bates Motel was a proper band: bassist Leslie Boehm, guitarist Bob Haag and drummer David Kendrick. Kendrick was born in Chicago, where he began playing in local bands in his teenage years, including one that Kendrick unbelievably persuaded to cover 'Talent Is An Asset' from *Kimono My House*. And that *wasn't* a Fleury/Mael scam. Kendrick relocated to LA in the mid-Seventies to play in Venus and the Razorblades, a band put together by scenester Kim Fowley, who was then running high on the success of The Runaways. After leaving Venus, Kendrick got himself a gig with Continental Miniatures, who were signed by London Records. Soon, Bates Motel followed.

The union of the two bands came through the Maels' only real vice: coffee and pastries.

David Kendrick: "We used to hang out separately at the Farmers' Market in LA. It was the only place in Los Angeles that you could get Espresso and we were all coffee fiends. There was this Belgian waffle stand there and we would end up there at the same time."

Kendrick and Boehm – the duo at the core of Bates Motel – impressed Ron and Russell with their prior knowledge of Sparks, something not many young Americans had. "We just got talking and it was clear that we liked a lot of the same stuff," says Kendrick. "We got to know each other that way."

The brothers began to open up about their situation, as Kendrick says: "They said that *Terminal Jive* frankly was a pretty bad album and they weren't too crazy about it. But they always seemed to have something happening somewhere in the world that would enable them to survive. Due to the success of 'When I'm With You' in France, they really wanted a live band again as they had this chance to tour there."

After Ron and Russell went to see Bates Motel play, they hired the whole group. The tour, which ran through the autumn of 1980, was a blast and, for the brothers, it was a delight to be playing live for the first time in four years. Often Ron would simply write out the chords and the band would learn the songs from scratch. The list was a perfect hybrid of all eras of Sparks' career. Being something of an aficionado, Kendrick helped shape the repertoire and made sure his personal favourites from the Island days – 'Here In Heaven' and 'Hospitality On Parade' – were incorporated. Tellingly, there was only one song, 'When I'm With You', from the album the band was supposed to be promoting.

Chapter Thirteen

So You Better Have Fun Now: America

"There's something about the words on Angst In My Pants *that has Ron's unique combination of sarcasm, wit and earnest emotion."*

Steven Nistor, 2009

"They can compare us to Devo if they want to, all the bands we predate by ten years."

Russell Mael, 1983

During rehearsals for the French tour, the new-look Sparks learned all the songs that would become their next album. Immediately afterwards, the band decamped to Musicland Studios in Munich where they started work on what was to be *Whomp That Sucker.*

Musicland Studios – where bands such as The Rolling Stones and Queen had recorded – was situated in Munich's Arabella Hotel. One might think of Musicland as being on top of a mountain, or secluded in a forest, but it was underground.

David Kendrick: "This was definitely subterranean. The coolest thing about it was that through one of the back doors in the basement, you'd

177

head into part of an abandoned underground system. I actually banged on some wood and pipes and stuff out there because the echo was so amazing."

Although still overseeing the four-album production deal he'd entered into with the Maels, after *Terminal Jive*, Giorgio Moroder was no longer involved with the recordings, which gave Sparks the opportunity to work with yet another producer.* Rheinhold Mack was one of Moroder's production team but was also very hot in his own right at the time. Fundamentally a rock producer, Mack (as he was known) had worked with the Rolling Stones, but was best known for his work with two bands that had crossed Sparks' path back in 1972 – Electric Light Orchestra and Queen. Mack was able to effectively blend the synthetics of Sparks' last two releases into something far more band-like.

For the first time since *Big Beat*, Sparks worked in one room as a group. Boehm, Haag and Kendrick were there to support the brothers and be sounding boards for both Ron and Russell and Mack.

David Kendrick: "Mack was easy-going and I liked him a lot. We recorded well. We did the songs to a click track but essentially played live. Everyone was around the whole time."

The group stayed at the hotel over the studios, and were on call most of the time to go downstairs to record. Ron wrote his lyrics in his hotel room the night before recording, after Russell had improvised nonsense words in rehearsal.

David Kendrick: "There was always a title to the song but the lyrics were not necessarily finished. We'd learn the songs and the final lyrics would be done literally as we were due to start recording the next song. I thought it interesting as Sparks' songs are so conceptually based and it was funny that the words were the last step."

Moroder popped into the studio once or twice to see how things were progressing. "It struck me there wasn't a lot of intellectual depth there," Kendrick says. "[Moroder] just wanted stuff done quickly. He didn't want to bother with Ron agonising over his lyrics; he and Keith Forsey took the view that lyrics didn't even matter! They worked well

---

* By now Sparks had had nine different producers and five different record labels, which, quite frankly, was going some.

together for a while but it didn't seem like he really, totally got where they were at. I was really glad that Mack was involved because he was a rock guy and liked the idea of a live band."

Kendrick remembers the sessions as a time of good humour, with Queen, who were painstakingly putting together their ill-received disco album, *Hot Space*, being around as well, adding to the freewheeling yet businesslike approach of the sessions.

Sparks' tenth album, *Whomp That Sucker,* was released in May 1981 on the Why-Fi label in the UK and Ariola for the rest of the world. The thanks list on the album's inner bag listed at least seven pastry shops around Munich, reflecting a shared love of coffee and cake that had helped the band through an intense recording period.

David Kendrick: "Quickly Imbiss was a fast-food pastry place we frequented near the hotel. We went almost daily to the Cafe Reitschule [riding school], a great cafe in the 'Englisher garden' overlooking the park and a dressage horse-training ring for the Munich elite."

After two records of Giorgio Moroder and Harold Faltermeyer-directed disco synthesiser experimentation, guitars and electric pianos were suddenly a major part of Sparks' world again. *Whomp That Sucker* updates *Kimono My House* with a nod to modernity as opposed to *No. 1 In Heaven* and *Terminal Jive*'s wholesale rejection of the past. It may not be one of their all-time greats, but it still contains 'Tips For Teens', 'Upstairs' and the simply smashing stupidity of 'The Willys' and 'Wacky Women'; after the meandering, phoned-in triteness of *Terminal Jive*, here at least was a little flesh on the bones. Sparks sounded like a band again and, importantly, on 'I Married A Martian' and 'Wacky Women' it sounded like they were having tremendous fun.

"Harmonies were back again," Russell said. "As were songs about girls who suffer from overly beautiful exteriors and their ensuing suicide attempts. Followed by new-found happiness as a result of their total facial disfigurement."

The song in question, 'Funny Face,' also featured the first proper Sparks guitar solo since *Big Beat*, courtesy of Bob Haag. Five years since their last permanent unit, and less than two years after denouncing bands in the press, Ron and Russell Mael rather enjoyed being part of a band again.

"That album was an explosion for us," Ron said in 1982. "We had been working in tight little ways with session people and real bourgeois types. We wanted to rebel against that and make an album that had real character to it – a lot of songs, really rocky. This album is important to us. We've always liked working in a band format. It gives you a certain set of rules and keeps you from being too cerebral. It gives you an element of looseness."

"This is a favourite because we felt liberated after the constraints of *Terminal Jive*," Russell told Paul Lester in 2008. "It didn't feel like a step back for us, even though it was working with a band again. We really felt free to work within what for us are traditional song frameworks, but with other people. There's a support system working with a band."

There was something dumb and accessible in this new Sparks sound. It sounded like Devo, for sure – 'Upstairs' especially has the breezy, wheezy synthesisers of 'Whip It' – but then didn't *they* sound like Sparks? Despite Devo's undeniable influence on *Whomp That Sucker,* it remains unclear if the influence was mutual.

In a 2009 interview in *The Wire* magazine, Devo vocalist Mark Mothersbaugh commented, "Even after I met him I was still a big Ron Mael fan. I just had this whole idea of who he could have been. Just from seeing him on TV… Somehow they got on TV with this stuff… I remember him with his really stern Adolf Hitler look, and it was so not rock'n'roll, in an unexpected way, that you just couldn't help but think that there was something there. I only met him in public situations, which weren't his forte as much as his brother. His brother was the flamboyant… or irritating-looking, poofy version of the two of them. And I really liked Ron and I always said, 'Well, I don't care what Russell's doing, I'm sure Ron really runs everything and it's really his band…'" *

Whomp That Sucker is funny, muddy and loud, and its cover reintroduced the humorous style of the early Island albums. After the strange, dispassionate dislocation of *Terminal Jive's* sleeve, *Whomp That Sucker* finds Sparks retreating to the broad comedy of *Propaganda* and

---

* In all probability most of Mothersbaugh's comments were made tongue-in-cheek as their paths have crossed over the years and Kendrick would later go on to drum with Devo.

Indiscreet, a pattern that was to last for the next three albums. Taking the title literally, we see the brothers in a boxing ring. Russell is out for the count, unconscious on the floor, while Ron is seen behind, victorious with both arms aloft, ribs on full display.

The sleeve marked the start of the Maels' collaboration with designer Larry Vigon, which set about making the brothers a cartoon of themselves. It worked very well; emphasising the brothers as a comedy double-act, with the fall guy alternating between covers. LA-born Vigon, who got to know Sparks through Moroder, would regularly meet the pair at the Farmers' Market.

Larry Vigon: "I was really happy to get a call from them. I really enjoyed working with those guys because they were smart; a good sense of humour, well-educated." Vigon draws similarities between the brothers and Lindsay Buckingham for whom he designed the hand-drawn Fleetwood Mac logo on *Rumours* and the intricate artwork of *Tusk*. Both share the focus and eccentricities of musical geniuses.

Although *Whomp That Sucker* was not to be a chart success in the UK, its launch in the second week of May at the London Hilton in Park Lane marked one of the final appearances of Ron and Russell in Britain until 1985. A re-creation of the boxing match between the brothers was staged for the press and guests who included Viv Stanshall, Clem Burke, Tony James and Judge Dread.

Something curious happened – whether it was the publicity generated by their new American band or whether the world had caught up, but the album, with its broad-based B-movie comedy, began to be picked up by the burgeoning student radio movement in America.

David Kendrick: "There was a new radio station in LA, K-ROQ, and it was actually playing local, newer music; modern rock or new wave. It was one of the few stations that played Sparks. They were one of the first groups they really picked up on and there were a number of songs from *Whomp That Sucker* that got a lot of radio play in Los Angeles specifically. The group got really well known, really quickly."

MTV, too, had begun broadcasting and if ever a band were suited to repeat video screenings, it was Sparks. Promos were prepared for 'Tips

For Teens' (a re-creation of the boxing match) and 'Funny Face' (Ron appears to be waiting behind a tree to offer sweets to little girls before being beaten about the head by one of their mothers). *Rolling Stone* and *Trouser Press* were favourable in their reviews.

"A new young audience was attracted that was virtually unaware of our British and European past careers," Russell said. "We were a brand new band with nine albums that few of our new fans were aware of. Dick Clark welcomed us back."

Indeed, it wasn't long before Sparks were back on *American Bandstand*, the show that they had first appeared on almost a decade earlier. After all the attempts to break America, it now seemed to be happening. The band and Joseph Fleury were absolutely delighted when the album climbed to number 182 on the US album chart.

Sparks toured throughout the West Coast and played key dates in Europe. Like 'Sir' Peter Oxendale a decade before, a second keyboard player, Jim Goodwin, from John Cale's band, was drafted in to flesh out the band's live sound. One of the more bizarre appearances in Sparks' career came on December 9, 1981. A year on from John Lennon's death, the band appeared in a televised tribute concert at Bayerisches Femsehen as part of Eberhard Schroeder's *Rock & Klassik* series. An ad hoc ensemble performed what can only be described as a 'loose' version of Lennon's 1969 hit 'Give Peace A Chance'. On stage, being ever Stentorian with his vocal is the English eccentric performer Peter Hammill, the cult artist's cult artist, and over to the right, Sparks. Ron, in his sunhat, hits some claves apologetically and Russell shakes his maracas aimlessly. Around them, heavyweight performers such as Brand X percussionist Morris Pert, ex-King Crimson saxophonist Mel Collins and guitarist John Miles plod into the leaden groove. The very fact that any of these people were on stage with Sparks was frankly unusual. "Peter Hammill was there alongside Tangerine Dream," Kendrick laughs. "That was the end of the show. We were all playing. It was strange to say the least."

For Sparks' next album, RCA, which had represented them in the States, declined to pick up the option, so the band signed to Atlantic, one of the most respected companies in the world. Although Island had the romance and Virgin the status of maverick outsider, this was not just any old record company, *this was Atlantic*. The label, founded in 1947 by Ahmet Ertegun, the son of a Turkish diplomat, and student Herb Abramson, was named as a response to the West Coast jazz label, Pacific. Atlantic had an incredible soul, R&B, blues, jazz and rock tradition, and it was now going to include Sparks, too.

Angst In My Pants had a gestation period almost identical to its predecessor. Recorded at Musicland, it is the sound of players totally at ease with one another. 'I Predict', the Maels' tribute to the *National Enquirer*, is probably the greatest example of this new approach. Building on the new-found sense of play, everything sounds a great deal more relaxed than anything the band had recorded before. Russell began to sing out of the falsetto he'd been singing in since 1974. This new muscle to his voice could be heard especially on material such as 'I Predict'. While recording, the band played three nights of gigs in Munich and threw themselves into attendant press and promotion with gusto.

"This [album's] based around really good songs," Russell said in 1982. "I don't think there's any filler on it; it's just doing what we should be doing. As an after-effect, it turns out the album's been played on radio infinitely more than any other Sparks record in America. So we can do something that maintains the essence of what Sparks is, retaining personality and character, and still get airplay."

Angst In My Pants is one of the most charming of all Sparks albums and their best LP from the Eighties. It's daft, anthemic and full of great, funny, danceable songs. The grinding power-pop was so very of its moment, evoking 'Centerfold' by The J Geils Band or Toni Basil's 'Mickey', but adding lyrics that bordered on hilarious.

'Instant Weight Loss' strays close to vigorous, enjoyable rock. "Weight is an obsession with both of us," Russell continued. "Ron carries a scale with him on tour; he takes it about as far as you can get without seriously damaging your health. I really like sweets, so there's a real dilemma cos I also want to maintain the same appearance I had 11 albums ago."

'Sherlock Holmes' manages to weld Joy Division and doo-wop, while 'Nicotina' has a dramatic punch, referencing the same Cossack songbook that 'Goofing Off' had done five years previously.

With its fun-packed backing vocals and frantic synthesiser playing from Jim Goodwin, 'Sextown USA' became a live favourite. The album's title track was made from a tape loop of Kendrick's drumming, over which Ron added his keyboard parts. Mack encouraged Russell to go over the top, using a lyric that Ron was going to use for another song. The final track to be recorded for the album, 'Angst In My Pants', packed a mighty punch. Writing on allmusic.com, Dave Connolly encapsulates the album by saying, "Throughout the record, Sparks succeeds not by pushing a pipe full of music through a thin straw (as they did on classics like *Propaganda*) but by giving their ideas the space they need to succeed." And most of the ideas did succeed.

Larry Vigon perfectly realised Ron's next "purposely tacky" concept for the album's sleeve. People had been commenting for years about the duo's inseparability, that they weren't brothers at all, or could even be secretly romantically involved with each other. Remember there were those who even suggested that the geishas on the front of *Kimono My House* were the brothers in drag. All absolute nonsense, of course, but toying with genders and masculinity all added to the fun of creating a sleeve image. Photographed by Eric Blum, Ron is dressed as a demure bride, with long flowing veil, flower bunch and rock twinkling on his ring finger next to a beaming Russell, the epitome of a smiling rock'n'roll groom, wearing a silver lamé suit (and Blum's shoes, no less). The inner bag develops the theme even further – the happy couple are now at Niagara Falls; Ron in his polka dot honeymoon outfit smiling, while a Hawaiian-shirted Russell looks less sure than he did on his wedding day. Presumably, they had consummated the marriage by this point. For the first time since *Indiscreet*, the full line-up of Sparks appears on the album's rear sleeve. All six members stand in Elvis poses playing acoustic guitar in their lamé suits, undoubtedly serenading the newly married couple.

With material this visual, it was obvious that Sparks should do a lot of television. On May 15, 1982, they appeared on *Saturday Night Live* as the guests of host Danny DeVito. For a generation of Americans, this appearance was similar to Brits seeing the group on *Top Of The Pops* back in 1974. Ron delivered a speech about the cultural significance of mice before opening the show with 'Mickey Mouse'. For 'I Predict', Ron wore his sunhat, and, when not playing behind his keyboard (now with the 'Roland' brand name altered to state 'Ronald') he was eating in front of it or being hugged by his brother, who, in his crimson lamé suit, was going ape throwing athletic shapes. The band, too, were all resplendent in different shades of lamé. It was a great, 'in your face' performance, projecting the cartoon as large as possible for nationwide US TV.

David Kendrick: "We were a little wary of playing 'Mickey Mouse'. We worried if we'd need Disney's permission to use it but we went ahead. It was a brand new audience again for Sparks and it was a pretty young crowd. We even started to attract some celebrity fans while in New York. We were at the same hotel while we were doing *Saturday Night Live* as Muhammad Ali. We met Andy Warhol. Danny DeVito came to see us a few times."

'I Predict' came with a striking video that fell foul of the conservatism of MTV. Directed in the style of David Lynch by group friends, identical twins and occasional actors Doug and Steve Martin, it is crammed full of strangeness. Shot in a dimly lit bar outside LA, Ron, in drag, develops the bride theme from the album's cover with Russell still wearing the cover's wedding suit. And Ron is stripping. And Russell is watching. Something is clearly not quite right. With the attendant promotion and the video's notoriety, 'I Predict' reached number 60 on the *Billboard* Hot 100. Sparks had finally achieved a US Top 100 single after a decade of trying.

Ira Robbins wrote warmly about the album: "They have synthesized their past into a newly impressive whole with the current *Angst In My Pants* LP" and published a Sparks retrospective in *Trouser Press*. The piece was one of their first major career overviews and introduced this 'new' band's audience to the previous ten albums.

K-ROQ kept the group high on their playlist. Around half of *Angst In My Pants* was played on the network and, as a result, the album went to 173 on *Billboard*. Everything was moving in the right direction. Clearly delighted at how his charges were finally getting a soupçon of recognition in their home country, Joseph Fleury looked after his charges with care and diligence. What he may have lacked in managerial distance was made up for by still being their number one supporter.

David Kendrick: "He was very much a fan. I really liked him a lot. He was a good person. He was a fan of the band and he wasn't a super high-powered manager type. He was a good liaison between labels because the times I was [in Sparks], we were probably on at least four different record labels."

Fleury helped put together a tour that would capitalise on Sparks' new-found American success. The band returned to the Whisky A Go Go, which gave them a slightly more rapturous reception this time round as opposed to their previous visit in 1973. As well as large clubs in the Midwest and Texas Sparks even returned to perform a televised concert at Magic Mountain, where, in a previous life, they had filmed *Rollercoaster*, which by now was a television staple. At an outdoor gig at LA's Greek Theatre, the support act was a new band that welded funk to heavy metal. The Red Hot Chili Peppers, like previous support acts Queen and Van Halen, would eventually eclipse Sparks commercially.

One territory that failed to host a Sparks resurgence was the UK. The publication *The Rock Album* perfectly summed up in its review not just *Angst In My Pants* but this whole period of Sparks with the line, "clever European feel tinged with Californian surf-like teenage anxiety subject matters". With Duran Duran, Culture Club and ABC, Britain had shiny pop of its own. As a result, Sparks albums were quietly released and then slipped by unnoticed.

"We were going to do a *Whistle Test* at some point and it didn't happen," says Kendrick. "There was just nothing happening there for us at that time."

Angst In My Pants would go on to have a huge influence on future Sparks members. "My 'in' was *Saturday Night Live,*" Jim Wilson recalls. "I had heard 'I Predict' on Philadelphia radio and I thought 'Wow, those guys are great'." It sent Wilson off on a jamboree of Sparks collecting. "I had an *Encyclopaedia of Rock* with a photo of *Kimono My House* so I knew what the cover looked like. I'd heard it and it was so completely different to *Angst In My Pants*. I was just fascinated. I'd just never heard anything like it before. I would buy old Sparks albums from the vinyl store in Delaware at $1.99 each."

"*Angst In My Pants* is my favourite Sparks album," says Steven Nistor. "It's the strangest-sounding Sparks record. It has some of the coolest drum parts I've ever heard, from any band. I love all of Ron's lyrics but there's something about the words on *Angst In My Pants* that has Ron's unique combination of sarcasm, wit and earnest emotion. Every song is cohesive in that way. I have many favourite Sparks records but for some reason this one really stands out for me."

David Kendrick: "As someone who really liked the *Kimono My House* period, I really think *Whomp That Sucker* and especially *Angst In My Pants* are among their best. I was really happy to have been part of it."

The union between Sparks and Bates Motel had come at exactly the right time, and the fact they could enjoy some success at home felt good. Les Boehm, David Kendrick and Bob Haag's band were now known as Gleaming Spires. Ron and Russell would often see the band live and gave them their seal of approval by penning the tongue-in-cheek sleeve notes for Gleaming Spires' debut album. It was a mutually beneficial friendship where Ron and Russell met friends such as producers Greg Penny and Stephen Hague, who would both go on to work with Sparks.

There had now been a period of stability for three years, something Sparks had never experienced before. "They were never the hearty type," Kendrick says with a chuckle. "Russell was kind of the social one and Ron was always a little more introverted and he was more the intellectual half, if you will. He wrote all the words, pretty much to everything, his brother sang and they were absolutely inseparable. On tours and off the road, they would get together like every single day. It was unusual. They almost never did anything apart. It was always like Ronandrussell."

There was still a divide between the Maels and the others, but the band knew their place and, as they were all LA residents, there were no cultural barriers.

Sparks In Outer Space, their 1983 album, finds Ron receiving a custard pie on the cover, the ultimate comedy pay-off and very apt as the album is one big pie-in-the-face of a record. The first Sparks record to be entirely self produced by the Maels, the album – full of goofy, mid-Eighties US rock with a twist – was recorded at Synsound in Belgium at the studios of Telex – Marc Moulin and Dan Lacksman – with whom Ron and Russell had struck up a friendship in 1980.* Ron and Russell are pictured by the Atomium in Brussels on the album's inner sleeve – the latest stop in the group's nomadic career.

---

* In 1982 Ron and Russell provided lyrics for Telex's *Sex (Birds And Bees)* album.

"Unlike the two preceding LPs, *Outer Space* had no rehearsals before recording; just a bunch of rough versions sung by Ron on his Walkman," Russell said in his *Profile* notes. The record contained two tracks not recorded in Belgium; one of these was even more remarkable in that it finally delivered Sparks a US Top 50 hit single. 'Cool Places' was a duet with Jane Wiedlin, the co-leader of LA girl-punk pop act The Go-Go's, who had allegedly been the secretary of her own non-authorised LA Valley Sparks fan club, although that seems another piece of Fleury-Sparks hokum. As Russell said in the *Profile* notes, "rather than sue her, we asked Jane if she would like to do a duet together". Another story has it that The Go-Go's all wanted to enrol in Sparks' fan club, and their legendary International Fan Club Secretary, Mary Martin, aka the Maels' mother, personally passed the letter to her sons. Russell sent back a note suggesting they collaborate – possibly for a Russell Mael solo release.

"What finally helped [Sparks] was Russell's friendship with Jane Wiedlin and doing 'Cool Places'," Robbins says. "Suddenly it's like, 'Oh they're friends with The Go-Go's.'" And in 1983 The Go-Go's were one of the biggest groups in America. From a selection of proposed songs, Wiedlin and the band recorded two tracks for *Sparks In Outer Space* at Giorgio Moroder's studio in the living room of his Beverly Hills home. 'Cool Places' was completely of the moment: chugging synths, Ron's conversational writing and a perfectly matched duet between Russell and Wiedlin. It headed up an album that, although not as good as its immediate predecessors, was sufficiently strong to maintain the interest of fans who had been won over by the single. It's the sound of 1983 technology, and although the band were again shown on the LP's rear sleeve, it is difficult to hear their input apart from the charming-yet-vacuous stadium grunge of 'Prayin' For A Party'.

Highlights include 'Rockin Girls', which allows Russell to pay vocal tribute to one of his heroes, Jerry Lee Lewis; 'A Fun Bunch Of Guys From Outer Space' develops 'I Married A Martian' from *Whomp That Sucker* to the point where it almost could be the same backing track; while 'All You Ever Think About Is Sex' is high-powered, witty hi-NRG, and the album's second single.

"'All You Ever Think About Is Sex' is my favourite Sparks single," states Steven Nistor. "I saw the video the first time I heard the song so it's ingrained in my memory. You know the video with Ron taking all those pies in the face? That made an impression on me." It was a development of one of Sparks' most hilarious covers, with Ron being the fall guy this time.

"Every time I think of *Sparks In Outer Space*, it makes me laugh," its designer, Larry Vigon, says. "I was lucky enough to be the one who threw all the pies – we had a stack of 12 of them. All these stylists, make-up people and photographer Jim Shea were all falling on the floor laughing. It was doubled-up, tears rolling down the face laughter. In between takes we had to clean him up and do it all over again. It literally happened 10 times in a row with hysterical laughing. Eventually we didn't bother any more and the final shot is actually a composite. We added a couple of pieces of pie and we had to retouch a few little specks here and there off Russell's clothing. It was a blast." Vigon, who also recalled Russell frequently going to the window during the shoot to make sure his green '57 Thunderbird hadn't been stolen or dented, is today a respected corporate designer and still has *Sparks In Outer Space* in his portfolio.

With a video shot by The Residents' film-maker Graham Whiffler ("any director who would incorporate a photo of Mary Jo Kopechne into a pop video was all right with us"), Atlantic put their weight behind 'Cool Places'. Sparks were put on a mammoth US tour supporting the Australian-born, Hollywood-residing actor-cum-singer Rick Springfield, who had just enjoyed a global hit with 'Jessie's Girl'. Springfield actually chose the group for the tour as he had been a fan of 'Wonder Girl', "He seemed pretty easy-going," Kendrick continues. "His manager was another story…" Sparks' scaled up their act – a rock band but with all Sparks' characteristics – and played a seven-song set. By the middle of the tour they were getting a great reception.

Fuelled by MTV, "We started getting screaming girls again," Russell recalled in 2008. "Only now it was in places like Kansas. There were huge concert favourites from this album [*Sparks In Outer Space*] that we played a lot in the Eighties." It was another world. "We were playing [places like] Madison Square Garden, these 20,000-seat places, for months," Kendrick recalls. "We got pushed into the Top 50. It was the one time when Ron and Russell reached out beyond their own fan base. A lot of people saw that tour but it was weird." However being Sparks, something was bound to happen that would prevent them from becoming really huge. They seemed to play the part of perpetual outsiders, forever tripping on the banana skin, wilfully snatching defeat from the jaws of victory.

The American honeymoon appeared to end abruptly. "Some of it had to do with business stuff at that time," David Kendrick says. "It was a question of how much money Atlantic was prepared to subsidise us with." Through no fault of their own Sparks were dropped from the Springfield tour to be replaced by Quarterflash.

Also, there was a question over how tough Fleury had to be on behalf of the group. Sparks had reached a lot of people, but there was uncertainty about how to develop this. Momentum was seemingly lost. The group went out on their own to smaller venues, playing festivals with The Go-Go's and Joe Walsh. Oscar and Miriam, who like their sons had long since returned from the UK, manned the merchandise stall when the band played locally. Although their next album would produce a single that made the dance charts, Sparks' dalliance with the mainstream seemed to be reaching its natural conclusion. It was off to be a cult band again.

"The only thing people paid attention to was Ron's moustache," Ira Robbins suggested. "No matter what Sparks did, all America would boil it down to was 'He's got a funny moustache. He looks like Charlie Chaplin'. Whatever you aspire to, or whatever you accomplish, it boils down to a gimmick, a trick or some attribute that people cling to."

That gimmick had gained the group far more exposure than if they had simply been po-faced rockers. And now, the most familiar moustache in recent art-pop culture had gone. As a reflection of the changing times in the mid-Eighties Ron's toothbrush moustache finally changed shape into something a little more Ronald Colman. After all the jokes about it and Russell singing about it on 'Moustache', there was the very real underside that some people found the 'tache extremely distasteful.

"I really saw it as a fun thing to do and I just thought it looked cool," he told *Seconds* magazine in 1995. "It had a really strong effect especially when we first moved to England. There were problems with people who took it in a non-Chaplinesque way. We got cancelled from a show in France because there was a bombing of a synagogue in Paris [the October 3, 1980 Rue Copernic explosion that killed four people] right around the time we were doing a TV show. I probably should have made a change earlier on, but I was pretty naïve about the effect it was having."

Ron and Russell seemed unsure what to do with their new level of recognition. They were regulars now on a variety of film soundtracks, and talk of film roles and film opportunities was on the agenda. However the music they were making was now becoming too samey, with a law of diminishing returns. It was clear by the time of *Pulling Rabbits Out Of A Hat,* Sparks' final release on Atlantic, that the company was losing interest in them. There had also been a change in personnel – John Thomas joined the group as keyboard player, replacing Jim Goodwin.

Pulling Rabbits Out Of A Hat was the first Sparks album since 1977's *Introducing Sparks* to be recorded solely in America. It was produced by British producer and engineer Ian Little, who was in vogue thanks to his work with Duran Duran on 'Is There Something I Should Know' and the album *Seven And The Ragged Tiger.* Little received his first credit working with Roxy Music as production assistant on *Avalon* and, of greater significance, his engineering on one of the Eighties most unusual albums, Orchestral Manoeuvres In The Dark's *Dazzle Ships.* It made him an interesting candidate to produce Sparks.

However his reliance on sequencers and the Fairlight made *Pulling Rabbits Out Of A Hat* too homogenised, and it lacks the personality that the previous three albums had. It was clearly the era; Sparks weren't the only band sounding like this at this time. In a way, that's the problem, Sparks fans were too used to each album sounding different. 'Everybody Move' is a case in point. While everything is in the right place, it sounds like something off the *Footloose* soundtrack. 'A Song That Sings Itself' could be *Flashdance,* the keyboard sound is so generic.

David Kendrick: "There was a slight tapering off, really. We were still very popular live then but I don't think we played as well on that album. It wasn't quite as intriguing to me. There were a couple of good songs on it. Ian Little was an engineer-type producer. There wasn't like an amazing session. It was a little more elaborate production-wise with mainly sequenced keyboard parts. To me, it wasn't as immediate and wasn't full of the good things I loved about Sparks."

Of course, *Pulling Rabbits Out Of A Hat* was not without its moments – it was a Sparks album, after all. The title track is classic Ron Mael. In the style of 'Angst In My Pants', it is a tale of a lover trying to impress his partner with a series of audacious feats. The touching 'With All My Might' was a standout. "When we would do a song that was softer in tone, people often wondered what our motive was," Russell said. "They wanted to know what the punchline was for Sparks doing such an atypical song. There was no punchline." (Released as a single, it reached number 28 on the *Billboard* club play chart. Its striking video was set in a studio backdrop of the American West.) 'Love Scenes' has a riff that borrows from Joy Division's 'Love Will Tear Us Apart' and 'Pretending To Be Drunk' is like a lesser version of 'I Predict'. 'Kiss Me Quick' has a lovely, understated feel to it, amid the standard, mid-Eighties handclaps. It's not without its charms, but expectation levels were now higher as Sparks hadn't made a bad record since 1980.

Although claims are made for *Terminal Jive*, *Pulling Rabbits Out Of A Hat* is, to these ears, the weakest Sparks album, almost totally bereft of any personality. The machines whirr and whine, and the band seem lost within them. The best thing about it was the Larry Vigon-designed sleeve. Moving away from the twisted portrait shots of the last three albums, Ron and Vigon commissioned an illustration from American artist Stan Watts. Brightly coloured and unnervingly realistic, the drawing develops the theme used in the 'When I'm With You' video, showing Russell as a glove puppet on Ron's right hand.

Released in the US in October 1984, the album failed to chart and became the first Sparks album not to get a UK release. The experience convinced Ron and Russell that they had no need to use outside producers again. "*Pulling Rabbits Out Of A Hat* was the last album that we had a formal producer for," Russell said in 2008. "We decided that from the people we'd worked with – Giorgio, Tony Visconti, Todd Rundgren and Muff Winwood – we'd learnt a lot of techniques, and we felt we could best interpret how we wanted to be perceived and what we wanted to do musically. We wanted more control."

After a period of three albums on one label – their greatest stability since Island – the group again found themselves label-less. "The thing I remember at one point was realising that between them and Graham

Parker they'd been on every single record label that had ever existed," Ira Robbins says. "They reached a point somewhere in the Eighties where they had been on something like seven or eight labels, which is kind of unthinkable, especially given that Warner Brothers when they started had been a label that people were born and died on".

Chapter Fourteen

A Rainbow Over The Freeway – The Path To Retirement

"This is where the brothers do the bulk of their work nowadays, enabled by new technology to bypass the expensive recording studios of yore, another factor contributing to their survival. The downside: they have to halt work on Thursday mornings when a neighbor's gardeners fire up the leaf blowers."

The *LA Times*, 1988

With all the success they had been enjoying in America, Sparks had all but disappeared from their core market, the UK. "We didn't intentionally leave the British music scene, it was just circumstances," Russell said in 1986. "One of the problems was that we were with an international record company that had no personal enthusiasm to champion Sparks in the UK."

It was time to rectify that situation. After leaving Atlantic, the brothers looked to find a deal for the new material they had been working on in Belgium. Working again with Dan Lacksman of Telex, they'd written a song called 'Change' – one of their best to date, and a marked swing away from the heavily manufactured beats of the last two albums.

Sparks were a group who embraced transformation. It may have meant that a lot of their releases sounded different but, admirably, they understood the need to keep moving forward. As a result, the aptly named 'Change' represents a watershed in Sparks' career and their best release of the Eighties. For the first time ever, Russell sounds weary. Half spoken/half sung with a sparing use of falsetto, ostensibly it is a break-up song. However, the passing of Paradise, Greece and Rome, the old west and vaudeville are discussed, with an unerring belief that golden days still lie ahead.

It was a prophetic moment as Ron and Russell had already seen more changes in the group's 15-year career-span than most. It was almost a biography in song, with implied acknowledgement of all the people that had passed through the group and the considerable twists and turns of their saga to this point. It also showed how accomplished Ron Mael was as a songwriter. It has long been one of Russell's favourites. "We wanted to try something that was epic in scope; something that was really involved," he has said. "The lyrical spirit of everything we had done to this point was probably better connected by Ron in this one song than in anything else we had done. And from a sonic standpoint, we couldn't do any better than the instrumental passage in the middle of this song. We're especially proud of it."

'Change' was a mighty track – big and bold, updating all the grandiosity of the past by giving it a definite mid-Eighties feel. Although it bears a lot of the hallmarks of that era's production, it emphasises Les Boehm's bass and Bob Haag's treated acoustic guitar before Ron's Fairlight stabs appear. The basic song had been written before going into the studio, where much time was spent refining the arrangement. (The band also recorded 'The Scene' at these Belgian sessions.)

After the disappointment that had been *Pulling Rabbits Out Of A Hat*, 'Change' was a grown-up record that found the Maels not wanting to be wacky Californians, but relaxing back into their occasional role as old world aesthetes.

In June 1985, 'Change' was released in the UK as a one-off single as part of a new deal with London Records; their seventh label, backed with an acoustic version of 'This Town Ain't Big Enough For Both Of Us'. Ron and Russell, accompanied by Kendrick and Fleury, did a European promotional tour. With their by now familiar understanding of how these things work, the brothers subjected themselves to the interview and lip-sync treadmill. In early July, they appeared on Terry Wogan's prime-time early evening chat show – the first time that they had appeared live on the BBC since 'Tryouts For The Human Race' in November 1979. It was a wonderful performance, with Russell and Ron going head to head on the timpani breakdown and then Ron introducing his dancing on British television.

They next appeared on TV AM, where presenter Julie Brown, sitting next to an amused Thomas Dolby on the sofa, read out the opening verse of 'Change' to Ron and Russell, asking for clarification. Ron replied with, "It's a lot of the usual pseudo-intellectual garbage." He then went on to say that London had allegedly signed them for £500,000, which all went on the recording of the song, leaving a tight budget for the video. Ron then holds up a cut-out of a TV screen to Russell, who performs the 50p version of the promo.

Although London Records put a great deal of marketing muscle behind it, the single stalled at number 85, lost in all the global hoo-hah for Live Aid. What 'Change' did do, however, was to establish the kernel of the musical direction and ideas that would ultimately become *Lil' Beethoven*, 17 years later.

After the artistic triumph of 'Change', Ron and Russell again repaired to Synsound, and called on their supporting team of players when the need arose. Boehm, Kendrick and Haag were involved for what would be their final recording with the group, along with John Thomas and, on their spirited cover of Stevie Wonder's 'Fingertips', the former Swinging Madisons' guitarist, Robert Mache. *Music That You Can Dance To* was recorded in Brussels over 1985 and 1986. "We spent longer on the recording of this LP than we had done on any previous one," Russell said. "It was a great luxury for us to be extravagant with studio time, and so far from home."

London Records suggested that the brothers give the public something that was a little more danceable. The idea was that they could then add 'Change' and – presto – an album would be made. "As it happens," Russell said, "we had written quite a lot of dancey new tunes, including a song called 'Music That You Can Dance To'." However, it did not go down well with the record company. "When we took it along to play it to them," Ron said, "they thought we were making fun of them."

For the seventh time thus far in their career, the brothers were without a label. In the end, the album was picked up by Curb Records, run by the charismatic Mike Curb, the former MGM executive who had sung in The Mike Curb Congregation before producing The Osmonds and getting involved in Republican politics.

Music That You Can Dance To finally appeared in November 1986. Although it was ultimately flawed, the album established the template for Sparks' next phase as a duo, and has a lively, sprightly sound that is the epitome of '86. On 'Music You Can Dance To', a Fairlight replicates the sound of a saxophone just like the mellotron had done 12 years previously on 'Equator'. Same idea, different technology. * Released as a single in February 1987, 'Rosebud' sounds like a hundred other ballads that were released around the same time (although it owes something melodically to Talking Heads' 'Life During Wartime' from 1979). Its reliance on the noises a machine could produce would be overpowering were it not for the fact that Ron and Russell had actually written a really good tune and performance. At least they were trying to move out of the completely homogenised sound that dogged *Pulling Rabbits Out Of A Hat*.

Although the cover of Stevie Wonder's 'Fingertips' was largely pointless, it's great to hear the band stretching out with a less-than-obvious cover version. The rest of the album, including a duet of sorts between Ron and Russell on 'The Shopping Mall Of Love' and a reworking of 'Modesty Plays', which the band had first attempted at the time of *Angst In My Pants*, brings invention back into the Sparks mix.

"*Music That You Can Dance To* was dance music for people that don't like dancing," Russell said in 2008. "The title track was really popular in the underground clubs. But we were more interested in the sound, the electronics. We thought that the combination of that and my singing and Ron's lyrical slight would be interesting."

"It's got more depth than other records with that sort of sound," Ron said in a *Record Mirror* interview. "Compared to Bananarama's 'Venus',

---

★ The song was featured in the 1986 Hal Needham film about BMX banditry, *Rad*.

for example." Had it been recorded a decade earlier or later, it could have been one of Sparks' very best albums. As it is, its clanks, crashes and whirrs leave the listener somewhat numb, but always engaged. The main disappointment lay in this most visual of groups' latest cover. Rocky Schenck photographed the band extensively, and ended up using a drab silhouette as the front sleeve.

Music That You Can Dance To had a muted reception, limping out without making any significant commercial inroads. *Record Mirror* called the album "one of the freshest I've heard all year. It's punk disco but with melody. There's an underlying horror beneath the deadpan seriousness of it all."

After *Music That You Can Dance To*, Sparks stopped being a band altogether. "'Change' had a little bit of success but they tried more of a dancey tack," Kendricks recalled. "The whole record had a stamp of Sparks as much as some of the early ones from my time. Honestly, when they stopped having guitar live and more people were in it, I thought it definitely lost a little bit of its energy."

After four years of relative stability, Sparks were once again at a crossroads. Gleaming Spires began to split apart behind the band: Leslie Boehm went off to Hollywood to become a scriptwriter. Bob Haag moved back to the desert and disappeared. Jim Goodwin worked occasionally in TV. David Kendrick, who at that point was the longest serving non-Mael Spark, saw it was time to move on.

"They were really getting a little more insular, the two of them wanted to kind of just be doing more or less everything themselves. So when the live thing stopped, even a couple of years before any records came out, they tried to get involved in doing music on film projects."

Kendrick gained an impressive resumé, going on to play in Devo and Wall Of Voodoo. "I had quite a good run," he says today. "Ron and Russell were at my wedding and they've met my son, so we keep up. I'm very pleased I was involved with them because being part of Sparks' story is a worthwhile part of rock history."

Although they could not seem to achieve hits at the time, Ron and Russell's location on the cultural radar was still gently blipping away. In

February 1987, Siouxsie & The Banshees released *Through The Looking Glass*, an album of covers that had influenced them over the years. The opening track was a cover of 'This Town Ain't Big Enough For Both Of Us'. It was also around this time that the Maels realised that Morrissey, the lead singer of The Smiths, had been a huge Sparks fan of old. Long-term admirer Martin Gore of Depeche Mode released a solo album of cover versions called *Counterfeit,* on which was a touching rendition of 'Never Turn Your Back On Mother Earth'.

A few years later, as Island Records embarked on its Island Masters CD series, a new 20-track overview of Sparks' mid-Seventies career was released. *Mael Intuition: The Best Of Sparks 1974–1976, It's A Mael Mael Mael Mael World* (to give it its full title) has been a strong seller ever since. Designed garishly by Trevor Wyatt, it had sleeve notes by Gummo Mael, a knowing pseudonym for UK writer Paul Morley.*

The most significant step forward in Sparks' career came with the final installation of the studio at Russell's cottage in Coldwater Canyon initially affectionately dubbed 'The Pentagon' by the brothers. John Thomas, their most recent keyboard player, was on hand throughout the build and took up his role as studio engineer. The relief of having their own place was palpable. Working without needing record company permission was possibly the best thing that could ever happen to the brothers. Separated from the bureaucracy of a record company, they could work up songs at their own leisure. It also suited the brothers' work ethic. Except when they were on the road, Ron would travel from his nearby apartment to set about the daily work at Russell's studio.

"We have finally put together our own studio after always having been at the mercy of record company-imposed recording budgets to determine when and for how long we would be allowed to record," Russell enthused. As an article in the *LA Times* was to say, "This is where the brothers do the bulk of their work nowadays, enabled by new technology to bypass the expensive recording studios of yore, another factor contributing to their survival. The downside: they have to halt work on Thursday mornings when a neighbor's gardeners fire up the leaf blowers."

---

* Morley reprinted the essay in full in his 2005 book, *Words And Music,* as an example of one of his best. And it is. The affection and knowledge are there for all to see.

The leaf blowers couldn't stop *Interior Design* being the first Sparks album to be recorded at The Pentagon and the second to be self-produced. With help from guitarist Spencer Sercombe and Pamela Stonebrook adding vocals to 'Just Got Back From Heaven', it is in many respects a dry run for *Gratuitous Sax And Senseless Violins* in 1994, but with more primitive instrumentation. It is a whirring, clanking and very late-Eighties record with that clunky synth bass that was preserved on every single record of the period.

After the deal with Curb had lapsed, Fine Art Records, a subsidiary of Rhino Records, picked up *Interior Design* for US and UK release, and it was trailed by the single 'So Important'. Although the album can be viewed in some respects as an experiment with new equipment, fine writing is still to be found and a unified sound that has light and shade, not simply the monotony of droning machines. There's "walking, talking holy grail" on the anthemic 'Lots Of Reasons'; Russell still wishing to hang round with 'The Toughest Girl In Town'; and 'Madonna' about a man picked up for a night of love with Madonna. 'Let's Make Love' is touching in its twinkly Eighties way, while 'Just Got Back From Heaven' is probably the most successful tune, a gorgeous, luxuriant recording, with all the rattles and clanks in the right place. Its sound certainly was reminiscent of Pet Shop Boys, the most recent group in Britain to sound 'a bit like Sparks'. By the time of Sparks' next public appearances, these similarities would become a frequent talking point.

The *New York Times* suggested that "Sparks makes entertaining, danceable and very clever music… these guys from Pacific Palisades are back with a record that is so much fun that it would be easy to take for granted the originality at work in the music. Intelligent dance music is not exactly a crowded field and this disc is the best we have." *Goldmine* said, "Who even knew these guys were still together and working? Well, they are, and this recording is superb."

In its retro sleeve (a hark back to the first Halfnelson album), photographed by future Sparks drummer Christie Haydon, *Interior Design* was released without fanfare to a modest response. Some 14 albums on, perhaps it was time to take a break from being Sparks.

However, there was simply too much to do to retire completely. Sparks found that they had big fans in the Parisian art-pop double act

Catherine Ringer and Fred Chichin, alias Les Rita Mitsouko. Russell was flattered when he heard that their name was chosen with the "same spirit of mind as the title of our album *Kimono My House*". After meeting in LA, a call came through to collaborate, and Ron and Russell, ever the Francophiles, warmly embraced the opportunity to decamp to Paris as, for once in their career, they had no firm plans. Ringer and Chichin appeared with Sparks on French TV miming the guitar and drum parts to 'So Important', while Sparks returned the favour, playing on three tracks for Les Rita Mitsouko's album *Marc et Robert*.

Ringer and Chichin happened to be working with an old friend of the Maels, Tony Visconti. "I had no idea that Ron and Russell and Les Rita were friends with each other," says Visconti. "Russell spoke the language fluently as he learnt it from a girlfriend. I thought he'd gone to university as his French is so good. It was great hanging out with them; I actually got to socialise more with Russell and Ron when they were in Paris than we did in 1975."

The brothers, Les Rita Mitsoukos and Visconti spent three days together working on the songs, including the Maels-composed 'Singing In The Shower', which became a European hit.

What Visconti truly got to appreciate this time around was Ron's love of wordplay: "He would joke with us, using language that Les Rita Mitsoukos couldn't understand. Their English is really good but he was doing this high-browed stuff that was going over my head, let alone theirs. I had to rewind a bit and realise he just said something incredibly funny but it was all punning metaphor." Perhaps this wordplay could be better used in film as there seemed to be little call for it in music at that time.

With a career now approaching two decades and with no recording commitments, Ron became obsessed with cinema and reportedly returned to film study. The medium of film had always played a strong role in Sparks' career, and, in the Eighties, there had been several opportunities to hear their work used in a variety of films; 'Singing In The Shower' featured in *Black Rain*; 'Mini-Skirted' was in *Where The Boys Are*; *Heavenly Bodies* had 'Breaking Out Of Prison'; while 'The Armies Of The Night' played in *Fright Night*.

A project that came to dominate the brothers' attentions during this juncture was a film of Japanese manga comic *Mai The Psychic Girl.* Written by Kazuya Kudo and illustrated by Ryoichi Ikegami, *Mai The Psychic Girl* was about a 14-year-old girl with extraordinary extrasensory skills, on the run from an organisation that strives to control the world. The film was to be produced by *Beetlejuice* and *Addams Family* writer Larry Wilson and Walter Hill and co-written by Caroline Thompson.

Various directors were linked to the assignment, most notably Tim Burton, whom the brothers had met in a restaurant and invited back to Russell's studio to listen to the music they'd been working on for the film. Burton loved it but lost interest over time.

The brothers spent around five-and-a-half years trying to get the project commissioned with potential names such as Francis Ford Coppola and Tsui Hark in the frame to direct. Trying to get the $15 million raised for a real-life manga adventure proved difficult. "We actually found a business that is more disgusting than the music industry," Ron commented in 1993.

Although Wilson optioned the rights to the comic book, the final nail in its coffin was when Carolco, the company that was to fund the enterprise, foundered after the 1995 release of the Renny Harlin-directed, Geena Davis-starring *Cutthroat Island.* At the time, it was the biggest flop in the history of cinema. Apart from a mooted collaboration on a stage version of the Fifties cult film *The Amazing Colossal Man,* it was another moment when Sparks got close but yet so far from realising their Hollywood aspirations. Still, there was always *Rollercoaster* to fall back on.

On March 2, 1991 Joseph Fleury died of an AIDS-related illness at the age of 37. As their original supporter, fan-club runner and manager for the best part of a decade (as well as being John Hewlett's assistant for the years preceding), his death was greatly felt.

One of his last tasks had been to oversee *Profile: The Ultimate Sparks Collection,* a 40-track double-disc set compiled by Warner staffer (and Sparks fan) Gary Stewart, coordinated by Fleury and released by Rhino. For the first time, curios such as the Bearsville version of 'I Like Girls' were heard on a career-spanning journey that went from 'Wonder Girl' to 'So Important' (from *Interior Design*). Released within a month of Fleury's death, the already printed sleeve contained the legend in block capitals, "A VERY SPECIAL THANKS TO JOSEPH FLEURY FOR BEING THERE FROM THE BEGINNING".

John Hewlett: "I spoke to him in the months prior to his death. I called him to put matters to rest. We fell out because I hadn't paid a bill and he got ousted from the house that we had been sharing in the late Seventies … It was good to talk but he was pretty much in denial about his illness."

Fleury's panache with words and his ability to create dreams and smokescreens around the brothers was absolutely central to their success. In losing him, Ron and Russell lost an unerring supporter. What he may have lacked in business acumen was more than compensated for by his friendship and putting the brothers' needs first at all times.

Ironically Fleury's passing occurred when Sparks' influence was being acutely felt. The Pet Shop Boys went on to be one the biggest pop groups the UK had produced, working with Sixties diva Dusty Springfield arguably in the same way Sparks had wanted to work with Marianne Faithfull. From America, They Might Be Giants certainly would not have looked too out of place at a Sparks convention. In the much-vaunted *NME* Christmas edition of 1991, fondly remembered Manchester act Intastella dressed as Ron and Russell re-enacting the sleeve of *Kimono My House*. Spencer Birtwistle (later of The Fall) dressed as Russell and leader/singer Stella Grundy dressed as Ron. "In many ways, the spirit of Sparks is alive in what we do. They were smart, they were fun and they were a little bit strange."

There was vague talk of the Maels and Morrissey, who had recently relocated to LA, working together, but Morrissey thought that Russell was singing better than ever and should sing the songs that Ron had proposed for collaboration. The three met when Morrissey played LA's Great Western Forum in June 1991. They also met David Bowie who got up to duet with Morrissey on Marc Bolan's 'Cosmic Dancer'. "Someone else, Morrissey's biggest influence, wasn't invited on stage," Russell wryly told *Q* in 1993, "but we're just being bitchy now."

With this new-found respect, it was somewhat inevitable that not all would be so reverential. In the updated 1992 *Rolling Stone Album Guide* (at this point, only *Music That You Can Dance To* and *Profile* were available in the States) Mark Coleman wrote: "Does the following prospect sound enticing? A long-running cult band that combines Bryan Ferry at his most adenoidal – make that a falsetto Bryan Ferry – with the music hall indulgences of Queen at its most rococo, a group whose career spans more than half-a-dozen record labels and more than a dozen [deleted] albums. Well, brothers Ron and Russell Mael are your men."

Coleman concluded with the amusing line, "Docked a notch for inspiring the grossest excesses of both the late Seventies skinny-tie new-wave movement and the early Eighties haircut pop movements. Talk about a double whammy!"

In 1993, further Sparks' retrospectives appeared with the *Heaven* and *Hell* collections. These compilations, which originated from France, were designed to show the band's commercial work on one disc with out-takes and oddities on the other. Legendary sound engineer Bruce Swedien, who had worked extensively with Quincy Jones (and therefore Michael Jackson), was enlisted to work on some mixes for the *Hell* disc.

"Those guys! They were nuts, and they were great!" Swedien recalls. "I remember them so well… I have an unlisted phone number and I am very difficult to find. But they found me. We had a ball… Really good though – I made it sound like music, that's really what I do. Oh yes, they were very good at what they did."

Sparks *were* very good at what they did. So, towards the end of 1993, they reappeared. It was Scottish dance band Finitribe that sought the Maels out and effectively ended the longest hiatus in their career. Finitribe initially wanted to cover 'When I'm With You', which came to the attention of the brothers. Soon, the two groups had made contact and it was decided to make a new record together.

"We just liked the spirit of what they were doing musically," Russell said in 1993, "the entrepreneurial spirit of having a record company that is not like a record company."

Sparks sent over a DAT of the raw elements of a new song. Finitribe then sampled and reconstructed it. 'National Crime Awareness Week' is the tale of a criminal who derives pleasure from seeing his name in the papers after his latest exploits, thinking that a week that is supposed to make people vigilant will actually act as an advert for himself.

In November the first new Sparks recording since 1988 was released. The spoken word-meeting-rave nature of 'National Crime Awareness Week' located Sparks again on the edge of a relevant underground. Sampling Dick Dastardly's laugh, the mixes of the single were incredibly *a la mode*. The record gained positive reviews: *The Face* said Sparks "were back with a track so weird it's almost normal". *Record Mirror* compared the heaven mix to the then-current touchstone in techno, 'Rez' by Underworld. *Time Out* said "better looking than Peters and Lee, funnier than Wham!, the brothers Mael have been the best double act in pop for 20 years. Go on, make it number one."

The brothers were interviewed by Richard Madeley and Judy Finnegan on ITV's *This Morning*, and talked about how British bands would look them up in LA. "We had only done that single with Finitribe, 'National Crime Awareness Week'," Ron said in 2003. "We were bowled over by the reaction it received – it was hugely inspiring – and finally, we had a way to seamlessly mix the old and the new material."

It was enough to bring the brothers back over to the UK for their first promotional visit since the Eighties. They found that there was still a great deal of love for them and also a whole slew of acts, many of whom were now well established, who had been influenced by them but had perhaps not paid enough lip service. Feathers were ruffled as Ron and Russell suggested a little too heavily that the Pet Shop Boys and in fact all the synth duos owed them rather a lot. "Tell them we're really pissed off," Russell said, half-jokingly. "We've got our lawyers on the case."

The prevailing feeling that Sparks had somehow constantly been usurped floated to the surface. "We're supposed to be flattered," Ron told Q magazine. "But you're in a band and therefore an egotist, so when you see people taking our surface element and – because they are not so stylised – selling more records, you get pissed off. Especially when you know how difficult it is to sustain a career. It's hard to talk about because you don't want to come across as bitchy, but I think we've written a lot of Pet Shop Boys tunes. 'Bohemian Rhapsody' really pissed me off because we'd had 'Get In The Swing'. Look at Cheap Trick – two wacky guys, two pretty guys."

Rudderless since Fleury passed away two years previously, Sparks found themselves a manager in German-born Londoner Eric Harle at

DEF Management. The Maels had originally approached Harle, who was a huge Sparks fan and had all of their work, to see if one of his acts, The Progress, would do some remixes for them.

"Suddenly I ended up with their management too," Harle told *Music And Media* in 1994. They had asked to set up a label, but as Harle was a manager not a label owner, he went out to broker a deal for them. Harle approached Achim Fehlau from Frankfurt-based Logic Records and publisher Beate Geibel for support. After hearing six tracks that Ron and Russell had been working on at home, the trio, led by Harle, got behind them. Advances in technology meant that if Sparks were to return to the stage they could put on a proper Sparks show with all eras being represented.

"We detest nostalgia," Ron told *Melody Maker* in November 1993. "For us to re-emerge now with something which wasn't vital and relevant would be pointless. The only thing that interests us is trying to do something that doesn't fit in."

Chapter Fifteen

Not So Senseless, But Quite Gratuitous – Gratuitous Sax & Senseless Violins

"Sparks are still big. It's the world that got small."

Melody Maker, 1994

"If we're a novelty act then we're one of the longest-standing novelty acts in history."

Ron Mael, 1995

And so, it was time to come back. It was as if Britain had completely abandoned Sparks. "The irony! It was probably our most successful period in the States, the whole Eighties, it's practically unknown over here," Russell told the author in 2002. "When we played here at the time of *Gratuitous Sax & Senseless Violins*, all the questions were 'Where have you been?' They had simply missed an entire swathe of our output. For reasons we still don't know, it didn't translate and there seemed to be no communication between the UK and the US record people. We even started doing well in LA – we thought it's working somewhere, so we were content to go with that."

There would be no such issues with *Gratuitous Sax & Senseless Violins*, which was released on BMG through the German company Logic. The team of Eric Harle and Achim Fehlau added additional production and remixes to the tracks Sparks had worked on.

Eric Harle: "In a way, they were the first electro dance outfit, a fact for which they have always been credited by New Order and Depeche Mode. Embracing modern technology is their second nature, so they had no problems updating their music."

The management hooked the brothers up with Mark Stagg, who had mixed Björk and Linus Burdick, who was later to co-write Sonique's global hit 'It Feels So Good', to give half of the album a contemporary sheen.

Realising the way of the current market, the lead track 'When Do I Get To Sing "My Way"' – originally titled 'The Punch And Judy Show' – was given a makeover by Sparks fan Vince Clarke from Erasure and The Grid, the latter outfit featuring Dave Ball from Soft Cell – one of the Eighties synth duos erroneously said to have been influenced by Sparks. "Yes, we had a flamboyant frontman and I stood motionless behind a keyboard with my moustache, but we were much more influenced by Suicide and northern soul," Ball told the author in August 2009.

On October 17, 1994 'When Do I Get To Sing "My Way"' was released. It was exactly the right calling card for the group, with all the wit and texture of recent dance acts taken on board, yet remaining resolutely Sparks, showing that although two decades had passed since *Kimono My House*, the band were moving forward, forging a sound that was a perfect fit for the mid-Nineties. The video, which parodied and homaged Hollywood simultaneously, was directed by Sophie Muller and produced by Rob Small of Oil Factory. By the end of the month, the single was number 38 in the UK chart, Sparks' first Top 40 placing for 15 years. An aggressive regional radio campaign saw the single played through-out the UK and northern Europe. BMG, the parent company of Logic, put money behind the album and indulged in some aggressive co-op spending with retailers. This was proper support at last for a new Sparks album.

On November 7, Sparks emerged from their temporary retirement with the release of *Gratuitous Sax & Senseless Violins*. By consciously playing themselves as a synthesiser duo, the Maels were able to reclaim some of the ground the Pet Shop Boys had made their own.

Gratuitous Sax & Senseless Violins is an accomplished piece of work and the first real moment in Sparks' long career when their past caught up with their future and present. The new recordings were sleek and minimalist with enough flourishes to sound like the best of the most recent electro-pop. Few acts could disappear for quite so long and return with such a potent brew of material. As a result, the record was little short of a triumph. The former *Melody Maker* 'Best Newcomers of 1974' produced a work that was full of their trademark melody, hooks and irony, yet was still completely fresh and different. The album is rich with references, reflecting the Maels' cinematic and popular cultural obsessions – there can be few albums that namecheck Frank Sinatra, Sid Vicious, Charlie Parker, *Gone With The Wind,* Ted Turner, Tsui Hark, Liberace, Hillary Clinton, Madame Mao, Richard Wagner and William Shakespeare, and do so with such élan.

The album is chock full of highlights, with the *a cappella* overture evoking *Propaganda*, the celestial introduction of 'When Do I Get To Sing "My Way"' being pure *No. 1 In Heaven,* the Depeche Mode-*Violator* styling of 'Frankly Scarlett, I Don't Give A Damn' and the amusing high energy of '(When I Kiss You) I Hear Charlie Parker Playing'. The filmic nature of the material is highlighted by 'Tsui Hark', where director Hark – dubbed 'the Stephen Spielberg of Asia' – reads through a list of his credits over a sliver of mesmeric trance played by Ron. This track at once encapsulates the group's irony, cleverness, intelligence and simplicity and is one of the album's standouts. For the first time since *No. 1 In Heaven* they sounded effortlessly contemporary.

Gratuitous Sax… also had another great sleeve, their first classic since *Sparks In Outer Space*. Designed by Louis Flanigan, Alexandra Jugovic and Eilke König, it was the first to fully utilise the CD format as opposed to shrinking a traditional LP 12" × 12" image to fit. With photography by German fashion photographer Dieter Eikelpoth, it re-created a *National Enquirer* scandal sheet, capturing the brothers in a variety of poses as if shot by paparazzi. The pictures were supplemented with headlines such as 'The lowdown on the lyrics you'll never hear!', 'Are those break-up rumours true?' and 'EXCLUSIVE! Room service cover-up!' It was hot but it wasn't on the menu.'

The album was well received by the UK press: *The Face* heralded "a glorious return"; *Q* gave it four stars and called it "a triumph"; *NME* said "Plug in. You might just get a nice shock"; while *Time Out* was probably the most explicit saying, "You can keep your cardboard cut-outs, your Pet Shop Boys, the real thing is back." *Select* demonstrated their arch approach by saying that "they invented the novelty record and 14 years later are still doing that old trick wherein John Waters invites Bob Stanley round to DJ at his Casio-sponsored PWL convention."

As had happened with *Kimono My House, No. 1 In Heaven* and *Angst In My Pants*, the Maels were having fun while breaking new ground. Their timing seemed to be right – *Melody Maker* was desperate to try and get Romo, the music paper's attempt at reviving new romanticism, off the ground. (There would be better luck when electroclash bubbled up in the early 21st century.) Sparks were, of course, one of the 11 things that were chosen in the November 1995 piece *Synthetic Culture – The Iconography And Ideal Of Romo-ism,* published in the paper.*

Although Romo was clearly manufactured and got seen through almost immediately, the list description of Sparks, a band virtually every journalist wished to paint a picture of, was suitably florid. It said that Sparks "believed firmly in the blessed, redeeming qualities of disorientation and lively deadpan absurdity. Laughing Dada. American and heterosexual, they somehow tapped into what had been previously an exclusively gay, European aesthetic, and in doing so, blurred borders, defied orders and hauled 'over the top' overground."

Sparks toured to support the album, receiving rapturous receptions wherever they went. Technology had finally caught up with Sparks, and Island, even Bearsville, material could be placed next to Moroder-era or

* The other 10 were: F. Scott Fitzgerald, Nick Rhodes, Modern Art 1918–1939, Roxy Music, the Burschenschaften, Andy Warhol, Rasputin, *Under The Cherry Moon,* Kraftwerk and Quentin Crisp.

the new album – it now all sounded as one. The tour and the album's success proved that Sparks could always remain contemporary, even if a huge section of the audience hadn't bought a Sparks record since 1979.

With Christie Haydon as their new drummer, Ron and Russell played their first UK comeback gig at Shepherd's Bush Empire on November 17. For the encores, the UK's then-hottest guitarist, Bernard Butler, of Suede fame, came on to play. In a largely positive review, the *NME*'s Johnny Dee suggested that "Their electro pomp preceded the new romantics, their deadpan stage act a direct prototype of Pulp, their image was very Mute Records, the Freddie Mercury meets Dame Bowie, a bit Suede even." Commenting that they now looked younger than when Tony Blackburn introduced them on *Top Of The Pops* in the Seventies, the article was one of the first to point out that the group had, by now, acquired a huge gay following.

When Ron and Russell walked into the after-show party, they were greeted as if they were returning heroes. Long-time supporter John Aizlewood listed it in *Q* as being among the Top 100 Greatest Ever Gigs: "Strangers hugged each other, howling with excitement and relief. The sound was that of gods. They played everything and Bernard Butler's cameo was the best thing he's ever done. I've never felt so emotional at a concert."

Among the night's surprises was an invitation to none other than estranged Sparks bassist Martin Gordon who, of course, had bigger issues on his mind. "I actually tried to address the legal thing in 1994 when they played at the Empire and somehow weirdly, when we were not yet on completely non-speaking terms, I received an invite," Gordon recalls. "I went to the after-show too. Then we sat down and I thought 'This is now 20 years later almost to the day. What a good opportunity to try and discuss something on an adult level' and proposed a deal, whereupon they both stood up and said, 'We're really sorry, we have to go now. We have to go back to the hotel'. I wasn't very impressed by that. That was the last time we met."

Gordon decided to write a review for *Mojo*. "The following day, I then devised a method of revenge. I pitched my review of the show, which pleased me. I mean, it wasn't any more vitriolic than was appropriate but I felt better for having written it certainly."

The review – which was published in the February 1995 edition – was jammed with Gordon's scabrous wit, overpraising the *Kimono My House* material ("I should, however, declare an interest as I played bass on the thing, arranged it and was rewarded with a tiny black and white picture on the back, nicely balancing the brothers' expansive full-colour two-shot. But I digress into bitchiness") and remaining cool about the remainder. "The brothers performed to a relentless, computer-driven backing that [it must be said] became rather colourless over time." Of the role reversal they performed onstage during this tour, Gordon asked whether they were "post-modern or pissed, guru or gaga? No-one knew for sure. At the reception afterwards, an outwardly-normal landscape gardener from Jersey told me this event was a lifetime ambition achieved, as he went off to get a telephone directory autographed by one brother or the other."

Although his tongue may have been firmly lodged in his cheek, Gordon was being unfair as the set list was an incredibly well-balanced mixture of hits and album tracks from across the years.

The letters page in the following month's *Mojo* edition carried the following riposte from one Richard Banham. "Whose idea was it to get a sad, bitter old sideman like Martin Gordon to review Sparks?... Ron & Russell continue to make marvellous records. They deserve more than these embittered ramblings." Gordon's embittered ramblings would find much more of an audience as the internet culture was about to explode.

Gratuitous Sax... got lost during the Christmas rush in the UK but, unlike previous record companies, Logic was committed to its act and had a proper campaign planned, with subsequent single releases, expensive video promos and European touring. After the tour, some specially selected festival appearances could be planned. The brothers threw themselves onto the treadmill again; they arrived back in the UK on February 1 and stayed in Europe for two months. They did all the things necessary: German promo, Canadian phone-ins, shot electronic press kits and rehearsed at Nomis Studios on London's Sinclair Road. The duo were on BBC's *Live And Kicking* on February 25, and appeared on Channel 4's *The Big Breakfast* with Paul Ross and Zig and Zag, where Ron paraded his collection of snow domes.

Logic was rewarded with a series of Top 40 placings, Sparks' greatest consistency since 1979. There were the obligatory part-work releases

– 'When I Kiss You (I Hear Charlie Parker Playing)' was released on February 27, 1995 with another Sophie Muller video and mixes by Red Jerry, Oliver Lieb and The Beatmasters; other editions had an acoustic piano version of 'This Town Ain't Big Enough For Both Of Us' and a remix by Bernard Butler. The single received a mixed reception. "It's just Euro-techno, which I'm not into," said future collaborator Jimmy Somerville in *Top Of The Pops* magazine. "Sounds like the Pet Shop Boys after a helium binge," scoffed *Time Out*.

A six-date tour was scheduled to tie in with the new single, commencing in Wolverhampton on March 18 and concluding at London's The Forum on March 25, while the album itself was re-released on March 20. The shows were rapturously received; if anything, the reception at Wolverhampton Civic was more uproarious than the previous November's show at Shepherd's Bush.

David Cameron-Pryde from the band Eskimos and Egypt saw how well the new arrangement was working when he went for a Chinese meal with the Maels, along with Eric Harle, after the brothers' Manchester Academy show on March 22.

"It was a very odd evening for me as someone who watched Sparks do 'Beat The Clock' on *Top Of The Pops*," Cameron-Pryde recalls. "First of all Ron was very reminiscent in both looks and dress style of my deceased father – who was very dapper and always dressed like a well-to-do gent."

The evening was somewhat slow starting. "I thought I'd break the ice so proceeded to tell them about a recent one-caption joke that I had seen in an edition of *Viz*, the adult cartoon rag," Cameron-Pryde continues. "It was set at an airport and showed a taxi on the tarmac with a plane in the background ready to take off. The driver is pulling a suitcase from the boot and Ron and Russ are standing watching him lift it out."

The table was now enthralled. "The caption underneath read ... 'When this comes out, Sparks will fly'. Their very polite laughter afterwards was totally to spare my blushes."

It was easy to see why the brothers may have been somewhat non-plussed at this gag, as virtually every article on the group had, at some point, used the line 'Sparks Will Fly'. As this tour was seen as a comeback, they were getting asked the same questions over and over. It was almost time to start telling stories about their mum, Doris Day, again. On March 30, after the tour had concluded, the Logic press office issued a press release entitled 'Mael Out' showing how writers were actively encouraged to use terrible puns in the name of promotion. The 'Just For Fun Pun Top 10' was full of 'Sparks Fly Again', 'Sparks Plug', 'Bright Sparks', 'Vital Sparks', 'Sparks of Inspiration'. They had all been used; and in the case of 'Sparks Will Fly' overused. This sense of fun showed how far everyone was working together to make this a success.

"If we're a novelty act then we're one of the longest-running novelty acts in the business," Ron said to *Keyboard Review* in February 1995. "That's one area of the British music industry that we like in a detached way, the fact that things can happen very quickly. What we were doing in the beginning was so stylised, with our offbeat image and everything, and there were people who thought we were a novelty act and a one-line joke. There is humour attached to our music but we never considered it one dimensional because we always like to have different layers beneath the obvious humour."

Humour aside, one thing that was making them angry were the continual comparisons to the Pet Shop Boys that seemed to follow them around Britain. "Especially when we had 'When Do I Get To Sing "My Way."' When the song was first heard by radio, they all said it was like the Pet Shop Boys, which blew us through the roof, for obvious reasons," Russell stated.

It certainly sounds like both duos influenced the other – Sparks, obviously, on the Pet Shop Boys, but through similar technology, wit and songcraft, the Pet Shop Boys had also had some effect on the new Sparks, subliminal as it may have been. Listen to 'Being Boring' from the Pet Shop Boys' 1990 album *Behaviour*, which sounds like *Gratuitous Sax & Senseless Violins*. But then 'Just Got Back From Heaven' from 1988 sounds like a dry run of 'Being Boring'. *

After a brief sojourn back in LA, the brothers returned to Europe for a German tour, which began on May 5. Whereas England fell in the

---

* Coincidentally *Behaviour* was produced by Harold Faltermeyer, who, after producing Sparks, had gone on to have a worldwide hit with 'Axel F' from *Beverly Hills Cop*.

Seventies, and France in the Eighties, the next country on Sparks' slow-rolling conquest of Europe was to be Germany, where 'When Do I Get To Sing "My Way"' sold over 650,000 copies.

"It was our biggest single to date in Germany where we hadn't had much success before," Russell said in 2008. "We started getting really young audiences again, like we had in the States in the early Eighties and in Britain in the early Seventies. So we're arguably pop history's longest-running teenybop idols."

"They've sort of stayed between 30 and 40," ex-bass player Ian Hampton, who saw the London shows, recalled. "They've stood still. I took my son to see them at Shepherd's Bush Empire. He thought Russell looked like Tim Henman only with more energy. His energy is incredible. I wish I had half of that."

On June 17 1995, Sparks were on the bill at one of the most defining gigs of the era: Blur's concert at Mile End Stadium in east London. To tie in with the shows, 'When Do I Get To Sing "My Way"' was re-released with new mixes, to see if it would fare any better than its number 38 placing from the previous year. It got six places higher. Unfortunately due to new rules with *Top Of The Pops* and the volume of new entries, the UK charts at this time were all about the first week placing. With all the hard work everyone was putting in, Ron and Russell unfortunately didn't make it back onto their old stamping ground.

The Blur gig coincided with the crest of Britpop, a short-lived phenomenon that celebrated bands such as The Kinks, The Who and especially The Beatles, whom Sparks had once worshipped from afar. A Beatles v Stones war had broken out between Oasis, the Manchester-based working-class terrace boys who made obvious anthemic music that was obsessed with mid-period Beatles, and Blur who were southern, middle class, arty, educated. Blur Leader Damon Albarn loved being a cultural dilettante and their current look was a swirl of ironic shell suits. In *Parklife*, Blur had released one of the great albums of the Nineties.

Sparks had a big crowd to entertain and torrential rain to contend with. Sparks' set was a brief selection of present and past hits with an album track or two thrown in and, as from the onset of their career, the group could split a crowd. Ryan Gilbey, writing in *The Independent*, said: "The synth duo Sparks brightened matters when Ron Mael, a man so

217

square and sinister you imagine he'd do your accounts then murder your pets, broke into an incongruous tap-dance. But their pulsing pleasures were lost on all but a crazed ginger backpacker who was either on acid or bad tofu."

The audience were really only there to see one act and none of the other supports – John Shuttleworth, The Cardiacs, Dodgy or The Boo Radleys – fared a great deal better. Everett True in *Melody Maker* wrote, "Ten out of 10 for panache, wrinklies" but *NME* countered "There is doubtless a time and a place for tap dance routines and techno versions of *The Sound Of Music's* 'Do-Re-Mi' (a pile of Von Trapp, as they say round these parts) but this, quite frankly, is not it, and no, I am not making this up."

Andy Ross, Blur's co-manager and the head of Food Records, remembers the Mile End gig as an extravagance, most probably on his part. "I was once a badge-carrying member of the Sparks fan club and, in the mid-Eighties, I co-interviewed them with Stephen 'Tin-Tin' Duffy at Fortnum & Masons. I'm not sure how Sparks ended up on the Mile End bill, but I was a strident Sparks flag waver at the time. I actually considered trying to sign them to Food and met with them with that purpose in mind at a cafe near the BBC in Portland Place. I resisted that Alan McGee-esque conceit of vanity signing and did not pursue the deal.

"The Mile End show connection was one of those indulgences where the show was a sell-out from the minute tickets went on sale," he continues, "so the support acts were a bit of an indulgence/representation of how Blur chose to be perceived. Sparks went down like a lead balloon and the weather was awful."

Sparks received greater acclaim for their performance at Pride, back when it was still called Gay Pride. On June 24, Sparks played the festival at Victoria Park in east London, where it was reported that they upstaged Erasure. *NME* were far kinder here, saying that "the camptastic Sparks are dramatically, gloriously, silly." They may not have been able to win over the Britpop crowd, but the more open-minded Pride audiences loved them.

The year ended with a concert at London's Forum on December 20. Logic/Arista really did keep everything afloat – the album's third single, 'Now That I Own The BBC', was released in February 1996, 16 months since the first release of 'When Do I Get To Sing "My Way".' Unlike the previous three releases, it only reached number 60. Whatever was said, the album had truly been worked by the record company. This time mixers such as Motiv 8 had been brought in but no matter how hard they tried, the album resolutely failed to enter the UK Top 75.

Gratuitous Sax & Senseless Violins was released in the US in January 1996. The *LA Times* said that it contained "clever eye-winking words … warbled with a cooing falsetto over a festive trance carpeted hi-NRG groove". The *New York Post* passed an offhand compliment by saying "if you're going to dance, or do aerobics for that matter, this is a fine collection". *Cashbox* said that "the duo have given a valiant comeback effort". *America Online* accurately assessed, "After reconquering Europe, their US success was limited to their most loyal outlet, the nightclubs. It deserves another shot." 'When Do I Get To Sing "My Way"' even rekindled interest in the group in their traditionally indifferent home country, after it reached number nine on the *Billboard* Hot Dance Music/Club Play Chart. However, although valiant attempts were made to break the album in the US, America was again resistant to Sparks' charms.

Chapter Sixteen

So Close, So Real; The Look,
The Feel *Plagiarism* and *Balls*

"We were never comfortable with the general direction."

Russell Mael, 2003

"Our problem's always been we've had a foot in both the pop and experimental camps, so we just end up annoying both parties."

Ron Mael, 2003

For the third time in their career, Sparks had new ears eagerly awaiting their next work. Logic/Arista could sense there was a fresh audience waiting to embrace Sparks, who had absolutely no idea of the breadth and depth of the band's past. As Russell said in 2008, "We'd had this big success with *Gratuitous Sax & Senseless Violins*, and a lot of the audience, especially on the continent, thought we were a new band."

The mid-Nineties was the age of the tribute album and for their 17th album, Sparks would be their own tribute act. As all the interviews since 1993 had banged on about who they were supposed to sound like, the ultimate concept was to pay tribute to themselves if po-face duos like Pet Shop Boys weren't going to do it officially. And like all tribute albums of that era, some of *Plagiarism* works, some of it doesn't.

"We were really opposed to the idea of doing that album as we'd opened up this whole new audience – especially in Germany," Russell said in 2003. "It was suggested to bring these people up to speed. Although we were initially ambivalent, we were excited to be working with Tony Visconti again. We were never comfortable with the general direction."

Plagiarism was the first album since *Interior Design* that was partially recorded away from Sparks' studio. Recording at Russell's house was supplemented with sessions in San Francisco and London – the first time the group had recorded in the capital since 1975 with *Indiscreet*, coincidentally produced by Visconti who, instead of producing, looked after the orchestral and choral arrangements.

Tony Visconti: "I went to Russell's home in Los Angles and we worked on *Plagiarism* for a bit in their home studio. I was used on about six titles and it took me *ages* to write them. We spent a long time discussing what they wanted. The concept was amazing. It was wonderful to work with them at this level."

The Maels' main proviso to Visconti was that the songs were not to sound like the originals. It was to be "drastically different versions of our songs", Russell said. "For 'This Town' he [Visconti] came up with these aggressive small-string arrangements. And he did a version of 'Change' that had a *Threepenny Opera* sort of arrangement with a pit band." Visconti went back to Stan Getz' album *Focus,* with its pared-down string sections, for inspiration for his arrangements.

Tony Visconti: "The version of 'Something For The Girl With Everything' that I orchestrated is my favourite track on *Plagiarism*. I did that in the style of Scott Bradley, the guy who used to write for *Tom And Jerry* cartoons. In the middle part you can actually see Tom and Jerry being chased around the studio – that was my image for that. It nearly crippled the string players!"

Visconti was again astounded by Ron's abilities: "Ron wouldn't say really what he studied, he might say Gilbert and Sullivan. I wouldn't put it past him if he studied every one of their operettas. It's definitely in 'Pulling Rabbits Out Of A Hat'. We did it flat-out Gilbert and Sullivan. He never told me what his sources were!"

The level of collaboration was high. While Ron and Russell threw in ever more ambitious ideas to Visconti, they also drew up a list of potential collaborators. Admirers like Erasure and Jimmy Somerville were approached and were delighted to join in. There was only one problem – the budget was tight.

Tony Visconti: "I was only allowed 16 string players, which wasn't quite the right size. The engineer, Chris Dibble, would say that we needed more cellos, but that was all we could afford."

Once again there was a sense of what might have been, but there is still plenty to revel in on *Plagiarism*. Unsurprisingly, the tracks that come out the best are the ones originally recorded in the Eighties, when the machines had been out in force. 'Change' was turned into an incredible slice of woozy, big-band circus music without a Fairlight in sight. 'Funny Face' was reworked as a tender ballad (albeit about someone who has an accident in order to have reconstructive surgery so that they no longer look beautiful). The orchestral introduction of the long version of 'The Number One Song In Heaven', complete with celestial choir, is simply remarkable, while the strings on opening track 'Pulling Rabbits Out Of A Hat' point towards what would later burst into flower on *Lil' Beethoven*.

Of the guest appearances, Eskimos and Egypt, another band from manager Eric Harle's stable (featuring David Cameron-Pryde) play on a powerful rock version of 'Angst In My Pants', while the involvement of Faith No More on several tracks was a pleasant, if abrasive, surprise. The San Franciscan band got involved after Sparks heard they were big fans and established a link with guitarist Dean Menta that continues to this day.

"I saw Sparks play on *American Bandstand* in 1975," keyboard player Roddy Bottum told *Time Out New York*. "My sister and I immediately went out and bought *Indiscreet*. For *Plagiarism* they asked if we would collaborate on a song – and we ended up recording three."*

The hi-NRG of the dance half of *Plagiarism* simply wasn't enough. The quicker tempo benefits 'When I'm With You', but there's a hint of

---

* Faith No More's storming version of 'This Town Ain't Big Enough For Both Of Us', featuring Russell, reached the UK Top 40 at Christmas 1997.

regret by the end of it: exactly what was the point? Similarly, Erasure's version of 'Amateur Hour' was not their finest hour.

Overall, *Plagiarism* was not a great success. The album was as musically schizophrenic as Sparks' career – the dramatic baroque orchestrations jarred with the high energy reworkings of 'Beat The Clock' and 'The Number One Song In Heaven'. Also, the wittily designed sleeve with Ron and Russell's heads transposed onto bodybuilders' torsos did not augur well as a commercial proposition.

Again, Sparks had followed up great success with a commercial stall as a lot of the UK audience that had recently been won over by *Gratuitous Sax...* were not that interested. If anything, Sparks' 2000 album, *Balls*, should have appeared first, as hard-edged dance music was all the rage in the UK at this point with The Prodigy, The Chemical Brothers and Fat Boy Slim all in the charts with their abrasive hybrids of techno, funk and rock. Although instigated by Logic, by the time the album came out, it had been picked up by Roadrunner Records, a label synonymous with heavy metal releases. Ron and Russell's initial misgivings had proved correct. The project, however, is not without considerable merit, if only for showcasing Ron Mael as a songwriter.

Sparks supported the release of *Plagiarism* with a short UK tour in December 1997 and joined Faith No More on stage on the final night of their 1997 European tour in L'Aéronef, Lille, France on December 10. It marked the introduction of Sparks' new live drummer, Tamera Glover replacing Christi Haydon. With her striking bob and broad smile, 'Tammy', who had been playing with LA group Chewy Marble, would prove a most welcome addition to the line-up.

The final project of the 20th century for Sparks was to provide the soundtrack to Tsui Hark's film *Knock Off*. Hark's credentials were impressive, having been a leading light of the new wave cinema coming out of Hong Kong since the mid-Eighties. Ron and Russell had first encountered the Vietnamese director while working on the unrealised *Mai The Psychic Girl* project. Billed as 'an explosive thriller set in Hong Kong's shady manufacturing scene during the handover to China', it was another attempt by Hollywood to capitalise on Hark's considerable Asian success, and one of the few productions that was granted filming rights while the former British colony was handed back during July 1997.*

As evidenced by *Gratuitous Sax & Senseless Violins* highlight 'Tsui Hark', the brothers held the director in high esteem. As committed cineastes, the Maels wanted to work with him so much, they didn't stop to check if the production was to be Tati or simply tatty.

Opening in September 1998 to damning notices, *Knock Off* died quietly at the box office, along with hopes of a soundtrack album to house the selection of atmospheric instrumentals that supplemented Hark's visuals. "It probably wasn't the best decision, creatively, that we've made," Russell was to say in 2008. The title track, however, would be one of the key tracks on Sparks' forthcoming album.

Engineered and mixed by John Thomas and produced and written by the Maels, *Balls* was recorded over a period of 10 months at Russell's home studio. After the ornate strings and special guests of *Plagiarism*, this was to be a back to basics album in the vein of *Gratuitous Sax & Senseless Violins*.

With Tammy providing live drums to fill the largely synthetic backings, it is a record with edge and showed a group restless and ready for new challenges. "We're really opposed to the idea that at a certain point in your career, you're supposed to mellow things down. For us, it's almost the opposite," the brothers told David Hemingway in *Record Collector*.

Their rhythmic side needed greater emphasis as the whole music world seemed to have gone dance crazy in the late Nineties. "*Balls* is a techno album," Russell said in 2008. "It's pretty electronic... it has elements that were very reflective of 2000 – like The Prodigy. We really liked the stuff they were doing and some of the rhythmic elements might have seeped into what we were doing, at least subconsciously."

With another sniggering title to rank alongside 'T★ts' and 'Goofing Off', *Balls* is a record inspired by travel and opulence – very much the zeitgeist – alternating with the Maels' take on banging techno with

---

* The actual storyline was a shipment of bombs getting mixed up in a container load of counterfeit jeans. Only one person can be called upon to avert disaster – the muscles from Brussels himself, Jean-Claude Van Damme, as 'king of the knock-offs' Marcus Ray. High art this was not.

surprisingly tender interludes. Although ultimately viewed as a minor addition to the Sparks canon, the album is full of highlights. The title track, especially, is a Ron Mael classic – full-pelt electro behind a double-tracked Russell. A fantastic statement of intent to open their fourth decade in the business, the song's faux-aggression pays homage to The Prodigy's controversial 'Smack My Bitch Up'. ('It's Educational' was also in The Prodigy mode.)

The smooth dance of the album's lead single, 'The Calm Before The Storm' takes the 'When Do I Get To Sing "My Way"' formula to its next level; it is most interesting for its vocal breakdown two and a half minutes in, where Russell accompanies himself as a barbershop quartet (an alternate version that was recorded emphasised this section). 'The Calm Before The Opera' gave the clearest indication how this idea could be developed in the future. 'Aeroflot', with Aksinja Berger providing the voice of the hostess, was to become a live favourite, while 'How To Get Your Ass Kicked' features a beautiful, mellow setting with extremely repetitive lyrics; another idea waiting to be developed.

There was one simple treat left for the end: 'The Angels', which became the album's second single. One of Ron's unequivocal love songs, unusually for Sparks, it openly uses a profanity ('fucking', if you must know).

The Roadrunner distribution deal had now lapsed, and for their 11th label Sparks went through Independent Recognition Records, distributed by Universal. Released on August 22, 2000, *Balls* came and went. The album's main criticism was that it all became a little familiar after a while, with the uptempo numbers lacking the killer kick drum, the big beat that defined the very best millennial dance music. The sleeve didn't add to the project either – arriving in a choice of four coloured CD jewel cases, with a silver slipcase, which frequently tore in retail racks, featuring a circular cut-out that emphasised the album's title. The four-page booklet emerged from the coloured sleeve – bearing a moody soft-focus shot of Russell. Designed by Dave Park from an original concept by Ron, it was art but it was anonymous, something you could never accuse previous Sparks designs of being.

Unlike Sparks' reappearance in 1994, there seemed to be no head of critical steam. Although *The Independent* said *Balls* was "tongue-in-cheek, disco friendly glam-techno crossover", long-time champions Q decreed that it was "a profound disappointment ... few songs lift themselves above pedestrian tedium." However, what was clear was that Sparks were still committed to being original in their choice of lyrical matter and, even though they were using similar beats to many at this time, they were still adding their own particular invention. Beyond the hardcore however, it seemed that no one cared as *Balls* sold less than half the number of its predecessor. After the love for *Gratuitous Sax & Senseless Violins* and the ground lost with *Plagiarism,* it appeared that Sparks were performing to a void. The situation seemed clear – if you wanted cutting edge techno, you could buy, by way of example, *Everything Everything* by Underworld; if you were a lapsed Sparks fan, you could always pick up a best of.

Yet in the background, Sparks' presence could be felt; whether being sent up by Vic Reeves and Bob Mortimer on their UK TV show *Shooting Stars* or being namechecked by Morrissey, their gentle glow in left-field culture shone on. One thing that positively developed as the new millennium got underway was the Sparks fan community. Thanks to the growth of the internet, information and opinion could be scuttled around the globe with a minimum of effort. The sites have been tremendous in promoting the band, and the warmth of the community is evident from the level of welcome and friendship they offer to new fans. Sparks may remain a well-kept secret, but it is one that many are prepared happily to share.

However opinion is something that the sites are most definitely full of – the sort of place where rumours can be propelled, half-truths propagated, and old folk devils are made even more devilish. One of the latter is Martin Gordon, whose position as Sparks' pantomime villain seems secure.

"If you ever had the pleasure of looking at the Sparks Fan Forum thing, you will find that any mention of my name immediately produces either a torrent of abuse or a torrent of non-interest," Gordon says. "At one point there was a thread called 'Who is Martin Bleedin' Gordon?' and this went on for some weeks and there were some really impassioned pros and cons. If anything pisses me off, it's that! It's as if nothing else has ever happened in my life. If that's what the fan wants to believe, then that's what the reality is for the fan."

Ron and Russell had started to think about where to go next. Their live shows had now become a definite fixture in their approach, and working with Tammy Glover suited them greatly as they had formed a tight playing unit. Sparks' current live show was a slam-banging mix of greatest hits and over half of the new album, introduced by a witty new anthem, 'It's A Sparks Show Tonight'. They took it around the globe – playing LA, London, Germany, Japan and, in January 2001, Australia, where Sparks had enjoyed a good level of success since the mid-Seventies.

Serendipitously, Knott's Berry Farm, the long-established amusement park in Buena Park, California, used 'Cool Places' in its advertising campaign that year, and provided a well-needed spike in the brothers' income. With studio time no longer a problem, and thanks to Ron's intermittently uncanny ability to sixth-sense a situation, Sparks retreated to Russell's studio to start work on what was to become the greatest album of their career.

Chapter Seventeen

Practising Makes Perfect: *Lil' Beethoven*

"Commercial suicide has seldom sounded more joyous than it does here."
Duncan Bell, *Muzik* magazine 2002

"Do you want to do something for that A&R guy that you loathe so much or are you going to do something for yourself?"
Russell Mael, 2003

With its flurry of sequencers and machines, the commercially disappointing *Balls* had been a brave work, but it simply felt as if the end of a line had been reached. Even though Sparks played to rapturous crowds, for once, the novelty seemed to have gone. "*Balls* had the mild air of retread about it," David Buckley accurately assessed in *Mojo*. It was clear that for Sparks to develop in their fourth decade together, a radical change of approach was needed.

"We've never been able to bask in the glory of our multi-platinum selling albums, despite being the most influential pop band in history," Ron stated sardonically. "The situation sucks, but after 30 years we've got used to it. It means we can't be complacent, we have to be progressive." And progressive was what Sparks were about to be.

"We actually had a whole album of songs ready to go that was a natural evolution from *Balls*," Ron told the author in 2002. "We were seeing what other people were doing – we don't work in a complete vacuum. We're aware of the general pop music context, but it seemed that nothing was going on. It's hard as a songwriter to scrap songs you have written, because each one is a precious gem – but we thought in order to come up with something that was impossible to pigeonhole we had to break out into an area that was uncomfortable."

Working for most of 2001 and into 2002, with John Thomas, Tammy Glover and Dean Menta, the brothers sweated and obsessed to find something different; to get the right sound. They decided to dispense with the thing their songs had been synonymous with since the late Seventies – the backbeat. Instead of working with songs and from drum loops, they started from scratch.

No stone was to be unturned and all clichés were to be avoided. The songs were going to be based around piano, vocal and orchestra. "We eliminated a lot of the rhythmic elements that most people use in pop music," Ron told the author in 2002. Taking the lead from the choral work on *Plagiarism* and 'The Calm Before The Storm', Russell's vocals became one of the key instruments on the album – around 75 voices were overlaid. "We wanted to replace the songs' drive with vocals," Ron continued. "We wanted it to be aggressive with rhythms and replaced the drums with these massive, aggressive vocal choruses."

It was as if he had returned to his 1974 list of how to jam-proof your composition as there was no idea that could have remotely developed from a jam session. Ron was determined to get everything just right. "It was important that the string parts weren't Moody Blues type-things and that they were driving and edgy."

The going was hardly easy with the brothers spending tortuous hours in the studio. "I find that whole process of working excruciating; it's horrible; they are in the studio for 14 hours a day," Glover said in 2007. "They love each other, they have harmonious lives with each other and they care deeply about the music but because they care so deeply, there's huge conflict. It's not easy at all and it goes on for an incredibly long period of time. These albums take a year, 18 months to record and during this time it's excruciating. They work seven days a week, 14 hours a day. If you could see the two of them, they are just wrung out by the end of them." On the final evidence, there was no other way to work. "*Lil' Beethoven* was hard to make – it was intense and it sounds it," Ron said.

The album was ready by early 2002. As the brothers listened to the finished work, they actually considered releasing it simply under the group name Lil' Beethoven in order to give it a chance without being pigeonholed. "We wanted to make it consistent, with no concession songs to the outside world," Russell said. "Then we had to bring variety within that area, to avoid nine songs that were exactly like 'The Rhythm Thief'. All these things floated around for a solid year. There's no turning back now. We've gained something really strong. We have to just move forward."

Everything on *Lil' Beethoven* sounded like the most extreme examples of Sparks' previous work, developed further. 'The Rhythm Thief' opens the album and sets its template. For a group that was frequently referred to as a 'dance duo', the opening words bade farewell to the rigid beats that had been behind their recent work. The album is not a complete break with the past; 'I Married Myself' echoes 'Falling In Love With Myself Again' and there is a return to the wild west with the cowboy metaphors in 'Ride 'Em Cowboy'. But these tales and observations of life in the 21st century, using classical orchestration, violins, oboes and celestial choirs, made for an unnerving yet melodious experience. The listener is immediately surprised by the album's texture, which fundamentally consists of walls of voices and keyboards and overall oddity.

There are so many layers to the album with each song presented as a mini-opera. 'Your Call Is Important To Us. Please Hold.', 'Ugly Guys With Beautiful Girls', 'What Are These Bands So Angry About' and 'How Do I Get To Carnegie Hall' have their titles repeated, aggressively and melodiously, occasionally to the point of distraction. Ron and Russell write about the frustration of being kept on the telephone, 'complaint rock' bands and unattractive men with hotties, all surveyed with an amusing weariness. 'Suburban Homeboy' is an affectionate swipe at white guys pretending they are from the 'hood.

The simplest song on the album, 'My Baby's Taking Me Home', is the best, in a dumb-ass way, and a perfect example of the album's craft, consisting of the title repeated 104 times with a brief monologue by Russell in the middle. For those who criticised Ron for overwriting in the past, it is almost the ultimate no-brainer while being staggeringly beautiful. It's like *Singin' In The Rain*. It does Busby Berkeley; it does 'Martha My Dear'. It does poetry and beauty.

Lil' Beethoven plays like a concept album in as much as it is difficult not to hear one track without hearing the whole work. "We see it that way," says Russell. "It isn't a concept album in terms of narrative, but it does seem you can't separate any one track. It holds together well as a whole piece. When we were recording it, we didn't have nine pieces of music prepared; we just went in blindly. We'd done 'The Rhythm Thief' and we thought have we shot ourselves in the foot doing something like this? Is anybody going to respond to this? All these things roll around your brain – we weren't sure if we should follow up on it. We thought we'd do it like *Kimono* or *No. 1* – have that spirit. Do you want to do something for that A&R guy that you loathe so much or are you going to do something for yourself? Musically, things are really bland now – and it's not just a case of age – it's not that there's nothing, but the bar rises higher and higher on your threshold for being inspired by something. We didn't want to leave anyone hearing it unmoved – whether in a good or bad way."

The album was certainly going to move people.

Lil' Beethoven was released in October 2002 through John Lennard's Artful/Fulfill label, in a white hardcover CD sleeve, featuring Dave Park's illustration of the German composer in the bottom right-hand corner and nothing else apart from the simple wording: **LIL' BEETHOVEN An Album By SPARKS**

For the first time since *Gratuitous Sax...*, the press was in raptures. "Time to give Sparks their due surely," said *Mojo*. The now defunct *Muzik* magazine opined "We doubt whether they've ever made a better – or odder – record than this. A fanciful, Gilbert & Sullivan on Quaaludes disco-rock operetta, no less" before presciently suggesting that "commercial suicide has seldom sounded more joyous than it does here". Ireland's *Hot Press* described 'Suburban Homeboy' as "the kind of record that the Bonzo Dog Doo-Dah Band would be making if they were still around". In *The Independent,* Michael Bracewell called *Lil' Beethoven* "A masterpiece of pop art – part manifesto, part, vitally, a critique of pop itself and sounding as though George Gershwin, Philip Glass and the Mothers of Invention had sat down with Tim Burton and decided to write a musical." David Cheal proclaimed in *The Telegraph* that "[Sparks have] just made one of the most extraordinary albums of the year."

For *Uncut,* writer Ian McDonald, who in 1974 had written so favourably in *NME* about *Kimono My House,* in one of his final reviews, wrote in August 2003, "It's a bravely avant garde endeavour ameliorated by a continually dry irony that raises the occasional smile. Mostly, though, the results are mystifying. Be warned. It's challenging stuff." Long-time champion Martin Aston said in *Q,* "This is the first Teutonic glam-rock chamber-classical cabaret opus, and uniquely, brilliantly, Sparks."

When first hearing *Lil' Beethoven,* this author was as bewildered and delighted as the next reviewer. "It's all a bit like Laurie Anderson's 'O Superman'," I wrote in *Record Collector.* "Brecht and Weill's 'The Threepenny Opera', 10cc's 'Une Nuit A Paris', the second side of *Tubular Bells* with vocals and the 1970 England World Cup Squad's 'Back Home'. Only, of course, it's nothing like these reference points. At all."

My contention at the time, and it still stands today, was that "If anyone else can give me evidence of a group 32 years into their career writing and performing an album as interesting, inventive and accomplished as *Lil' Beethoven,* I will personally come down and buy them a very hearty luncheon."

Lil' Beethoven received its live premiere at London's Royal Festival Hall on October 19, 2002. The souvenir programme explained the concept Ron and Russell had devised: of how the elusive musical prodigy Lil' Beethoven – a descendant of the composer and the daughter of an ear doctor Beethoven used to frequent – lived in the town of Heidelberg, and had been approached by various musicians for years. He had always turned them away – until Sparks arrived, of course. The closing paragraph of the programme notes made many fans realise why there could be few groups as interesting and creative:

"Why Sparks? Perhaps it is their mutual love of language, of pushing boundaries of popular music, of experimenting in recording to bring new excitement to a moribund field. Perhaps it is Lil' Beethoven's love of 1970s Hollywood disaster movies, such as *Towering Inferno*, *Earthquake* and *Rollercoaster*, the film in which Sparks make a brief appearance (an appearance they have regretted for 25 years) – a film that Lil' Beethoven has seen 127 times. Whatever the reason, the long awaited results of the meeting between Sparks and Lil' Beethoven can be heard and seen this evening."

It was as if the ghost of Joseph Fleury was hanging over the proceedings. It was pure drama. Whatever was to happen, people were not going to ignore this album.

To bring *Lil' Beethoven* to the stage, the Maels realised they had to do something special. With the brothers facing the crowd and Menta and Glover away to the side, they created 50 minutes of pure theatre, playing the album in its entirety (the second half of the show was a greatest hits set), using the whole stage as a blank canvas to visualise these audacious pieces of music. For example, Ron wore false arms during 'How Do I Get To Carnegie Hall?' and strolled with a model in 'Ugly Guys With Beautiful Girls'.

At year's end *Lil' Beethoven* ranked at number 25 in *Uncut*'s Best Of The Year's Albums poll and in *Record Collector*'s Best New Albums of 2002 ("possibly the most exciting and interesting release ever from such a long established act"). However the album hadn't received proper distribution through the tiny Fulfill label. As it was such a slow-burner, there was still plenty of work involved to make sure people were aware of its glory. For that, Ron and Russell began to rely heavily on Sue Harris, who, in 2003, became their sixth manager.

Although Eric Harle had done an incredible job of restoring Sparks' reputation in the UK and Europe, by mutual consent, the agreement with DEF Management ended after the release of *Balls*. Harris, who like virtually all of Sparks' UK supporters first became aware of them in May 1974 via their *Top Of The Pops* appearance, had trained as a nurse before moving into PR with the PWL stable in the Nineties. Her PR company, Republic Media, had been employed by Recognition, who distributed *Balls*.

Sue Harris: "We'd loosely kept in touch by email. [Sparks] had finished recording *Lil' Beethoven* and had arranged the gig at the Royal Festival Hall to premiere it. They wanted some help to PR the gig. They didn't have anyone representing them in any other way over here so over the next few months I started filling the management gaps."

Harris was to oversee Sparks' greatest period of consistency since the Seventies, and coming from a press background, made sure that no PR opportunity would be missed.

In March 2003, Sparks returned to London's Royal Festival Hall to perform the album again. It was little short of a tour de force. Again, the first half was *Lil' Beethoven* in its entirety, the second a sprightly jaunt through the catalogue including tracks from *A Woofer In Tweeter's Clothing* ('Here Comes Bob') up to *Balls* ('Aeroflot'). Their reputation found at least a dozen notable writers and editors of the UK music press – some of whom had even paid for their tickets – all standing for an ovation. The invention, the humour, the – in the words of *Times* writer and pop boffin Michael Bracewell – *otherness* of Sparks made them more than merely survivors – anyone can *survive* – but to still be leaders – albeit in a very defined niche – was truly something.

The hits half of the show had the audience on their feet and dancing. Simon Goddard, writing in *Uncut,* said, "From the first throb of 'The Number One Song In Heaven', bodies and bad hairdos of all shapes and sizes are a-bouncing, hands clapping above their heads 'Radio Ga-Ga' style to every metronomic beat. You could almost forget Sparks were ever a 'rock' band since this, ducky, is pure 21st century gay disco."

As word of mouth about *Lil' Beethoven* spread, there was no shortage of those who declared their love for it, including old cohorts. "I really love the album," Tony Visconti says. "I think they've got a sense of what's classic. They'll never lose that – they can take a genre and make it their own. They can still sound like Sparks and the songs will still be completely further out than anyone else's writing."

"I really love *Lil' Beethoven,*" David Kendrick says. "I'm so happy that came around, I thought it was one of their best albums ever." Even John Hewlett thought it their best for years, saying the album was "a stroke of genius".

Ironically, it was another name from Sparks' past that was to provide a much-needed hand in pushing the album in their most problematic of territories, America. Since Chris Blackwell had sold Island Records to Polygram in the late Eighties, he had gone on to found Palm Pictures, a multimedia entertainment company. Blackwell had heard *Lil' Beethoven* and, unlike his initial view towards the group in the Seventies, he absolutely loved it.

"We've just signed with Blackwell's Palm label for the rest of the world," Russell said in 2003. "A strange set of circumstances brought us together again. A friend was talking about us to Chris. We spoke with him again and sent a copy of *Lil' Beethoven* to him – within a couple of days we'd done a deal for the whole world. It reminded him of when he first heard Procol Harum's 'A Whiter Shade Of Pale'. He's now really involved."

Blackwell's involvement was to be significant, as Palm Pictures were to market and distribute the album in America. "We can't remember when there's been so much interest in our stuff in the States," Russell continued. "It's ironic we're all back together again."

"The record to them is a challenge rather than a problem," Ron said. "We've always had respect for these kinds of people. It's an honour to be back with him [Blackwell] in a non-nostalgic kind of way."

Released in America on July 8 *Lil' Beethoven* attracted a string of positive reviews. *Billboard* called it "the best soundtrack to a film that does not exist". David Fricke in *Rolling Stone* trumpeted its arrival: "Ron and Russell Mael, the brothers and brains of the eclectic, enduring Sparks, spare no buffoons or expense on *Lil' Beethoven*: nine songs of lethal grandeur built from Ron's swollen waves of strings and fistfuls of piano and Russell's one-man operatic chorales. Ron fires up his ivories and piles on the orchestra like the real Beethoven running amok in the Brill Building, and Russell's quivering tenor – a perfect cocktail of Noël Coward and Freddie Mercury – is a deadly thing."

It was high praise indeed and there was no denying the support the album deserved. The group threw themselves – as always – enthusiastically onto the promotional treadmill. To cater for MTV a video for 'The Rhythm Thief' was shot by Olivier Kuntzel and Florence Deygas, with whom Sparks had worked on the 1999 short film *A Cute Candidate*. The brothers paid a visit to Tower Records in Manhattan, where Ron recited the album's lyrics in front of the crowd, including all the repetitions. For the first occasion they had played the city in 20 years, in August, Sparks took the show to New York by way of a free concert in Central Park. Russell talked of the possibility of *Lil' Beethoven* being turned into a film with Hollywood producer Don Murphy.

Unfortunately, despite the considerable buzz, the album simply didn't ignite. It was odd enough for the European market, who were much more open to this kind of thing, but America? Weren't Sparks that dance group?

Chris Blackwell: *"Lil' Beethoven* was such a huge disappointment to me. I thought the record was such a masterpiece. I thought we would do so much better than we did. It was nothing to do with them – they'd done their work, the record was masterful. We just weren't able to get it going."

The year 2003 was a bad one for Palm; Blackwell was ill and the company was having financial problems. Blackwell also realised the music industry was now a world apart from the business he knew in the Sixties and Seventies. "The thing with Island, in the mid-Seventies when we first signed [Sparks], we had such great momentum that people would give us the benefit of the doubt if we released something a little left of centre; the label actually helped them. Later when we signed them, Palm didn't have any of that kudos attached to being a respected brand. I was very disappointed. [The album] did nothing, nothing, nothing. We took 'The Rhythm Thief' everywhere that we could. I liked them a lot and we did what we could and we really tried to do whatever we could for them. It was different and so brilliant, it just didn't fit anything."

In the old days, Island could guarantee support from record shops. Now, in America especially, record shops were big boxes where you had to pay a fortune to get price and positioning. *Lil' Beethoven* was simply not a Wal-Mart record and although it was making inroads, the digital revolution, lead by iTunes, had yet to fully take hold. With every will in the world, and high-powered support, America again didn't seem to be interested.

After having a difficult time with Artful, the label that had originally put the album out in Britain, Sue Harris and the Maels set up Lil' Beethoven Records after the UK rights reverted back to Ron and Russell. Immediately the white-sleeved hardback edition was removed in favour of a black-sleeved Deluxe Edition, released on March 15, 2004. Blackwell gave permission to use the Palm Pictures-funded 'The Rhythm Thief' video, and some other oddities – 'The Legend Of Lil' Beethoven', 'Wunderbar' and an instrumental version of 'The Rhythm Thief' were added to make the show even more elaborate. To celebrate the new edition, the brothers played two nights at The Ocean, East London's short-lived state of the art music venue in Hackney on March 20 and 21.

The band then went over to Stockholm for three nights, returning to the States for a gig on April 9 at the Independent in San Francisco and then, to bring *Lil' Beethoven* home, at the 1,300-seater Henry Fonda Theater on Hollywood Boulevard the following night. However Sparks' next major show gained them arguably the most publicity for a gig they had enjoyed in their entire career. The press hoo-hah surrounding Morrissey's curation of the Meltdown Festival on London's South Bank in June 2004 was hard to believe. For the preceding month, it seemed that every arts section and magazine pored over his choice of line-up, which included Sparks.

David Sefton had put together the first Meltdown Festival at London's Royal Festival Hall in 1993. When he departed to take over the UCLA's arts programme in 2000, his role was taken by Glen Max, who developed the idea further, making it a key event in the UK arts calendar. Each year a series of weekly events in June would be brought together by a certain individual in the arts. It quickly moved on from its classical and serious-minded origins until it became a badge of honour for every left-leaning musical name; Scott Walker, David Bowie, John Peel and Patti Smith would all get to 'curate' their own Meltdown. It also propelled the word 'curator' into the mainstream for any potential booker/organiser of events.

In 2004, it was the turn of one of pop's most contrary individuals, who, as a teenager, wrote to the *NME* extolling the virtues of *Kimono My House*, to curate the festival. Having already set his sights (successfully) on persuading his beloved New York Dolls to reform (despite two key members being deceased) Morrissey approached Sparks to perform *Kimono My House* in its entirety. "All they could think was 'Why?'" says Harris. "Why would a band that was making some of the best music of their career suddenly revisit an album from 1974, with no reference to the 'now?'" When the invitation was met with a refusal, Morrissey, who was on record as saying the album was one of his most important influences, asked again.*

"It was agreed to add *Lil' Beethoven*, and that made sense," Harris continues. "It meant the show referenced the past, but was all about the present. They had revisited the past but it was always in context."

There were those who suggested that Morrissey had played it safe with his line-up, which also included his LA neighbour Nancy Sinatra and Alan Bennett. The London *Metro* even considered that "pop enigma Sparks are the most avant-garde choice".

On June 12, Sparks took the stage with a one-off line-up to play the album. Tammy Glover and Dean Menta were joined by Redd Kross' bassist Steve McDonald and Jim Wilson, the sometime guitarist with Henry Rollins. Wilson's path had crossed with the brothers after Tony Visconti invited the guitar player along to his birthday party to meet them, knowing he was a Sparks fan. Through a twisting chain of events, including making a copy of a Dean Young cartoon of Sparks that Wilson had bought at a convention and a further chance meeting in a Mexican restaurant, Wilson was in.

The Delaware-born Wilson told the brothers with only slight exaggeration that he had been rehearsing for the show since the age of 14. "I went to Russell's house/studio and I plugged in and kind of just played through *Kimono* to the CD and he said 'Wow, you really do know it'. I was a *huge* Sparks fan growing up," Wilson says. "My Sparks infatuation began as a teenager when I first got into their music. I just kept getting deeper into the catalogue." His love for the group was shared with Marcus Blake, his school-friend and future co-founder of Mother Superior.

The Royal Festival Hall, sometimes a difficult venue to set alight emotionally, went up in flames. It was an intense and remarkable evening. "It was so exciting," Wilson recalls. "I was so nervous. We hadn't played

---

* In his notes to a *Songs To Save Your Life* CD he compiled (featuring 'Barbecutie') given away free with *NME*, Morrissey took the opportunity again to say that Sparks were "Very, very clever. Ahead of their time. Lyrically astonishing."

Kimono My House for anybody and didn't know what the reaction was going to be."

The band members dressed in matching red shirts and black ties with Glover dressed as a geisha. The reviews were unanimous in their acclaim. The author wrote in *Record Collector* that "by the time of 'Suburban Homeboy', the audience were on their feet and Ron's heartfelt thanks for prolonged UK support brings the evening to a touching close. A memorable occasion." In *Mojo* Keith Cameron compared Russell to a "dapper and talented version" of Bombardier Beaumont (played by Melvin Hayes) from Seventies UK TV show *It Ain't Half Hot, Mum* and said that, "Separated by 20 years, neither set of songs sounds remotely precedented, nor wants anything for charm or pure excitement." Ryan Gilbey in *The Independent* said there was no time to dwell on the past as "the vigour with which the songs are invested leaves no room for nostalgia. Who has time to reminisce about the 70s when the band's drummer, Tammy Glover, is dolled up as a geisha, incongruously bashing her way through 'Hasta Mañana Monsieur' like Keith Moon in a black bob and lippy?"

The concert successfully showed that Sparks were about *now* as much as then. They continued to take the *Lil' Beethoven* show around Europe, and the Stockholm show was filmed for a DVD released in August. David Buckley in *Mojo* said the concert showed that "Ron Mael is funny; his brother Russell's live vocal is simply angelic". It concluded two years of work that had repositioned Sparks less as novelty and more as high art.

Lil' Beethoven had provided the fillip to the career Sparks had been carving over the past decade. Although it sold broadly in line with all of their other recent releases, what the album had done was spread the word. The group hadn't really had a buzz on this scale since *No. 1 in Heaven*. While there had been a palpable sense of delight when *Gratuitous Sax & Senseless Violins* was released, as good as it was, the music was not ground-breaking. *Lil' Beethoven* was ground-breaking and then some.

It was during this period that another indie act came forward to declare their undying admiration. Franz Ferdinand had erupted in early 2004 with their angular art-rock and a breakthrough single, 'Take Me

Gered Mankowitz's studio, London, August 1979. (GERED MANKOWITZ)

"You're laying in my space!" – a tramp admonishes Ron during the guerrilla photography for the sleeve of *Terminal Jive*, Victoria Station, London, 1979. (GERED MANKOWITZ)

"The new album's a hoot, I'll tell you." Ron grins and bears it. Unused photograph from *Terminal Jive* sessions, Safeway, Kings Road, Chelsea, London 1979. (GERED MANKOWITZ)

Ron and Russell Mael at Sparks' unofficial LA HQ, the Farmers' Market, 1980s. (BARRY SCHULTZ/RETNA)

Sparring before *Whomp That Sucker* launch, Park Lane, London, 1981. (SIPA PRESS/REX FEATURES)

Taking it to the (big brass?) ring, May 1981 at the launch for *Whomp That Sucker* at the Hilton Hotel, Park Lane, London. Viv Stanshall and Clem Burke were among the onlookers. (RICHARD YOUNG/REX FEATURES)

Ron and Russell, back as a duo around the time of *Music That You Can Dance To*. (GEORGE DUBOSE/LFI)

As years passed, Ron's caricature became more extreme on stage - a fun guy from outer space. Ron in his early Eighties stage outfit of his dressing gown ...(BOB LEAFE/FRANK WHITE AGENCY)

...doing his on-stage strip, 1983. Les Boehm can be seen in the background ... (BOB LEAFE/FRANK WHITE AGENCY)

Rock, Rock, Rock. Ron's miming of Jim Wilson's off-stage guitar solo was a highlight of the *Hello Young Lovers* tour. (LIVEPIX)

… Practice man, practice! Ron finding out the way to Carnegie Hall, *Lil' Beethoven* tour 2003. (RICHARD C MURRAY/LFI)

Ron Mael, dicking around on stage, 2006, on the *Hello Young Lovers* tour. (LIVEPIX)

Ron Mael and Russell Mael, Cambridge Corn Exchange, October 2006.
"They are charming gentlemen … I don't need to know anything else about them than
what is on the record." – manager Sue Harris. (CHRIS BOLAND/REX FEATURES)

"It became world-wide news – no-one had ever done anything like that before." – Sue Harris.
Sparks onstage at the 21 Nights, 2008. L to R: Marcus Blake, Russell Mael, Ron Mael, Steven Nistor.
(ELLIOTT FRANKS/LIVEPIX)

(ANDY WHITTON)

Out', a metallic update of Led Zeppelin's 'Trampled Underfoot'. With their asymmetrical haircuts and breezy Scots attitude, the band was everywhere. Alex Kapranos, their lead singer, did a piece in the *NME* entitled 'Why I Love Sparks'. "It's only after a few listens you really get into it. That's what Sparks were like. You can go back and listen again and again. Then you really fall in love and bands change your life. Now I can't imagine life without them." When Franz Ferdinand were in LA, they had lunch with Ron and Russell. "We heard they liked our record," drummer Paul Thomson told *The Daily Record*. "They didn't eat anything and were so polite, while we stuffed ourselves with burgers. We've always liked them, because they are great songwriters." *

After the indifference that met *Plagiarism* and *Balls*, it was a period of intense activity and fun. On Orbital's *Blue Album,* released that June, two 'synth duos' met when Ron and Russell made a guest appearance on the track 'Acid Pants', described by the *London Metro* as being "goofy, faintly hysterical". Another oddity at this time was Sparks' cover of 'We Are The Clash', a very much unloved song from that band's final album, *Cut The Crap,* for a free *A Tribute To The Clash* CD in *Uncut* magazine. "A delicious rock'n'roll irony," as the magazine put it.

In October, through the internet, fans mobilised to attend the International Sparks Conference 2004, held at The George and Pilgrim Hotel in Glastonbury and organised by fan Lynn Bastian. The brothers sent a filmed message and former members Trevor White, Martin Gordon and Ian Hampton turned up in person. Also in 2004 the publishing deal with Island Music, which John Hewlett had negotiated 30 years before, lapsed and saw the rights of over 200 Sparks songs revert back to the Maels. The brothers subsequently arranged a new deal with Warner Chappell on all their albums aside from *Lil' Beethoven, Balls* and *Gratuitous Sax...,* which remained with Universal.

The relationship between the brothers and Sue Harris had proved an astute management choice for the brothers: "Managing Sparks is not something you undertake lightly," she says. "It's like a marriage; you put your heart and soul into it. They are extraordinary and unique. I don't

---

* It was said that Franz were going to compile a Sparks collection but aside from Sparks presenting Franz Ferdinand with their 2005 Brit award, nothing has since happened.

think anyone else in the world is like them — to manage them can't be like managing anyone else. We have very defined roles. I don't get involved in their recording process, their A&R process, to me it would be like working with Van Gogh and saying 'I don't like what you did with that sunflower, can you make it a bit yellower?'"

Chapter Eighteen

Can I Invade Your Country?
Hello Young Lovers

"We've drawn a line in the sand with our new album. If you're coming with us, step right over the line!"

Sparks, 2005

"They make great art that is extraordinary."

Sue Harris, 2009

At the outset of 2003, Ron Mael was clear that he would not be content to bask in the critical accord with which *Lil' Beethoven* had been garlanded, stating, "We would like to elaborate on the general direction of this album." In the past detractors had attempted to undermine Ron and Russell's talent by suggesting that their best work had relied on outside collaboration: that it had been Martin Gordon's arrangements or Adrian Fisher's guitar playing that had sealed *Kimono My House,* or Giorgio Moroder's co-writes and production that had made *No. 1 In Heaven.* Now they had released an acknowledged masterpiece that was down to no one else.

The Maels had devoted an unprecedented four years to one project – writing, recording, promoting and touring behind *Lil' Beethoven*. In the same period, three decades before, Sparks had released six albums. With celebrity fans and critical respect, if their shows were not sell-outs, they were certainly operating on high-percentage capacities with new markets, such as Japan, opening up.

However, from Roy Silver's efforts in the early Seventies to Chris Blackwell's later endeavours, widespread success in their homeland still eluded the brothers. But, for once, Ron and Russell didn't seem to be that concerned. The seam they had struck in the late Eighties with their home recordings seemed to be bearing fruit so the pair retreated back into their LA studio to begin work on a follow-up, working with the regular supporting cast of Dean Menta and Tammy Glover with touring bassist Steve McDonald and guitarist Jim Wilson helping out. Working largely without demos, the brothers expanded the spectacularly singular sound crafted for *Lil' Beethoven*.

In May 2005, a press release was issued updating fans on the album's progress: "No time for play these days… Ron and Russell are feverishly working like mad scientists on their follow-up to *Lil' Beethoven* [which is quite frankly, very hard to follow up!] However, the Maels are now fiercely challenging their former masterpiece and promise to equal, if not exceed, its brilliance. Dean and Tammy are working hard to make sure they out-do themselves on this one as well."

The advance word on the album *Hello Young Lovers*, taking its title from the Rogers and Hammerstein standard from *The King And I*, mentioned pieces that ran for up to seven minutes. Russell added it wasn't for the timid and that it would be "elaborate, excessive, adventurous, more extreme, with lots of vocals! And there is much more diversified instrumentation on the new album." For once, there was an air of expectation outside the Sparks hardcore.

In the interim, Sparks certainly benefited from their new, raised profile in the UK. On June 25, they took a break from recording to appear in London at the 2005 Meltdown curated by their one-time touring partner, Patti Smith. The evening was a tribute to Bertolt Brecht. Ron and Russell performed 'The Mandalay Song' from *Happy End*, accompanied by the London Sinfonietta, and returned for the encores of 'The Solidarity Song', joined by the rest of the show's performers including Marc Almond, David Thomas and Smith herself. The Maels also attended the Q Awards in 2005 and presented the best album award to Coldplay. Liam Gallagher approached the brothers and paid his respects for 'This Town Ain't Big Enough For Both Of Us'

Sparks' profile was boosted again by a cover of that very song by British Whale, a pseudonym for Justin Hawkins, the leader of British band The Darkness who had shot to fame in 2003 with their humorous-yet-sincere take on clichéd heavy rock. Hawkins' version of 'This Town Ain't Big Enough For Both Of Us' rose to number six on the UK charts.

"It's hard to cover a Sparks song," Sue Harris says. "When Ron writes, he's writing with Russell in mind, and Russell has this incredible ability to interpret Ron's writing in a way that no one else can – which is part of the reason they are so unique. Often when you hear covers of their songs, they aren't very good and frequently artists give up because it's too hard… Justin Hawkins took it to the most preposterous level with 'This Town Ain't Big Enough For Both Of Us'– he out-falsetto'd Russell."

Ron and Russell were touched by Hawkins' tribute and appeared in the video, which was set at that most un-American of events, the World Darts Championship. "We've plundered and plagiarised the Sparks catalogue shamelessly throughout our career," Hawkins admitted. "It's a true classic."

With the new album finished, Harris visited UK record companies to see if the goodwill of recent years could be turned into an attractive deal. Leading UK independent Gut Records snapped Sparks up. Founded by Guy Holmes, Gut had enjoyed great success with Tom Jones at the end of the Nineties, and had recently enjoyed a huge British hit with the novelty record 'Crazy Frog'. Although Sparks were less 'pop' than the label was used to, with Harris working the promo, it was obvious that the album would be launched with enough fanfare. Gut MD Steve Tandy agreed that "it would never be easy taking the normal routes with someone like Sparks in terms of radio and TV because they are obviously in a different genre, but so far we are really pleased with everyone that has come on board."

Hello Young Lovers was released on February 6, 2006, with a Dave Park-designed sleeve full of pink and fluffy rabbits (the 'young lovers' of the title). For the first time since 1983's *Sparks In Outer Space*, other band members (Dean Menta and Tammy Glover) were pictured in the booklet; more strikingly, the band were all shown in the same picture – the last time that had happened was 1975.

Ron and Russell had become two-man Tony Viscontis recording their own *Indiscreet*. With little modesty, Russell called it "the modern equivalent of *Sgt Pepper*". It *was*, in the sense that it followed a better record (*Revolver* in The Beatles' case), but it took that formula of progression to a higher plateau. The walls of vocals are not quite in such evidence as in *Lil' Beethoven*, yet the instrumentation is more complex and there is also a great deal more guitar and drums.

The album starts and finishes with epics – 'Dick Around' and 'As I Sit Down To Play The Organ At The Notre Dame Cathedral', which meddle with form and convention. The former, a paean to leisure time, was later released as a single. The tracks act very much as bookends to the whimsy and invention inside. To these ears, they work the least.

'Waterproof' contains a mixture of recorders, violins, thrash metal guitar and clattering drums. 'Rock, Rock, Rock' retains a similar theme to 'What Are All These Bands So Angry About' but everything seems more extreme and mannered. 'Metaphor' and 'Waterproof' too are complex, funny and innovative, while one of the best examples of vocal trickery on the album can be found on the cat's chorus of 'Here Kitty'. Most notably *Hello Young Lovers* contains two of the best songs – 'Perfume' and the remarkable '(Baby, Baby) Can I Invade Your Country' – that Sparks have ever recorded.

'Perfume' is gorgeous. A warm, synthetic pulse underscores another of the brothers' occasional love songs. Menta's nagging guitar propels it further, and Russell's understated vocals, singing through a list of some 30 perfumes, are among his best. '(Baby, Baby) Can I Invade Your Country' is a mass of overdubbed acoustics creating a marching rhythm (without drums), with Ron's synthesiser and Menta's guitar. The group overlay vocals while Russell sings Francis Scott Key's 'The Star Spangled Banner', before asking the title's question. Written at the height of America's War On Terror, the global campaign in the wake of 9/11,

Ron would introduce it on stage by saying that Sparks previously had 'apolitical' tattooed across their chests for years. With this song, it was removed, marking the first overtly political song written by the Maels. With its jazz trumpet breakdown and extreme use of repetition, it further demonstrates how far the brothers had come as producers/arrangers.

Although it may have not had the impact of *Lil' Beethoven*, *Hello Young Lovers* did not disappoint. The product of 18 months' work, it is a record that the group feel duly proud of. "We've attempted to push the parameters for those who thought *Lil' Beethoven* was about as far as things could get pushed," Russell said. "Yet, we think the whole Sparks world will now live in peace and harmony with the scheme of the new Sparks album."

A six-page special feature was published in industry magazine *Music Week* entitled "Sparks fly into the future". Elsewhere, the album received the now customary platter of glowing reviews. "Sparks retain a mythic corona which few other than Morrissey continue to possess. Sparks remain a puzzle, but how refreshing is that?" David Buckley said in *Mojo*. "The most out-there pop record by fiftysomething Americans... ever" long-term fan Paul Lester declared in *Uncut*. "Be prepared to be welcomed back into their parallel universe," the author wrote in *Record Collector*.

A British tour supported the initial release of the album – a six-date jaunt from Glasgow to London, commencing February 12, 2006. The live band – Steven McDonald on bass and Steven Nistor on drums – was augmented with the presence of LA legend Josh Klinghoffer, the producer/guitarist who has played with a variety of acts from the Red Hot Chili Peppers to Beck. A new concert was devised with *Hello Young Lovers* played in its entirety in the first half and the now customary 'Sparks Show' in the second.

When Klinghoffer had other commitments, Jim Wilson returned to the band. "At the same time we were doing our Mother Superior tour so Josh and I would cross over. I played in Paris for that tour, I played at Guilfest. It was weird because Josh and I were literally passing each other by. I went to Russia because he couldn't."

The band had formed into a tight touring unit and the balance of theatre and concert was by now near perfect. The show opened with

'Rock, Rock, Rock' in which Ron mimed to Klinghoffer's offstage guitar, throwing rock shapes. Behind his horn-rims and dressed in black, he had honed his nearly 40-year-old routine to perfection. This was the Chaplin of *The Great Dictator*, not of *Easy Street*. Projections by Shaw Petronio and Eiko Fujimoto were used throughout, most notably on 'The Very Next Fight' where Ron boxed with himself on the screen onstage.

On May 20, Sparks played LA's Avalon Ballroom, followed by various well-received festival dates including the Isle Of Skye Music Festival in June and Guildford's Guilfest a month later. The one misstep occurred when Sparks headlined the Saturday night of *The Big Chill* festival at Eastnor Castle on August 5. Despite great anticipation, the show didn't quite come off and the crowd dwindled. "The weekend was crying out for big names who could unite the 30,000 crowd for a defining moment," said *The Guardian*. "That was well beyond the capabilities of Sparks who topped Saturday night's main-stage bill playing their new album to a tiny audience." *The Daily Telegraph* added "Their arch and rather brittle sound jarred in the warm glow of the big chill ambience. By the end they were just playing to a handful." Perhaps headlining a festival whose whole reputation has been based on mellow vibes was not necessarily the most obvious fit for Sparks. In many ways, it was akin to them playing the Whisky on Sunset early in their career. The hardcore adored it, but the rest moved on.

As an interesting sideline during this time, the Maels selected tracks for a Motown compilation in its *Made To Measure* series. The brainchild of Universal's UK office, the idea was for compilations of personally selected material from the Motown vaults by artists not immediately associated with the iconic label. British actor Martin Freeman had the first go; Sparks were next. Released on June 6, 2006, Russell and Ron were interviewed by journalist Paolo Hewitt for the sleeve notes at their Kensington hotel. Theirs was a catholic selection that paid no mind to conventionally received wisdom and saw established Motown treasures such as The Supremes' 'Back In My Arms Again' and The Temptations' 'Get Ready' next to 'uncool' selections such as 'Ben' by Michael Jackson or 'Don't Leave Me This Way' by Thelma Houston.

The world of radio had changed beyond recognition from the days when Motown got singles played on the medium. Getting Sparks heard over the UK airwaves was a huge issue and a wall of indifference met 'Perfume', the first single to be taken off the album.

Sue Harris: "Back in 1974, people said that 'This Town Ain't Big Enough For Both Of Us' wasn't a hit. Then Tony Blackburn played it and off it went. German radio got behind 'When Do I Get To Sing "My Way"'. It doesn't matter if a song is off the 20th or the third album. If Sparks got airplay they would sell more records. No doubt about it. They might not be like James Blunt – but they do write pop songs."

With the album's critical support and its encouraging sales, Gut gave the green light to release another single. Great expectations were held for 'Dick Around', released as a double A side with 'Waterproof', which in itself suggests that there was possibly some initial reservations about putting a single out with the word 'dick' in the title. Ron and Russell admitted to *Mojo*'s Johnny Black that they were hoping for a chart position. "In our minds, that's the perfect hit single. We're still optimistic and we believe a song like that, in its spirit and sensibility, has the same thing that 'This Town Ain't Big Enough For Both Of Us' had in 1974. It should be a hit here and we'll be very disappointed if it isn't." *The Gay Times* called 'Dick Around', "Philip Glass played by *A Night At The Opera*-era Queen. No, really."

The Maels appeared on BBC Radio London's *Breakfast Show* on September 25, but the station refused to play the single, allegedly objecting to the title. This, of course, gave the brothers and the promotional machine an opportunity for a bit of old-fashioned smoke and mirrors. "The BBC has officially killed off our new single 'Dick Around'," a press release said, "ostensibly through rather childish objections to the title, an innocent reference to the idle life. That a piece of music can be condemned purely by its title without the decision makers even having the decency to open the CD case is a travesty and an insult to both us as the creators of the music and to the listeners of the BBC."

That the record may not have been commercial enough to the ears of the 2006 programmers was neither here nor there; here was an old-fashioned piece of hokum, straight from the Joseph Fleury stable.

Sue Harris is still furious. "It was ridiculous. We were promoting the single and then they said we'll have to play the previous single, 'Perfume'. We were told it was because of the word 'dick'. Then the presenter realised what was going on so it became this farcical conversation about how many times can they all say 'dick'. It's not about a penis; it's about a guy fooling around. It was embarrassing. Don't ask an internationally respected pair of musicians to come on a show and then insult them."

That said, it's no wonder that the remaining stiff-shirted BBC types may have been a little suspicious of a track from a record that makes a pun regarding 'invading your country' and from a group whose 2000 album was called *Balls*. Despite all this and predictable strap-lines in papers such as *The Glasgow Extra* ("Sparks fly after Beeb ban new single"), the single could not manage to make it into the Top 75.

It did, however, conclude a year that saw not only *Hello Young Lovers* make it to number 48 in the *Mojo* year-end polls, but the group's profile remained steady, with the Motown compilation and, in November, Universal Music Catalogue's release of superior '21st Century Editions' of their four Island albums. All had bonus material, essays by four sympathetic writers and memorabilia supplied by Sparks authority Auke Lenstra. All sold well, in the (chronological) order one would expect. The inner trays all advertised *Hello Young Lovers*, indicating that Sparks were still very much about the present.

At the start of 2007, another singer clearly influenced by Sparks appeared on the UK scene. Mika, a stunningly good-looking chap of Israeli descent, not only sounded like a hybrid of Russell and Freddie Mercury but, visually, he resembled Russell as well. While he was at the top of the charts, it was all good for business sending people back to Sparks' catalogue, most of which was now available on iTunes.

As the band completed their *Hello Young Lovers* touring commitments, Ron and Russell returned to Russell's studio to start work on the next Sparks album. On January 20, 2007 BBC Radio 2 presented an hour-long documentary, *This Town Ain't Big Enough For Both Of Us – The Story Of Sparks*, hosted by Mark Radcliffe with a variety of contributors from Giorgio Moroder to Alex Kapranos of Franz Ferdinand.

Russell took a break from recording to make a rare solo performance on September 21, 2007, when he played in Milan on a bill alongside

Jarvis Cocker, Beth Orton, Peter Murphy and Alex Chilton – supported by the band Baby Lemonade and augmented by the London Sinfonietta. The concert, *It Was 40 Years Ago Today,* was a birthday tribute to The Beatles' *Sgt Pepper's Lonely Hearts Club Band.* Russell sang 'When I'm 64'. The year closed with the November release of *Dee Vee Dee,* an enthralling visual souvenir of the group's September 30, 2006 gig at the Kentish Town Forum.

Hello Young Lovers had been another successful campaign, and for the first time opportunities were not missed in following up a key album. Writing in *The Times* back in early 2006 David Sinclair had said that "the recent revival of 'This Town…' by Justin Hawkins of The Darkness, under the alias British Whale, has doubtless jogged a few memories while an efficient PR campaign seems to have done the rest – although the album's entry into the chart at No.66 was something of a reality check after all the flattering profiles and glowing reviews."

At least it got into the chart, however – the first Sparks album to get a chart placing since *No. 1 In Heaven,* and that was approaching 30 years ago. The great thing with *Hello Young Lovers* was that they had actually built on the success of a preceding album, and for the first time since *Kimono My House,* it actually sold more than its predecessor.

This was due in large part to a combination of Ron and Russell making some of the best music of their career and Sue Harris' management and promotion skills.*

Sue Harris: "They're the genius. It's my job to help communicate that to the world. Sometimes, as with great art, it doesn't happen immediately – Sparks simply don't make the musical equivalent of Athena posters that will paper everyone's walls. They make great art that is extraordinary. And sometimes it's going to be more eagerly received and sometimes you are going to have to make a louder noise to get people to pay attention to it."

---

* *Hello Young Lovers* was the first Sparks album to be released solely under the wing of Republic Media.

Chapter Nineteen

"A toe-tapping, rib-tickling delight" 21 Nights and *Exotic Creatures Of The Deep*

"It became worldwide news – no one had ever done anything like that before."
Sue Harris 2009

After Gut Records folded, Sue Harris, as an unstinting champion of Sparks, went around the UK record labels with their new album to find another deal. "I heard *Exotic Creatures Of The Deep*, like *Hello Young Lovers*, when it was all done, mixed and mastered," said Harris. "I don't need to see the ultrascans of a baby – give me the finished child and I'll proudly show the world the most beautiful baby. How do we get attention, that was the big question? With *Hello Young Lovers* it was a matter of what labels do we talk to, with *Exotic Creatures Of The Deep*, it soon became a case of 'Shall we do this ourselves?' It's the industry discussion – you might get some better short-term results to give it to a label, but the long-term results will be better on your own. It's fabulous to have the might of a major, but it may come with a sting in its tail."

That said, *Exotic Creatures Of The Deep* was seriously considered by the tailor-made Universal Music Catalogue label, W14. Label MD and industry veteran John Williams saw the synergy between Sparks and some of his other roster, most notably original fan Siouxsie Sioux, who had recently struck out on a solo path. After serious and protracted discussions, the deal was not to be. Again, the band decided to release *Exotic Creatures Of The Deep* through their own Lil' Beethoven imprint. However, the album, scheduled for a May release, wasn't just issued; it positively shot into orbit thanks to the marketing strategy devised to promote not just the group's new album, but their entire career.

The idea – more like an event and a half – came out of a summer 2007 brainstorming session in Moscow.

Sue Harris: "We were in Russia and we'd just finished a show and we were talking about how to promote *Exotic Creatures Of The Deep*. Having just worked on the run of dates supporting *Hello Young Lovers* and presenting it in its entirety with a supporting greatest hits set, the crew and I started talking about what we could do logistically to present the new album in a live setting."

For an act with longevity but without stellar record sales to generate huge budgets, it was a case of getting maximum attention for a modest outlay. "We were saying that you can't just keep playing the new album and some hits," Harris continues, "but what if you take it to the next level and just play *all* the albums in their entirety? Everyone laughed. Ron and Russell don't just sit and stare back at their career and pat themselves on the back. They are always looking forward – they are not a retrospective band at all. The thought of them going on a 'Here And Now' tour; you simply couldn't imagine anything further from what they represent. The concept of revisiting the past has always been alien to them. So the idea of playing the whole catalogue – is it completely preposterous or is there some kernel of feasibility in there? I put the idea to Russell, and he chuckled."

After Russell passed it by Ron they thought the idea through. If something this audacious could be done to promote the new album, then it could be a fascinating proposition. "It was almost the scale of it that made it appealing, which gave them a reason to do it," Harris adds.

Ron and Russell got in touch with the band. They knew that if they were to pull off such a bold feat, they would need a great deal of loyalty and time from the players. They were aware that because of various commitments, Dean Menta wouldn't be able to do it, and Tammy Glover could only play certain shows. They also found that due to Redd Kross' tour dates, Steve McDonald could only make the early shows. Jim Wilson, fan-turned-guitarist, takes up the story.

"When Russell told me about it I thought that it was never going to happen. I just couldn't see myself in a room with Ron going over 'Whippings And Apologies'. I had mentioned to Ron and Russell that Marcus [Blake] could play the other nights if they needed a bass player. Marcus came down and played *Introducing Sparks*, which was the first one that Steve couldn't do. We played 'A Big Surprise'. Marcus and I were doing the background harmony vocals with Russell." Blake was in, playing every show in a utility role, either on bass, guitar or singing harmonies.

London, the city that had been so receptive to Sparks over the years, seemed the most suitable venue for this undertaking. Harris spoke with the band's agent, Dan Silver, at Value Added Talent, who then talked to the Academy group. The 800-capacity Islington Academy, a perfectly sized venue in the area's N1 shopping precinct, was ideal to play the 20 albums, while the magnificent 2,000-seat Empire Theatre overlooking Shepherd's Bush Green in West London, just around the corner from where the band recorded *Indiscreet*, was the choice to premiere *Exotic Creatures Of The Deep*.

The shows were booked in blocks of threes and twos to give the band a chance to rest. Each Sparks album would be performed in its entirety, adding in a period B-side or rarity as an encore. The first in the run was due to begin on May 16, before climaxing with the live unveiling of *Exotic Creatures Of The Deep* on June 13, 2008.

'21 Nights' – or 'The Sparks Spectacular' as it became known – was announced on November 28, 2007. For £350, there was a golden ticket, granting admission to all 21 shows as well as a poster and a CD single with a specially written track, 'Islington'. "We will be performing all 21 of our albums, which will mean a grand total of over 250 songs or 4,825,273 notes," Russell announced. "We counted twice just to make sure," added Ron.

"It became worldwide news," Harris said, "no one had ever done anything like that before."

The band began a strict regimen of practice. "They finished the album completely in the second week of January 2008 and then the next day started work on rehearsals," says Harris. "And then, they rehearsed for four months pretty constantly. The musicians were amazing – they weren't on the records, yet they embraced the challenge enthusiastically. They pulled the old albums apart and then put them all together again."

Wilson and Blake had a reputation for being hard-working, straight players – just like their bosses: "That's why they hired us to do the job," Blake, who has been friends with Wilson since the age of nine, says. "There are no drugs involved or anything like that, we're always on time and we do the job as best we can. If they want us in the studio at a certain time or on stage at eight, then we'll be there. We learnt all about professionalism early on from when we played with Henry Rollins. It was a good preparation for Sparks. It was an incredible experience. We were such big fans of their music to begin with; we wanted to treat the music with respect. So we rehearsed our butts off and I hope it showed."

Wilson found the first two albums the most unusual to come to terms with: "They were the craziest. Earle and Jim Mankey obviously grew up together, so it wasn't like session guys where you had to learn what kind of style they're playing. They were making up their own shit, so those songs were really unconventional and quirky. I spent hours trying to get the guitar right at the beginning of 'Nothing Is Sacred'. The first two albums were pretty hard to do together… we did it, though."

Drummer Steven Nistor agrees that the early material was the most interesting: "'The Louvre' from *A Woofer In Tweeter's Clothing* for me was my favourite from the process and the most difficult to learn. I couldn't get that song out of my head the entire four months we rehearsed for the '21 Nights' run."

Unlike Wilson and Blake, Nistor did not have an intimate knowledge of Sparks' repertoire. "I'm embarrassed to say that I only had *Kimono My House* and the *Mael Intuition* collection, so I had a surface knowledge of their catalogue," he says, laughing. "My love for it grew through being part of their rehearsal process, for the 21 Nights run in London." Nistor was to play on all but one of the nights; *Balls* featured Tammy Glover playing alone. On *Lil' Beethoven* and *Hello Young Lovers* Nistor played percussion.

Steven Nistor: "The sheer volume of the catalogue alone kept me awake for many a night. We're talking upward of 270 songs, so that was very intimidating. For me, there were also some technical challenges. I wanted to go above and beyond and be able to electronically trigger some of the signature sound effects live to make the performances sparkle. Like the gong hit you hear at the beginning of 'Falling In Love With Myself Again'. Triggering became essential with the records of the late Seventies and Eighties. I was triggering everything from the maracas on 'A Big Surprise' to the electro toms on 'Tryouts For The Human Race' to the crushing of the soda cans on the intro to 'All You Ever Think About Is Sex'. It was quite an undertaking."

Nistor was well aware of fans' love for former occupants of the Sparks drum-stool ("Sparks has had so many great drummers, so for me, at least academically, it has been a fantastic education to try and get inside the heads of 'Dinky' Diamond, Hilly 'Boy' Michaels or David Kendrick") and of following Tammy Glover, one of Sparks' most popular ever members. "It's tricky. We're totally different drummers. In a way, she reminds me of Larry Mullen Jr. from U2. They're both from a snare drum background, almost a marching kind of style. I'm from a jazz background, so it took a little while for me to adapt the drum parts from *Hello Young Lovers* to my playing. But that also worked to my advantage, as was the case with 'Perfume'."

As the first date got nearer, the whole thing then became an interactive circus, masterminded by Ron and Russell and Sue Harris, who had become Joseph Fleury and John Hewlett rolled into one. With each album being little more than an hour long, a support act would be needed. Requests went out on the allsparks.com site, which became a story in itself. Groups such as The Rumble Strips, The Young Knives, beat merchant Dan Le Sac with the Essex Gil Scott Heron, Scroobius Pip, and The Electric Soft Parade were found. Harris and her assistant Lucy Wigginton also drummed up the fan base to the band's advantage – a street team was put together of fans working to promote the shows.

There was a full-on media onslaught – radio and TV coverage, as well as a gallery show of Sparks' photographs on London's Brick Lane. Not every story was quick to acknowledge the graft involved in such an ambitious undertaking. *The Guardian Guide* showed its customary wit in May 2008: "This month, [Sparks] are playing all their albums live over 21 nights, a great conceit, though any right-thinking person would take a mini-break in Guantanamo Bay rather than going the whole distance." It showed that, like their first UK press feature all those years ago that Roy Silver had to smooth over, Sparks were at least getting the column inches.

Arriving in London, Ron and Russell went on BBC's *The Culture Show*. "We were looking for some conceptual way to put some focus on the [new] album and so we thought what is it that Sparks can do that probably no other band in their right mind would want to undertake, and that was to do live in concert all the 20 albums that led up to the 21st," Russell told hostess Lauren Laverne. "From song number one to song number 256. It was like going back to being a cover band doing Sparks songs." It was almost as if it had to keep being said out loud just to believe it was really happening.

While the brothers resided at their usual Kensington hotel, the band found some rooms in Islington.

Jim Wilson: "It was down the street from the venue. The band got to stay in a house. We each had our own room. It was like The Monkees. Get up in the morning and someone's making breakfast. It was pretty cool." The band had a whale of a time on their occasional rest days. Wilson went back to the States with 60 vinyl albums bought from second-hand shops in the area – pride of place was the UK pressing of Sparks' first album. One dealer was a huge fan and attended all of the shows.

There was little partying; the band were focused solely on the work, and the brothers often shunned any after show activity and took to wearing surgical masks to keep potential germs at bay.

Jim Wilson: "We had to finish a show and go to bed because we were very tired. We couldn't stay up and party, because we had to do this again tomorrow. You can't pose through it, you're dependent on it. We'd go to bed and then next day, I'd wake up and go to Starbucks listening to the album that I had to play that day on my iPod."

Marcus Blake: "We'd get back to the flat, and that night into the early morning hours I would listen to the next night's work to just refresh. We'd be getting back sort of midnight and I'd rehearse in my bedroom for the next night. It wasn't torture, it was a pleasure."

Blake was aware of stepping into his predecessors' shoes: "Ian Hampton's my favourite for sure. Martin Gordon set the precedent I think, so melodic. The notes didn't exactly match up to each other but they would work harmonically together. Martin Gordon is similar to McCartney in that they're both very melodic bass players. They don't just play the root notes all the way through their song. If you single out their work, it could be a song on its own."

The band would arrive at the venue at 2pm every day and soundcheck that night's particular album.

Sue Harris: "Every single musician probably had moments of trepidation, but once they were committed to it, they were extraordinary. Every day of the '21 Nights', they would come in, do a run-through and that was it – that was the production rehearsal, that was the refresher from the last time they played the album, perhaps weeks previously, and then, they played it that night."

The shows also proved a challenge for the small stage team of lightning designer Paul Birks, Simon Higgs on monitors, sound engineer Cristiano Avigni, Robert Garnham on the backline as well as the logistical team of Harris and Lucy Wigginton. "The crew were amazing," praises Harris. "They didn't know what was going to happen day-to-day and there were no rehearsals. *Plagiarism,* for instance, had strings and a horn section as well as Jimmy Somerville. All on that tiny stage."

Jim Wilson: "It was difficult and totally fulfilling. We all felt that there would be some lighter nights or nights that wouldn't be as important or as well attended and we were wrong about that. There was obviously a difference in crowds and things but people were reacting just as strongly for, say, *Pulling Rabbits Out Of A Hat* as they were for other albums. We really got into those shows, too, because it felt good to bring those albums to life."

There were never less than 500 in the venue during the run. The least attended was, as Wilson said, "either *Pulling Rabbits Out Of A Hat* or *Music That You Can Dance To.* Erm, maybe *Interior Design* might have been another light one."

Marcus Blake: "There's a gay pub across the street from the Academy. It just got overrun by Sparks fans. It became Sparks fan central for a month and we would *occasionally* pay a visit. Ron and Russell would never go but we did. It was cool, we got a lot of instant feedback and I was so impressed by their loyalty, especially the people who went to all '21 Nights' and went to the pub every night and waited in line from like noon onwards. That's dedicating your life to Sparks for a month."

The support given was testament to how devoted Sparks fans are. Each had an opportunity to sponsor that evening's show, and the souvenir programme included the names of each of those who had backed the relevant album/night.*

Sue Harris: "The most committed fan had to take a month off work, pay for accommodation for a month, some had the golden tickets for every show – it was a huge undertaking. *Kimono My House* and *No. 1 In Heaven* sold out very quickly. The attendance was still amazing for the lesser known albums – and the audience were there singing every word. It was so nice to be a part of it. There were lots of emotions on show – everyone was absolutely exhausted but this is something that will never be repeated. It's one thing to have a catalogue that size, but more importantly to have the will to do it and not even for financial gain. You wouldn't just do it for the sake of it, giving away six months of your life after spending a year recording your own album."

There were many highlights. "At the first night, Russell introduced the gig saying 'OK, my friends, number one,'" reported Andre Paine for the BBC. "In contrast to Russell, his brother Ron was a severe, slightly scary presence on keyboards who didn't react to the chants of 'Ron, Ron' from the crowd."

It was Wilson's own favourite that provided his happiest moment of the month. "*Indiscreet* was a great night. We had to switch around so much for the instrumentation and we actually had horns and strings and stuff. I didn't do anything on 'Under The Table With Her', so I went out to the front of the crowd and watched it and then I had to be back on stage for 'How Are You Getting Home?' It was too much, almost,

---

* Ron and Russell dedicated all 21 Nights to their oldest fan, mother Miriam, who was name-checked under her Mary Martin *nom de Spark* in the programme.

I should've just stayed there! I got back on stage and it was so exciting, it's hard to explain."

It was often the nights with least expectation that delighted the most. *Big Beat*, Sparks' 1976 flop, sounded as if it been recorded yesterday. Ron even stepped out from behind his keyboard to insist that 'White Women' should not be taken seriously. *No. 1 In Heaven* on Bank Holiday Sunday was as much of a jolt as the original album had been – the venue was seriously over-full, and being pinned into the back corner didn't suit this writer's dancing shoes. It sounded brilliant and the brothers appeared delighted at playing it live completely for the first time. Best of all was Ron's tribute haircut – a direct reprise of his pre-Phil Oakey 1979 Veronica Lake bubble perm. "When it came to that album," Wilson says, laughing, "I said, 'I don't want to be the guy that plays guitar in *No. 1 In Heaven* so I didn't even play, I just sang."

Watching the largely unloved *Interior Design* you knew you were among the most fervent of the hardcore. Hardly any of it had been played live before, and trimmed of its most Eighties excesses, it further proved that Ron is one of popular music's most consistent writers.

Jim Wilson: "I'm just happy to be playing Ron Mael's songs. That's something that never slipped away. Sometimes I'd be on stage and I'd look over and be like 'Ah man, I would be at this show if I wasn't playing here.'"

However, all of this would amount to nothing without Russell's delivery. His preening style, at once the very epitome and simultaneous deconstruction of a rock star, makes him as enduring as a Roger Daltrey or a Freddie Mercury. "Russell's pretty amazing," Wilson says. "I've never heard that guy have a bad voice night. Just an incredible singer, especially when you have to sing with him, you learn how much is actually going on."

Jimmy Somerville's appearance during the *Plagiarism* night, singing 'The Number One Song In Heaven' was described by *Scotland On Sunday* like "two men with their knackers in a vice trying to think of more pleasant things".

The live show moved to Shepherd's Bush Empire for the series finale of *Exotic Creatures Of The Deep*. The band arrived at the Empire at noon on June 13 and worked through solidly until seven o'clock, an hour before they were due on stage. For the second half, the B-sides set had still to be rehearsed.

Nistor provided an amusing blog for *Billboard* on the subject. "Of course, it turned into a pissing contest of who knew the most obscure Sparks songs, and we were to play them. We didn't even know what the set was going to be until the day before the show, and even after that, there were additions and substitutions. I assumed we were going to go over them in soundcheck, at least, just to run them, but we rehearsed the new album right until the doors opened." There was electricity in the air; a reunion of old friends combined with the meeting of new ones.

'21 Nights' was a remarkable undertaking, and one that will gain greater significance as time goes by. The exposure the shows gained for Sparks was phenomenal and while, like the best work in their career, it didn't actually help shift many units, the impact was felt throughout the music business.

"Bands get kudos for their past careers, but Sparks are unique as they are still doing it and are doing it better than ever," Harris points out. "We are all a bit obsessed with retrospectives in the UK – bands often play their album from 1960something but they haven't done anything since. That's fine, everyone has mortgages to pay, but Sparks are still making new and exciting music."

21 Nights' took the concept of the Don't Look Back idea – artists playing a notable album from their catalogue onstage in its entirety – and pushed it to the *nth* degree. If Sparks take on something, there will always be an additional twist.

"It was one of their most brilliant ideas," says John Hewlett. "That, to me, is genius. Trevor went, however, and he was disappointed."

Trevor White: "I was supposed to meet them afterwards, but we were in such a hurry, we had to run out and catch our train. I was there with Ian Hampton and Joe Elliott from Def Leppard, who is a huge fan. I didn't understand any of it."

Russell reflected on the shows some months after they had finished: "It was extremely daunting. It took four months of rehearsal. Luckily we have a band that's committed to those levels of preparation, and to the time we spent in London playing the show. We were pleasantly shocked that people gave up their time to come from all over the world."

Jim Wilson: "It happened so fast and you had one shot to get it right. It wasn't simple rock'n'roll songs like 'Jumping Jack Flash'. The hardcore

Sparks fans were watching our every move because everybody knows every little part."

If anything, the release of *Exotic Creatures Of The Deep* was overshadowed by the hype for the live performances. Released on Lil' Beethoven Records on May 19, 2008, it was put out by Universal's distribution arm Arvato. The sleeve concept was again very strong – available in a Ron or a Russell sleeve, it featured Susie the chimpanzee. On Russell's sleeve, she is playing the piano. On Ron's, she is at the microphone.

After a most impressive first-day chart placing, which saw it heading toward the Top 20, the album stalled at 54 in the chart. As consolation, the tide of critical plaudits that Sparks had ridden since *Lil' Beethoven* was ready to carry them away again: *Rock n Reel* said "Sparks are one of those delightful eddys in the cultural river, and they are a vital one." *Record Collector* thought that, although two songs too long, "The glam of 'I Can't Believe That You Would Fall For All The Crap In This Song' and Ron's wordplay on 'This Is The Renaissance' demonstrate, once again, that for a veteran band [a description the brothers would surely detest] moving forward, they are simply without equal."

Q suggested that the album was full of "elegiac and wry lyrics, durable tunes and unbridled adventurism". *The Word* considered "the real joy… is the unadorned pleasure of hearing two misfits not fitting in, in the most stylish manner imaginable". *NME* described the album as "a textbook example of the quirky falsetto disco that the Scissor Sisters would give their silver lamé leggings for". Even the *Daily Mirror* called it "a toe-tapping, rib-tickling delight". However, there were some dissenting voices; pitchforkmedia suggested that "This time, though, the premise has worn thin. Virtually every song enunciates its central joke, then repeats it and repeats it and repeats it. And repeats it. And repeats it. And so on, with the repeating. (And repeating.)"

Overall, the album maintained the standard of the previous two with ease. The synth glam of 'I Can't Believe That You Would Fall For All The Crap In This Song' is an absolute standout, and possibly the only time that the group have dabbled in the musical style that they were accused of practising in the Seventies. 'Let The Monkey Drive' was singled out by

Mojo as an "insidious gnomic joy, like The Goodies writing for Michael Nyman". The highlight was certainly the album's second single, 'Lighten Up Morrissey', a tale of a man whose girlfriend's Morrissey obsession is driving him to the point of distraction.

"He [Morrissey] actually loves it!" Russell told various interviewers in August. "We played it for him – we wanted to make sure he heard it before it was out and someone told him about it. He said he adores it… Morrissey understood the sentiment of the song beyond face value. The title alone one might think would be a dig at him. It's not at all, it's a relationship song."*

Exotic Creatures Of The Deep was led by the bright, buoyant single 'Good Morning', a real humdinger of an old-fashioned pop song about regrets after a one-night stand. However it only reached number 147, while 'Lighten Up Morrissey' didn't make the Top 200. That didn't stop them being great records. It was just that the brothers' natural home, even for men now both in their sixties, was still the pop chart. "In their heart of hearts they'd love to be number one. I can't ever see them doing it again, gaining that mass acceptance," Ian Hampton says. "They put such decent records out but they are just not gaining airplay. 'Good Morning' was on the playlist on Radio 2 but only got played twice. [DJ Terry] Wogan used it as a jingle but it didn't get any airplay."

It's a problem that many bands in a similar position face. "When I first heard *Exotic Creatures* I thought – 'Great, they've given us some pop songs'," says Harris. "'Good Morning' was such a great pop song but you discover that radio will simply play Mika instead. Well, we wouldn't have artists like Mika if it wasn't for Sparks. I've wondered whether we should do the sneaky and pretend it's not Sparks but some indie band from Sheffield with bad haircuts to fool the little skinny-jeaned kids dictating what the world is going to listen to. If you just based it on the music, what would the reaction be? On radio it should all be about the song. Radio 2 is great because they don't care about the press pack, they listen to it and they ask 'Will our listeners like it?' You go to Radio 1 or a

---

* The relationship between Morrissey and the Maels is still strong. When invited to play his favourite bands on KCRW's Guest DJ Project in August 2008, Morrissey chose the old *A Woofer In A Tweeter's Clothing* standard 'Moon Over Kentucky'.

commercial station and it's all about 'Do they think it would fit between Mika or Franz Ferdinand?' Of course it would because they sound like Sparks, so it should be played. That's the idealistic view, but it's not like that."

Soon after the close of '21 Nights', Sparks played various festivals around the globe before returning in July to Japan, where they had solidly been building their fan base. "Japan's really getting [Sparks] now," says Harris. "They have a great label that completely understands and a great promoter, Smash. The label works hard, puts out back catalogue and, well, 'gets it'."*

On July 26, the band played the second night of Japan's Fuji Rocks festival at Naeba, witnessed by an ebullient Harris. "At Fuji Rocks, Sparks were on the Orange Court Stage and took over all the projections and put on a full show – you looked out and there were thousands and thousands of young Japanese fans just going crazy. The stage was the far-end of the festival away from the main stage; there was a constant stream of kids pouring in and going mad. The feedback was that they were the buzz of the whole festival. Primal Scream, Kasabian were all there. And Japanese fans are supposed to be reserved. Not when Sparks play! There's hysteria."

A UCLA show in February 2009 was something of a coup. It was the brainchild of long-time Sparks fan David Sefton, UCLA's Director of Programming, who was one of the many who sat transfixed as 'Hitler' entered his British living room at teatime in May 1974.

Liverpool-born Sefton had moved from the small Millfield Theatre in North London's Edmonton to being the man who introduced the Meltdown Festival at the Royal Festival Hall. He had relocated to LA in 2000 to look after the arts programme at UCLA. "I was given a clean sheet and the basic brief – don't burn the place down, don't piss off too many old rich people; I came in with carte blanche. My major stipulation was that I was allowed to do what I wanted with the programming."

---

* This has further been demonstrated by the remarkable reissues in paper sleeves of the albums between *Introducing Sparks* and *Sparks In Outer Space* in 2009.

Having been an admirer for decades, having seen Sparks at the Liverpool Empire in 1975, Sefton was determined to present Sparks at the university.

"Sparks was absolutely a personal thing for me. Since the big mega-album thing in London, they had wanted to do something resonant of that here. Given that they are ex-UCLA students, there was an inevitability it would happen one day. The timing was perfect – they wanted to do something around *Exotic Creatures Of The Deep*, and I said that if you're doing it, the other one has to be *Kimono My House*. This job is a bit like playing your own records at a party – you *can* stipulate."

When first mentioning the idea, Sefton's team were unsure. "Most of my staff had no idea who they were. There was a fairly comprehensive lack of recognition. It gave me an opportunity to be unbelievably smug and say 'Don't worry, this will sell'. When it sold out, I was enormously full of myself! People were deeply sceptical about doing it in an 1,800-seat room; happily I was able to prove them wrong."

Sefton understands why Sparks are not an easy option for America to accept. "Sparks were loved by the eyeliner crowd in Liverpool. It partly is that arty thing that makes Sparks unacceptable to most Americans. I was thinking about this in relation to Bowie; it wasn't a slam dunk for Bowie when he first came out in the States, eventually it took off – the artier end of things struggles in this country. The UK embraces that ambiguity. How weird they seemed when they hit the charts but how weird must they have been when they started! That's why they would have come to Britain as it was more disparate; it wasn't about Woodstock."

A traditional music venue, set in an idyllic, green location, Royce Hall – modelled on the Cathedral of St Ambrogio in Milan – is one of the oldest buildings not only on campus but in LA itself, being 80 years old. It was a memorable night, with the Maels right back where they started, a few hundred yards from where Russell was next door to Ron in theater arts and graphic design respectively.

David Sefton: "It was packed out. People came in from all over the States. One girl had even flown in from Scotland. She'd never been to the United States before and had just come in for the one night. The band could not have possibly wished for a greater response. I have my favourite moments but [Sparks] breaking into 'This Town Ain't Big

Enough For Both Of Us' [at Royce Hall] is definitely going to count among those moments. It was a real scene."

It was good for Jim Wilson to be back on home turf: "It was just like every person I ever knew was there. It was a good night. It just went so smoothly. A Sparks show is not just going up and plugging in, there are sets and dancers and always something going on. I got to bring my own amplifier. It was amazing."

Steven Nistor: "The band was on fire by this point. It was fantastic. We have this mutual respect. I mean, after rehearsing as much as we have, especially after the 21 Nights thing, we feel sort of invincible up there. I think that event really made us 'a band'."

Marcus Blake: "I felt so good for them as it sold out because of word of mouth. Americans had never seen *Kimono My House* in its entirety. The album seems to have recently caught on there. It was good to see how well they took to *Exotic Creatures Of The Deep* too."

In attendance were a few special guests from the distant past – namely James Lowe and Harley Feinstein, who had reunited a few years previously when Feinstein played drums on several cuts on the reformed Electric Prunes album, *Feedback*. "Harley and I saw Sparks at UCLA recently and they were amazing. Not a move you could predict. I mean who has a monkey in the show? I guess they couldn't afford a kid," says Lowe, recalling the 14-year old Kip Tulin from *A Woofer In Tweeter's Clothing*. It had been a long journey.

The *Exotic Creatures Creatures Of The Deep* tour moved to London in March, for a rerun of the two biggest-selling nights from the Sparks spectacular – *Kimono My House* and *No. 1 In Heaven* – with *Exotic Creatures Of The Deep* taking up the first half of each night. Nistor, Blake and Wilson were match fit and blasted through the material. Wilson recalled how nervous he'd been for the first play-through of *Kimono My House* back in 2004 at Meltdown, when now it was all rather straightforward in light of all the events of the past year. The tableau of dancing ladies during 'This Is A Renaissance' was a sight to behold and for the final three shows in Japan in April, a local agency provided six dancing geishas.

For the celebrations surrounding the 50th anniversary of Island Records, Ron and Russell were approached to play the week-long series of gigs at Shepherd's Bush Empire at the end of May.* The show on the 27th would have had them playing with The Fratellis in a series of gigs that saw players as diverse as Ernest Ranglin, Grace Jones, Paul Weller, Cat Stevens, Tom Tom Club, Spooky Tooth and U2 take to the stage. After careful consideration, the Maels turned the opportunity down, as their next project was taking shape.

* *Kimono My House* was selected as one of Island's 50 albums of all time, and it received not only a vinyl reissue but the 21st Century Edition, released in 2006, was reissued in Japan in a full CD replica edition.

Chapter Twenty

Talent + Invention + Mystery × Fanbase = Longevity

"Not since eighties King Crimson has anyone made a trio of LPs so perfect they should use them in music schools around the world to educate young people to what real pop rock should sound like. Lil' Beethoven, Hello Young Lovers, Exotic Creatures Of The Deep *please look these up and save your ears today and the other 18 albums too!"*

Juicyjesus99, YouTube

"There are actually no creeps in the music business. We're just one happy family. Everybody's in it for the love of music and art."

Russell Mael, 1995

"They've really been a fringe operation who once struck it big."

John Taylor, 2009

"Sparks are still a new band as well."

Jim Wilson, 2009

W hen questioned about the future by BBC Scotland after their performance at the Hydro Connect Festival on August 29, 2008,

Ron came out with the prescient statement, "Every time you finish you think there is nowhere else to go, but we have such drive that I think that's what propels us and puts us in the position of trying to top each thing we've done."

Now with advances in technology and being proprietors of their own label, Ron and Russell can really be Sparks full-time, beavering away on the next project, not waiting simply for a record company to deem it possible. And their studio is, of course, Russell's house, where they go every single day to work.

The latest example of this is their Swedish Radio drama, *The Seduction Of Ingmar Bergman*, premiered on Sveriges Radio on August 14, 2000 (two days after Ron's 64th birthday).

Sue Harris explains the idea's genesis. "Sparks have played in Sweden a few times recently and they've had a nice relationship with the media there since *Lil' Beethoven*. Swedish Radio contacted them direct and asked them to write an hour show with Swedish content and lyrics."

The title itself is another Sparks movie in-joke, as it nods to the 1971 Swedish softcore film *The Seduction Of Inga*. This move into, for want of a better word, musicals has gone some way to scratching the itch that began right back with the Maels scoring Larry Dupont's film about the Goodyear blimp at UCLA, through *Confusion* and *Mai The Psychic Girl*. This was to take them into a different realm altogether. Being Sparks, it couldn't be straightforward.

"When Sveriges Radio approached us with the idea of creating our own musical for the radio," Russell said, "we were excited about the prospect yet hesitant at trying to figure a way to successfully fulfil their only restrictions with the project: that it incorporates the Swedish language in some manner. Once we came up with the idea of placing one of the ultimate Swedish icons and one of our favourite film directors, Ingmar Bergman, in a fantasy setting, we became extremely excited about this musical and knew we were on to something special."

Although there is still a strong tradition of radio drama in the UK, Ron was happy to resurrect a dormant form for Sparks' next work. "As Americans we have almost abandoned radio drama," he said, "and it was truly exhilarating for us to work in a medium where the imagination of the listener is so integral a part of the work. Aside from our love of Bergman, we have a love of Orson Welles and his use of the medium of radio was something that inspired us in this work." The story was a tale of the battle for artistic integrity against the demands of commerce that every great artist has to face at some juncture in their career, set in an imaginary time when the legendary Swedish director was being courted by Hollywood in 1956. It ends with his meeting Greta Garbo, who is sent as a messenger from God to help him return to Sweden.

David Sefton: "I went round to Russell's studio to hear the Ingmar Bergman project in its entirety… It's off the wall, but only in the way you'd want and expect. The hardcore Sparks fans are going to adore it. It's a singular piece of work. Only the [Maels] could come up with something like that."

The similarities between Bergman's pet subjects – "matters of death, faith, God's existence, and the struggle to find love and meaning in our lives" – and Ron's lyrics are easy to spot.

Both Jim Wilson and Marcus Blake were involved in the recording: "Russ was singing and he explained to us what it was going to be, we didn't see any lyrics or anything. Marcus and I sang almost two full songs as autograph hunters." Wilson and Blake also demoed the roles of the two policemen who try to capture Bergman towards the end of the play, but the recording was revoiced by Russell.

The mixture of song and dialogue has several familiar Mael traits. "The songs are so cool," Wilson says. "This is really intense stuff. There's some rock ones too. I've played on recordings with them before, but this is the first time that we were singing parts. We were listening to Russell's guide vocal and we were kind of replacing that but it still sounds strange to hear your voice singing a Ron Mael melody."

The listener also gets to hear, for the first time, Ron's vocals as a limo driver and Hollywood tour driver.

Jim Wilson: "When we first heard about it a couple of months ago, Ron said he had to start thinking about new songs. You just think that as it's not really a new album and it's just going to be broadcast on Swedish radio that he might not put that much into it, but when you hear it, it's like 'Wow, you've made a little movie.' It's like a story and it's the perfect follow-up for them because it's kind of the new Sparks album, and, at the same time, it kind of isn't.

"They didn't have to come up with ten funny song titles or whatever to make another *Lil' Beethoven*. It's something that's really different again and it fits into the Sparks mould because it's really heavily keyboard written, so the melodies are really fast."

Recorded on the soundstages of Hollywood-American Studios, California and at the Radio Drama Studio, Stockholm, *The Seduction Of Ingmar Bergman* was released in November 2009 on double vinyl and download in a variety of collector's formats including a box with Swedish and English versions. To coincide, a special preview, taped on October 28 at BBC Broadcasting House and including an interview and audience Q & A with Ron and Russell, premiered in the UK on Stuart Maconie's *Freakzone* BBC 6 radio show on November 8.

The Seduction Of Ingmar Bergman is a 64-minute opera, song cycle, whatever you want to call it. It is grand, late-period Sparks. It's esoteric in subject matter, but then so was *Evita* when it first appeared. It doesn't have a 'Don't Cry For Me Argentina' or even an 'Oh What A Circus' but it does have a surfeit of imagination and left-field delights. There are all the customary Mael tricks and devices on 'Mr Bergman, How Are You', an effective piece of heavy metal, fully utilising the band, and a duet between Russell as the studio chief and Swedish actress Saskia Husberg as Bergman's interpreter. 'The Studio Commissary' is Sparks in overdrive as they finally marry their love of Hollywood, European cinema and pop music in one song. Set in a studio canteen, it is a roll call of all Hollywood émigré directors, from Alfred Hitchcock to Jacques Tourneur, deliciously delivered by Russell, as if his whole life had been leading to this moment.

Obscure, of course, delightfully warm, naturally, *The Seduction Of Ingmar Bergman* underlines Sparks' greatness and importance. With a vocal cast of 13, and the extended version of the band – Glover, Menta, Wilson, Blake and Nistor – it has all the craft and tension of a Sparks work, naturally coming alive when Russell as the studio chief sings. Swedish actor Jonas Malmsjö plays Bergman with all the appropriate detached paranoia. Only the final song, 'He's Home', seems conventional.

Record Collector gave the work five stars and concluded "This review could read like one of those YES/NO flow diagrams. Did you love *Lil' Beethoven*? If YES – you will love this. If NO, return to *Kimono My*

House." Martin Aston wrote in *Mojo* that the album "plays to Sparks' strengths, finding that unique spot between artful kitsch and camp lunacy." For the first time since *Balls*, however, the praise was not unanimous. *The Observer Music Monthly* labelled the recording "strange", and Stephen Trousse in *Uncut* suggested that the album was "strangely unseductive: Ingmar's own horrified flight from Hollywood reflects the brother's own retreat from pop into something more sophisticated. But a lot less fun."

The Seduction Of Ingmar Bergman deals with the issue of providing a follow-up to three of Sparks most satisfying works to date. "There is always a 'what next' moment," says Harris. "I have confidence in them that they will go into the studio and come out with something incredible. They keep outdoing themselves. As [*The Seduction Of Ingmar Bergman*] took shape it seemed to be more than a musical for Swedish radio and so it was fortuitous that it came at the time that the band would be thinking about their next record.

"What form it takes in the future only time will tell. It could go on to be a stage musical around the world. They may initially be in it, but ultimately a good musical production can be put on by any theatre company. "

At the time of writing, the next step will be live performances in 2010. Ron and Russell have been talking to David Sefton about the possibility of more shows. Although undecided in November 2009, Sefton thinks, "I would turn it into a concert with knobs on with some visuals but quite minimal. Maybe it will be their great breakthrough moment." Canadian director Guy Maddin has also shown great interest in the work. Maybe the Maels will enter their sixth decade working together finally making the film they have always wanted.

Sparks have been in business now for over 40 years. It's one thing for artists with similar or higher tallies of studio albums – The Fall or Peter Hammill, for example – to have perennially inhabited the margins, but for a group that, in the UK at least, were borne from teenybop screams to be producing their best work 30 years later is unparalleled.

There is little shortage of theories about their longevity, from former band members to others whose paths the Maels have crossed. "They have held true to their concept all these years yet they keep coming up with something different," James Lowe says. "They are able to morph and change with the times. And their smart humour. These are some of the funniest records I have ever heard."

"They are a couple of talented artists, and it is impossible to compare them to an ordinary rock band," Harley Feinstein posits. "They tell their narrative well. Back when I met them, it was already in place; the intent was very interesting and intelligent. They are very astute from the point of view of art. I'd never heard about new wave cinema. Ron pretty much predicted MTV years before it happened; astute, culturally and artistically."

Brothers in bands are not normally noted in pop for lasting the distance in harmonious fashion. "The fact that they're brothers makes the likelihood of that taking place almost impossible," Ira Robbins suggests. "If you look at the stories and examples of brothers in pop music, there's very few that have lasted very long. Certainly Ray and Dave Davies and the Gallaghers – it just goes wrong down the line. Maybe the Allmans would've stuck it out if Duane hadn't died."

Jim Mankey has long worked out the formula: "They managed to get along. Almost everyone else in the music business would get into big arguments and get in a huff and break up. Ron and Russ worked out all their personal animosities while they were 12 years old."

The dynamic of the brothers' personalities remains the tightly knit mystery that it has done since 1970. Their singularity and determination constantly sees them producing high-quality work.

Larry Dupont: "They still want it. It is a passion. It is who they are. They aren't going to quit."

Sue Harris: "They go into their Sparks world, their vacuum and create. They never stop being Sparks. For over two-thirds of their lives they have been Sparks. I'm not sure how often they are not together creating. It's a unique relationship."

Gered Mankowitz: "It's a combination of things; because they work so well together, they clearly are incredibly bonded. Importantly, there is enough work to keep them together. Look at these dreadful Seventies revival tours that go round the summer seasons – you see people who are close to being desperate playing on an oldies platform. Sparks have always maintained a high originality and they have always been able to hold on to a very devout fan base; they have some very major records that have a huge impact on a lot of people and they have kept it up."

Ian Hampton: "They have a very loyal fan base who are always pushing them for more. More changes of direction, more innovation and they get very encouraged by the fans and take heed of what they are saying. They are streetwise, very literate, extremely well read. Ron is without question one of the greatest lyricists of his time. I think he's probably the most uniquely overlooked writer in the past four or five decades. He gets critically acclaimed, sure, but nothing mass."

Tony Visconti: "I think back in the day, everyone had a soft spot for Sparks, they were kind of revolutionary and 'This Town Ain't Big Enough For Both Of Us' was one of the greatest British singles ever made. I think the world of them. I always considered Ron Mael to be, besides a great musician, also a great poet. The lyrics are just unbelievably funny."

Rupert Holmes: "I have such tremendous admiration for how they've continued their artistry over the ensuing decades. I know how hard it is to sustain that creativity, and yet their releases up to the present always seem vital, fresh and absolutely original. It's a remarkable achievement for which, as a fan and listener, I'm also very grateful."

'Artist' is a word that keeps recurring. Chris Blackwell, a man who has worked with some of the greatest names in music, says this of the Maels: "I liked them because they are artists in the real sense. I am a big fan of talent and when you never know what an artist is going to do next, that's literally music to my ears. Sometimes you have a better record than others, but that's the main thing, you have a long career. They would not be able to live if they weren't able to do what they are doing – they are true artists."

"Their entire world is their music, that's what they care about to the exclusivity of everything else," Tammy Glover told the BBC in 2007. "The only thing that gives them a buzz is music. I mean, girls and cars to some extent, but it pales in comparison to playing music, composing music and contributing to a body of work that is unique, edgy and genre-defying."

Steven Nistor: "They're really of the same mind. Maybe two different halves of the same brain would be a better way to put it. If you look at Sparks' entire catalogue they are impossible to nail down. They've covered a lot of stylistic ground."

Although not claiming to have followed their entire oeuvre, Duran Duran's John Taylor still regards the group with high affection:"They have a big enough reputation and there will always be an audience for them. There's this artistic side to them; although they did their amazing 21-night thing, they are not hung up on *Kimono My House*. They seem quite self-aware to be artists. They can be philosophical about the curve they are on. They've always been quite left-field really. It's almost like their pop moment was the exception – there's always been a whiff of Zappa about them. They've really been a fringe operation who once struck it big."

Sue Harris: "They have always changed. If they had stayed as the Sparks of 'This Town Ain't Big Enough For Both Of Us' / 'Amateur Hour', they would have probably had more success at that time and carried on steadily into the Eighties but today they would have less critical respect. Possibly they have repeatedly shot themselves in the foot by changing, but I'm so delighted they did. If they hadn't, we wouldn't have had extraordinary music like *Lil' Beethoven, Hello Young Lovers, Exotic Creatures* or *The Seduction Of Ingmar Bergman*."

David Betteridge: "I find it amazing, here they are today, 22 albums later, and their longevity has been remarkable. There was no marker before. Ron and Russell still around today is extraordinary."

Another key to their longevity is down to the success of the band as a live force. From early gigs to recent live extravaganzas, for most of their career, Sparks have made music to be replicated in concert.

David Sefton: "They are the Gilbert and George of pop music. They have fully committed their lives to being Sparks. They do still appear to be good at it. To me, *Exotic Creatures Of The Deep* is their best record for a significant period of time. When I saw it live, I really got it. They've come back into their own. Maybe the world is ready for Sparks. They should be applauded for their tenacity."

And their appearance. From halfway down a concert venue it looks as though the brothers were cryogenically frozen in 1974. "They are both bone thin," says Sefton."You look up and think 'Bloody hell, you're both doing very well'. Russell still has that youthful thing going on. I'll have a pint of what he's had, or not had."

The mainstream will always elude Sparks because they are simply too clever. "It's hard to get away from that one since it is patently clear," says Ira Robbins. "Russell's voice may be too much of an acquired taste for people. They have been able to survive in the same way as Ray Davies who can still write a song that you want to hear 50 years later. I think Sparks just have found a way continually to develop and reinvent themselves. The music they have done in the last 10 years sounds very little like anything they did in the first 10 years and that's certainly to their credit. I mean, Russell's voice has changed, Ron's style of orchestration has changed. Their lyrical concerns have changed but they have never stopped making the effort."

Jon Savage: "Sparks' records created their own world and they have this ability to live in that world. Which every artist of note has to do. You set the whole thing rolling and you can just continue doing it and also be paid for doing it."

Jim Wilson: "I've always loved how they changed. Because if they'd stayed the same and kept making *Kimono My House* over and over, their audience would be full of old guys and they wouldn't have the audience that have been coming to the shows. Sparks are still a new band as well. Sparks is the only thing that means a lot to them whereas other people have ups and downs, but they're just real guys that are in it for the right reasons, because they love music and they want to make fresh music. It's an honour for me to have anything to do with them… The more I find out about them as people the more I think, 'Wow, they're great guys', which is refreshing in LA."

Marcus Blake: "I don't think their career was premeditated to be long lasting, it just worked out that way. They don't follow anybody's rules other than their own and I don't think they're much worried about pop chart success, but they are worried about making the best music that they can. That's number one to them rather than how successful it's going to be."

As we have seen, for the brothers, it has always been about moving forward, and it will remain so. Russell told *Clash* magazine in 2008, "We're proud of the past, but we're not wallowing in it because that's where you can run into trouble by dwelling on it, trying to re-create something even though the parameters have changed and it's not possible."

277

Former manager John Hewlett feels there should have been longer periods of stability in the quest for constant reinvention. "When you are rejecting something good purely for change, I don't agree with it. I have utmost respect for them, but as they are they are very focused on themselves, that's survival. Their talent is unquestionable, sometimes with a stroke of genius. When it was blended with that earthiness it was wonderful, a fantastic combination that could have taken them to the status of major rock. As it is, they are still a very interesting cult – enormous credit to them for sticking with it.

"In many respects, I think there is something tremendously positive about their attitude," Hewlett concludes. "This is this year's release, and then there'll be the next one. We will sell some records somewhere as we have a hardcore following around the world."

"We're genuine in our own way," Ron said in 2008. "There is a sort of pose to what we are doing, but it's a natural pose. A heightened version of what we are when we're not being Sparks. There is irony to what we do, but not to the point that we feel we are outsiders working within pop music, we really love pop. That's the reason we keep doing it."

Sparks remain 'musical Marmite'. Love them or hate them, you are certainly aware of them. This is a story to be continued. As long as there remains a 'y' in the day, Ron and Russell will keep on working. The novelty, the fairground ride, the carnie carousel; it is not without irony that their only significant film appearance was set in a fairground. It is still all lights and glitter.

Ron and Russell Mael are one of the great comic double-acts of all time. They made us laugh and intrigued us when we first saw them on *Top Of The Pops*. Think of Laurel and Hardy, Abbott and Costello, Morecambe and Wise – the relationship is symbiotic with instantly recognisable, defined personas. The comparison with artists Gilbert and George is telling as well. Their music and personas make people smile, and then their art challenges you. The Maels are rarely out of each other's company and now produce music that suggests that they have never listened to another record in their lives.

Rather like they did when they first appeared in 1970. They've been around a lot of scenes yet never really been part of them; original alliances

278

with Todd Rundgren, Albert Grossman and Jim Lowe and then their affiliation with the UK mid-Seventies glam rock movement, Giorgio Moroder later that decade and their LA associations in the Eighties.

Some 33 people have passed through the Sparks line-up; The Pheasantry on King's Road is now a *Pizza Express*; Cleethorpes' Winter Gardens – the scene of the opening night of their 1974 tour at the height of the mania – was demolished in summer 2007; Heron Garages and the Heron Stamps featured on the *Propaganda* sleeve are long gone. The South Kensington Hotel where the brothers stayed on their first wintry visit to the UK is now called the Brompton. Miss Christine, Albert Grossman, Joseph Fleury, Roy Silver, Norman 'Dinky' Diamond, Adrian Fisher and Jeffrey Salen are no longer with us. Disco has long been rehabilitated.

As for those questions about their personal lives or spare time, they remain largely unanswered. Mainly because they have no spare time. Is there any noticeable difference between them? "One sings and one plays piano!" says Sue Harris, laughing. "They are charming gentlemen. I don't know everything about their personalities or their personal lives. And I don't need to. It's not relevant. I don't need to know anything else about them than what is on the record."

The credits for *The Seduction Of Ingmar Bergman* show a pair of brothers who ultimately got their wish for complete and utter artistic autonomy:

All words and music by: Ron Mael and Russell Mael
Produced by: Ron Mael and Russell Mael
Story by: Ron Mael and Russell Mael
Orchestrations by Ron Mael
Recorded and mixed by Ron Mael and Russell Mael

Running their own record label, with a small and supportive team, suits the Maels down to the ground. Now they only have themselves to deal with. For those who mourn the democracy of Sparks' earliest outings, it isn't coming back. Russell was unequivocal about this in his comments to *Clash* magazine in early 2008: "Ron and I have such a clear vision of what Sparks should be, what a band should be. It's that thing of having a kind of purity about your music and we become very precious about it. And we want that purity to be conveyed by the people who play it with us. You can read that as purity equals dictatorship or a lack of democracy, but it has a purpose. Early on, there was more democracy among the people we played with. But as time has gone on we've become more insular about what we want."

Insularity. Singularity. Autocracy. The devil is now in Sparks' painterly detail. Since they took over their own career in 2002, they have become the artistic institutions that they have always wanted to be. Living small and thinking big. It is paying off. It is all about talent. And talent, as we know, is an asset. Musically, they married themselves. They're very happy together.

Living with Sparks is always a particular pleasure. When you assess their legacy, for all their foibles and missteps, thanks to a dozen stunning albums and over 100 truly memorable songs, it will always be something rather special.

As the late, great Derek Taylor concluded in his autobiography, *50 Years Adrift*: "And in the end… Sparks did well. They were good. They always had a certain *je ne sais quoi* but it took time for sufficient people to hear it. 'Twas ever thus."

Now for their next trick…

What Happened Next?

MIKE BERNS (manager, 1969/70): Whereabouts unknown.

MARCUS BLAKE (bass guitar, 2007–present): Still recording and touring with Sparks. At time of writing, has finished recording and mixing the tenth Mother Superior CD, to be released in 2010. www. mother-superior.com/ http://www.myspace.com/mothersuperiorrock.

LESLIE BOEHM (bass guitar, 1980–1986): Hollywood screenwriter. Boehm wrote *Dante's Peak* and *Daybreak* and the Steven Spielberg science fiction cycle *Taken*.

NORMAN 'DINKY' DIAMOND (drums, 1973–1975): Took his life in 2005. "When I look at it now," John Hewlett says, "there could be absolutely no other drummer to play *Kimono My House* but him. He was a clever drummer and a clever man. He had the perfect feel for every track."

LARRY DUPONT (friend, photographer and road manager, 1968–1973): Photographer and visual artist, working on album covers and film posters. Through Todd Rundgren, became involved in building train sets for people. "I started to build these large train set-ups for people who don't have the time but have the money and are willing to hire somebody to do it for them. This is the second time I succeeded in taking a hobby and turning it into work."

HAROLD FALTERMEYER (producer, 1980): Renowned producer. Wrote soundtrack for *Beverly Hills Cop* and its theme 'Axel F'. Producer of Pet Shop Boys' *Behaviour* album.

HARLEY A. FEINSTEIN (drums, 1970–1973): Became an attorney at law, currently practising in San Diego, CA. Recently playing drums again with James Lowe.

FRED FRANK (Urban Renewal Project, 1967): Frederic Gary Frank was born November 3, 1944 in New York. "Last place I think he lived was in Aurora, in the San Fernando Valley, California," ex-wife Ronna Frank says.

RONNA FRANK (Urban Renewal Project, 1967): Lived in England between 1973 and 2000. "In London, I composed five film scores for various documentaries. I also wrote and adapted children's books as stage musicals, including Roald Dahl's *Charlie And The Chocolate Factory* and *James And The Giant Peach*. I have two children's musicals published by The Dramatic Publishing Company: *Stuart Little* and *The Just So Stories*. I work with US playwright Joseph Robinette. He wrote the adaptations and I wrote the music, lyrics and full orchestral scores. I have also written three children's books."

JOSEPH FLEURY (friend, fan, wordsmith, manager, 1972–1991): Aside from managing Sparks, looked after acts such as Mumps and Milk'n'Cookies. Passed away in 1991.

CHRISTINE FRKA (MISS CHRISTINE) (brought Halfnelson to the attention of Todd Rundgren, 1970): Died: November 5, 1972.

ADRIAN FISHER (guitar, 1973–1974): Joined Boxer after leaving Sparks. Played with Trevor White, John Hewlett, Ian Hampton and Dinky Diamond in The Four Squares in the early Eighties. Relocated to Thailand where he made his living playing guitar. Died of a heart attack in 2000.

KEITH FORSEY (drums, 1979–1980): Produced Billy Idol in the Eighties and helped make him a superstar. Co-wrote 'Flashdance (What A Feeling') for the 1983 film of the same name and wrote 'Don't You (Forget About Me)' for *The Breakfast Club*. Idol turned it down, as did Bryan Ferry. Simple Minds scored the massive worldwide hit. Produced debut album for Rooney in 2003.

TAMERA 'TAMMY' GLOVER (drums, 1997–present): Still studio drummer for Sparks, Glover is also the Vice President of Production at US cable and satellite channel Comedy Central.

JIM GOODWIN (keyboards, 1981–1983): After playing with The Call (1983–1991), Goodwin started Eggchair Music (www.eggchairmusic. com) creating original music for all media. Is founder of Central Oregon School of Performing Arts in Bend, Oregon, a non-profit centre where young people can learn to express themselves through artistic performance with an emphasis on community and commerce.

ALBERT GROSSMAN (head of Bearsville): Continued supervising Bearsville, while overseeing the legacy of another of his artists, Janis Joplin. Died January 25, 1986 and is buried behind his Bearsville Theater in Woodstock, New York. As the Bob Dylan legend continues to grow, Grossman's place in pop history – as his manager throughout the Sixties – is secure.

MARTIN GORDON (bass guitar, 1973–1974): Currently pursuing a solo career after decades spent silently fuming while others spouted drivel and nonsense. Now, finally, he spouts his own drivel and nonsense at will. The fifth and final part of the *Mammal Trilogy (Time Gentlemen Please)* was released by Radiant Future Records in 2009, and all MG exploits and current affairs can be found at www.martingordon.de.

BOB HAAG (guitar 1980–1986): Returned to the desert. Current whereabouts unknown.

IAN HAMPTON (bass guitar, 1974–1975): Became respected session player. In his own words, "Still slogging on, and hanging out with old chums!" At the time of writing had been with Ian Hunter at Mott The Hoople's reunion show at Rockfield Studio, Monmouth. Hampton's recent activity can be heard at www.myspace.com/heavenscenther.

ERIC HARLE (manager, 1993–2000): Still a successful manager with acts such as Mylo, Robyn, Royksopp and Moby.

SUE HARRIS (manager, 2003–present): Manages Sparks and runs successful music and entertainment PR business Republic Media.

CHRISTIE HAYDON (drums, 1995–1996): Former regular extra on *Star Trek: The Next Generation*, she left Sparks to marry Larry Wilson, the scriptwriter of *Mai The Psychic Girl*. In 2009 the pair were co-writing and co-directing the film *Me & My Shadow*.

JOHN HEWLETT (manager, 1973–1978): Went on to manage The Dickies, before returning to A&R at A&M in the Eighties. Attended Kingston University in early 21st century to study music technology; currently developing ideas. "I am content living life as an art form, dealing with what each day brings forth," Hewlett says. "I will continue helping my aging family members; to work with Trevor [White] on music projects including creating a new band, The Zimmermen, hopefully with myself on vocals; to help develop a new record label; to visit the Caribbean following the England Cricket Team schedule on their next winter tour; possibly to record a blues album with Mick Jagger – he loves cricket, so maybe recording in the Caribbean; to help others and be a positive influence in the world."

RUPERT HOLMES (producer, 1976): Had huge solo success with his fifth album, *Partners In Crime*, in 1979. Its lead single, 'Escape (The Pina Colada Song)' became a US number one and a worldwide hit. Although a playwright, novelist and songwriter, has said that "no matter what I do, my tombstone will be a giant pineapple".

DAVID KENDRICK (drums, 1980–1986): Went on to drum for Devo (most recent stint 2002–2004) and Wall Of Voodoo. Founder of the band The Empire Of Fun, a ragingly eccentric melange with a core of two and many other players (sound familiar?). Kendrick is writer-lyricist-drummer with the music and voice of Steve Summers (www.empireoffun.com). He also drums with former Wall of Voodoo singer Andy Prieboy.

JOSH KLINGHOFFER (guitar, 2006): Musician and record producer, currently playing with Dot Matrix.

IAN LITTLE (producer, 1984): Spent most of the later Eighties trying to break new acts. Had a Top 40 UK single with 'Imagination' by Belouis Some on EMI/Trident. Moved to New York in 1989 and set up one of the first CPU-based pre-production studios. Returned to London and is currently working with drum'n'bass artist DJ Harmony and developing singer/songwriters.

JAMES LOWE (producer, *A Woofer In Tweeter's Clothing*): After a long career in television production, now writes and records with a reactivated Electric Prunes.

IAN KIMMETT (Jook leader, 1971–1974): Went to work for Bearsville Records. Currently lives in New York.

ROBERT MACHE (guitar, 1986): Guitarist in Steve Wynn and the Continental Drifters and The Swinging Madisons.

RHEINHOLD MACK (producer, 1981–1982): Hugely successful producer, working with Queen in the early Eighties and on their retrospective releases.

SAL MAIDA (bass guitar, 1976): Currently playing bass with Cracker – www.crackersoul.com.

EARLE MANKEY (guitar, 1969–1973): Became engineer for The Beach Boys at their Brother Studios. Worked on a variety of releases for them and others including engineering and playing guitar on Dennis Wilson's now legendary *Pacific Ocean Blue*. Set up own studio using the old Brother mixing desk that he bought when The Beach Boys upgraded. Recorded The Long Ryders, The Cramps, Mumps, Concrete Blonde, The Dickies and The Runaways among others.

JIM MANKEY (bass guitar, 1970–1973): Formed Concrete Blonde with Johnette Napolitano and enjoyed considerable US success.

JIM McALLISTER (guitar, 1976): Whereabouts unknown.

STEVE McDONALD (bass guitar, 2006–): Founder member of Redd Kross.

MEDIASOUND STUDIOS, NEW YORK (*Big Beat* sessions, 1976): Closed in 1989. Became the trendy club Le Bar Bat where, unwittingly, people would sometimes dance to music that had been recorded where they were standing. Now Providence nightclub.

JOHN MENDELSOHN (Halfnelson drums, 1969–70): Esteemed music journalist, now writer.

DEAN MENTA (guitar, 1997–present): Former member of Faith No More, Menta is a successful music producer and editor for television. Recent credits include *The Flight Of The Conchords*, *The Sarah Silverman Program* and *Extraordinary Measures*.

HILLY MICHAELS (drums, 1976): Released two albums in the eighties, *Calling All Girls* (1980) and *Lumia* (1981). Currently making music again.

GIORGIO MORODER (producer, 1979): Still hit-making producer. Wrote 'Forever Friends' for 2008 Beijing Olympics Closing Ceremony.

STEVEN NISTOR (drums, 2005–present): Currently working on records produced by Danger Mouse, Daniel Lanois, Scott Litt and Steve Albini. Has recently played drums and keyboards on the Danger Mouse/Sparklehorse collaboration, *Dark Night Of The Soul*.

'SURLY' RALPH OSWALD (bass guitar, Halfnelson 1969–70): Whereabouts unknown.

'SIR' PETER OXENDALE (keyboards, 1974): After working with scores of acts, most notably Chris De Burgh as musical director, producer and arranger, is also a forensic musicologist, working on many high-profile music litigation cases.

LEE PACKHAM (secretary, Island Records, part of Sparks team 1973–1976): Married and divorced from Dinky Diamond, Lee died in 1997.

THE PHEASANTRY, KING'S ROAD, LONDON (first UK venue, 1972): Now a Pizza Express.

TERRY POWELL (producer, 1977): Whereabouts unknown.

ROLLERCOASTER (film, 1977): Still showing somewhere in the world, right now.

TODD RUNDGREN (producer, 1971): Remains a Wizard, a True Star.

JEFF SALEN (guitar, 1976): Respected guitarist and leader of Tuff Darts. Played on countless sessions. Died of a heart attack January 26, 2008.

ROY SILVER (manager 1970–1973): Continued his many business interests, including managing Bill Cosby. Was filmed by Martin Scorsese for the Bob Dylan *No Direction Home* biopic. A bonus DVD of his footage was included in a deluxe package of Bob Dylan's 2009 album, *Together Through Life*. Died in 2003.

SPENCER SIRCOMBE (guitar, 1988): Whereabouts unknown.

DAVID SWANSON (bass guitar, 1976): Went on to form The Pop. Now a renowned painter.

JACQUES TATI (director of *Confusion*, 1975): Died in 1982. The *Confusion* project never reached fruition.

DEREK TAYLOR (Bearsville Records, 1972): Continued working for Warners before returning to The Beatles to work for Apple, putting together the *Anthology* series, and various other projects. Died of cancer in 1997.

JOHN THOMAS (keyboards, 1984–1988, engineer, 1988–present): Works in LA as esteemed engineer.

TOP OF THE POPS (Sparks UK TV debut, 1974): Bastion of the BBC's pop programming, the weekly show broadcast for the final time on July 30, 2006. It still broadcasts its Christmas special, and at the time of writing, it is rumoured it may yet return.

TONY VISCONTI (producer, 1975; arranger, 1997): Still a world-renowned producer. Reunited with David Bowie in early 21st century to produce *Heathen* and *Reality* – seen as Bowie's best albums since the Seventies.

TREVOR WHITE (guitar, 1974–1975): Currently working towards completing his solo album, a collection of home recordings entitled *Music Of White Origin*. Working with John Hewlett on various projects including The Zimmermen and John's Children (if Hewlett and Andy

287

Ellison agree to work on new material); to maintain his MySpace site, and to continue working with The DTs duo that he gigs with regularly.

JIM WILSON (guitar, 2004–present): Still recording and touring with Sparks. At time of writing, recently finished recording and mixing the tenth Mother Superior CD, to be released in 2010. In 2009, recorded sessions with Daniel Lanois for a forthcoming Robert Plant album and provided background vocals on the next Meat Loaf album. www. mother-superior.com/ http://www.myspace.com/mothersuperiorrock.

MERVYN 'MUFF' WINWOOD (producer, 1973–1974): Moved from Island to CBS in late Seventies and oversaw Adam Ant's rise to fame, and signed Sade and The Psychedelic Furs. Produced Dire Straits' debut album. Now happily retired.

LUKE ZAMPERINI (guitar, 1976): As a member of The Scooters made two albums for EMI (*Young Girls* and *Blue Eyes*) in London at Utopia Studios produced by Phil Wainman. The band broke up after little success. Zamperini is now a manager for The City of Los Angeles Department of Building and Safety. He still plays live for the enjoyment.

HAROLD ZELLMAN (UCLA friend, 1967): World-respected historian of modernist architecture and communitarian movements.

Sparks Discography

PART ONE: SINGLES

Original UK singles

Bearsville K15505 Wonder Girl / (No More) Mr. Nice Guys (11/72)

Island WIP 6193 This Town Ain't Big Enough For Both Of Us / Barbecutie (4/74, No. 2)

Bearsville K15516 Girl From Germany / Beaver O'Lindy (7/74)

Island WIP 6203 Amateur Hour / Lost And Found (7/74, No.7)

Island WIP 6211 Never Turn Your Back On Mother Earth / Alabamy Right (picture sleeve, 10/74, No. 13)

Island WIP 6221 Something For The Girl With Everything / Marry Me (1/75, No. 17)

Island WIP 6236 Get In The Swing / Profile (6/75, No. 27)

Island WIP 6249 Looks, Looks, Looks / Pineapple (9/75, No. 26)

Island WIP 6282 I Want To Hold Your Hand / Under The Table With Her (DJ Promo only, 3/76)

Island WIP 6337 Big Boy / Fill 'Er Up (10/76)

Island WIP 6357 I Like Girls/ England (11/76)

CBS A 5593 A Big Surprise/Forever Young (10/77)

Virgin VS 244 The Number One Song In Heaven / The Number One Song In Heaven (Version) (p/s, some green vinyl, 3/79, No. 14)

Virgin VS44–12 The Number One Song In Heaven / The Number One Song In Heaven (Version) (12", p/s, some blue/red vinyl, 3/79)

Virgin VS 270 Beat The Clock / Beat The Clock (Alternative) (p/s, 7/79, No. 10)

Virgin VS270–12 Beat The Clock / Beat The Clock (Alternative Version) (12", die-cut sleeve w/picture disc label, some blue/yellow/red vinyl, 7/79)

Island WIP 6532 This Town Ain't Big Enough For The Both Of Us / Looks, Looks, Looks (7/79)

Virgin VS 289 Tryouts For The Human Race / Tryouts For The Human Race (Alternative) (p/s, 10/79, No. 45)

Virgin VS289–12 Tryouts For The Human Race / Tryouts For The Human Race (Long Version) (12", die-cut sleeve w/picture disc label, some green/blue vinyl, 10/79)

Virgin VS 319 When I'm With You / When I'm With You (Instrumental) (p/s, 1/80)

Virgin VS 343 Young Girls / Just Because You Love Me (p/s, 5/80)

Virgin VS 343/319 Young Girls / Just Because You Love Me / When I'm With You/When I'm With You (Instrumental) (double-pack, p/s, 5/80)

Virgin VS343–12 Young Girls / Young Girls (long version) / Just Because You Love Me (12", p/s, 5/80)

Why-Fi WHY 1 Tips For Teens / Don't Shoot Me (p/s, 5/81)

Why-Fi WHYT1 Tips For Teens / Don't Shoot Me (12", p/s, 5/81)

Why-Fi WHY 4 Funny Face / The Willys (7/81)

Atlantic K11740 I Predict / Moustache (6/82)

Virgin VS590–12 The Number One Song In Heaven / Beat The Clock / When I'm With You / Young Girls (p/s, 5/83)

Atlantic A9866 Cool Places / Sports (6/83)

Epic A 6671 EVELYN KING: Give It Up /SPARKS: Armies Of The Night (p/s 4/85)

Epic TA6671 EVELYN KING: Give It Up / SPARKS: Armies Of The Night (12", p/s, 4/85)

London LON 69 Change / This Town Ain't Big Enough For Both Of Us (acoustic) (p/s, 7/85)

London LONX 69 Change (Extended Mix) / This Town Ain't Big Enough For Both Of Us (acoustic) (12", p/s, 7/85)

Consolidated TOON 2 Music That You Can Dance To / Fingertips (p/s, 11/86)

Consolidated TOON T2 Music That You Can Dance To (UK Extended Club Version) / Fingertips (Extended Club Version) (12", p/s, 11/86)

Consolidated TOON 4 Rosebud / Theme For Rosebud (p/s, 1/87)

Consolidated TOON T4 Rosebud (Extended Club Mix) / Theme For Rosebud (Cinematic Mix) / Rosebud (FM Mix) (12", p/s, 1/87)

Carrere CAR 427 So Important / The Big Brass Ring (p/s, 7/88)

Carrere CART427 So Important (Extremely Important Mix) / (Incredibly Important Mix) / So Important (p/s, 7/88)

Carrere CAR 431 So Important / Just Got Back From Heaven (p/s, 8/89)

Carrere CART431 So Important (Extremely Important Version) / (Single Version) / Just Got Back From Heaven (Heaven Can Wait mix) (12", p/s, 8/89)

Finiflex FFCD1004 National Crime Awareness Week (Psycho Cut) / Thirteen Minutes in Heaven / Highly Strung Hoedown (CD, 11/93)

Finiflex FF1004 National Crime Awareness Week (Thirteen Minutes In Heaven Mix) / Perkins Playtime (12", p/s, 11/93)

BMG/Logic 74321234472 When Do I Get To Sing 'My Way'? (Vince Clarke Remix) / (Progress Mix) / (Microbots Mix) (CD, 10/84, No. 38)

BMG / Logic 74321234462 When Do I Get To Sing 'My Way'? (Sparks Radio Edit) / (The Grid Radio Edit) / (The Rapino Brothers Extended Sola Mix) / (The Grid's Ron and Nancy Mix) / (The Grid's Frank and Kitty Mix) / (Men Behind Club Mix) (CD, 10/84)

BMG/Logic 7432134461 When Do I Get To Sing 'My Way' (Rapino Brothers Extended Sola Mix) / (The Pro-Gress Mix v.10.3) / (The Grid's Ron and Nancy Mix) / (Microbots Club Mix) (12", p/s, 10/94)

BMG/ Logic WAY 2 When Do I Get To Sing 'My Way' (Rapino Brothers Extended Sola Mix) / (The Pro-Gress Mix v.10.3) / (Microbots Club Mix) / National Crime Awareness Week (12", p/s, 10/94)

Logic 7432164262 (When I Kiss You) I Hear Charlie Parker Playing (Bernard Butler's Fashionable World Of Fashion Remix) / (When I Dub You Remix) / (The Beatmasters Full Blown Dub) (CD, 3/95, No. 36)

Logic 74322164272 (When I Kiss You) I Hear Charlie Parker Playing (Red Jerry Remix) / (Oliver Leib Vocal Mix) / This Town Ain't Big Enough For Both Of Us (BBC Session Acoustic Piano) (CD, 3/95)

BMG/Logic 7431264261 (When I Kiss You) I Hear Charlie Parker Playing (Bernard Butler's Fashionable World Of Fashion Remix) / (When I Dub You Remix) / (The Beatmasters Full Blown Dub) / (Red Jerry Remix) / (Oliver Lieb Mix) (12", p/s, 3/95)

BMG/Logic 74321274002 When Do I Get To Sing 'My Way'? (Sparks Radio Edit) / (Vince Clarke Remix) / (Total Fog Dub 1) / National Crime Awareness Week (Complete Psycho) (CD, 5/95, No. 32)

BMG/Logic 74321274012 When Do I Get To Sing 'My Way'? (The Grid Radio Edit) / (Sticks & Stones Remix) / (BBC Session – Acoustic Version) / Now That I Own The BBC (BBC Session – Acoustic Piano Version) (CD, 5/95)

BMG/Logic 74321348672 Now That I Own The BBC (Sparks Radio Edit) / (Motiv 8 Extended Vocal Mix) / (Legend B Remix) / Beat The Clock (Live) (CD, 3/96, No. 60)

BMG/Logic 7431348662 Now That I Own The BBC (Motiv 8 Radio Edit) / (Tony Catania & Ingo Kays Mix) / (Motiv 8 Dub) / She's An Anchorman (CD, 3/96)

Roadrunner RR2262–9 The Number One Song In Heaven (Sparks Radio Edit) / (Tin Tin Out Mix) / (Heavenly Dub) / (Tin Tin Out Instrumental) (CD, 10/97, No. 70)

Roadrunner RR2262–3 The Number One Song In Heaven (Sparks Radio Edit) / (Extended Version With Jimmy Somerville) / (Part Two) (CD, 10/97)

Roadrunner RR 2262–6 The Number One Song In Heaven (Tin Tin Out Mix) / (Part Two) / (Heavenly Dub) (with Jimmy Somerville) (12", die-cut p/s, 10/97)

Roadrunner RR2251–3 This Town Ain't Big Enough For Both Of Us (with Faith No More) / (Plagiarism Orchestral Album Version) / Something For The Girl With Everything (with Faith No More) / The Great Leap Forward (CD, 12/97, No. 40)

Roadrunner RR2251–9 This Town Ain't Big Enough For Both Of Us (with Faith No More) / (Plagiarism Orchestral Album Version – Instrumental) / Pink Panda (CD, 12/97)

Winney CD IFPI LAE 1 The Cute Candidate / This Town Ain't Big Enough For Both Of Us (1920 Archival Recording) / The Winney Empire / The Cute Candidare On TV / The Race For President (CD, fanclub only issue, /99)

Recognition Records CDREC14 The Calm Before The Storm (Radio Edit)/ The Calm Before The Opera / It's Educational (CD, 8/00, unreleased)

Artful LILBCD 2 Suburban Homeboy (Single Edit) / ('Ron Speaks' Version) / Wunderbar (Concerto in Koch Minor) (CD, 3/03)

Gut CDGUT 77 Perfume (Radio Edit) / Baby, Baby, Can I Invade Your Country (Alternate Lyrics) / Perfume (Clor's Eau De Perfume remix) (2/96)

Gut CD Gut 79 Dick Around / Waterproof / Change (Live) / Interview With Sparks By Steve Jones Of Jonesy's Jukebox / Enhanced CD: Dick Around (video) (CD, 9/06)

Lil' Beethoven LBRCDS102 Islington N1 (CD, 'Golden Ticket' Holder's Bonus, 5/08)

Lil' Beethoven LBRV 2 Lighten Up, Morrissey / Brenda's Always In The Way (p/s, 3/09)

US Singles

Bearsville BSV 0006 Wonder Girl / (No More) Mr. Nice Guys (1972)

Island IS 001 This Town Ain't Big Enough For Both Of Us / Barbecutie (1974)

Island IS 009 Talent Is An Asset/Lost And Found (p/s, 1974)

Warner Bros BEA15516 Girl From Germany/Beaver O'Lindy (1974)

Island IS 023 Achoo / Something For The Girl With Everything (p/s, 1974)

Island IS 043 Looks, Looks, Looks / The Wedding Of Jacqueline Kennedy To Russell Mael (1975)

CBS 3–10579 Over The Summer / Forever Young (1977)

Elektra EF 90157 Beat The Clock / Tryouts For The Human Race (1979)

Elektra E 46045 Tryouts For The Human Race / The Number One Song In Heaven (p/s, 12/79)

Elektra/Asylum AS114–12 Tryouts For The Human Race (Long) / Beat The Clock (12", 12/79)

Atlantic 4030 I Predict / Moustache (p/s, 5/82, No. 60)

Atlantic DMD325 I Predict (Club Mix) / I Predict (12", Promo)

Atlantic 4065 Eaten By The Monster Of Love / Mickey Mouse (1982)

Disconet MWDN511 SPECIAL REQUEST: Salsa Smurf / AZUL Y NEGRO: Mar De La Tranquilidad / NORMA LEWIS: Maybe This Time / GAUCHO: Dance Forever / SPARKS: Modesty Plays (6:54 mix by Jack Cardinal and James Pallares) / AMY BOLTON: Get Up And Get It / CHARLIE: I'm A Space Woman (2x12", p/s, 1983)

Atlantic 7–89866 Cool Places / Sports (p/s, 4/83, No. 49)

Atlantic 0–89863 Cool Places (12" version) / Sports (4/83)

Atlantic 7–89797 All You Ever Think About Is Sex / I Wish I Looked A Little Better (p/s, 11/83)

Atlantic 086990 All You Ever Think About Is Sex / Dance Godammit (12", p/s, 11/83)

Atlantic EPPR516 Sparks On Tour: All You Ever Think About Is Sex (Live) / Cool Places (Live) /Popularity / Praying For A Party (12", promo, p/s with sticker, 1983)

Morocco 66842 SPARKS: Get Crazy / MALCOLM MCDOWELL: Hot Shot (1983)

Atlantic 0–86939 Progress (Extended Club Mix) /Sparks In The Dark (Extended Club Mix) / With All My Might (Extended Club Mix) (12", p/s, 5/84)

Atlantic 7–89616 Pretending To Be Drunk / Kiss Me Quick (6/84)

Atlantic 0–86917 Pretending To Be Drunk (Extended Vocal Version) / Kiss Me Quick (Extended Vocal Version) (12", p/s, 6/84)

Atlantic 7–89645 With All My Might / Sparks In The Dark (1984)

Atlantic PR617 With All My Might (LP version) / With All My Might (LP Version) (12", promo)

Disconet MWDV702 SPARKS: With All My Might (Gary Otto Mix) / Real Rhythm Tracks / Master Mix Medley / ALIVES HIDDING: Hollywood Seven / M7M: Cooling The Medium / BIANCA BONELLI: Je Veux L'Amour / JAY NOVELLE: If This Ain't Love / GIORGIO MORODER: Machines (2x12", p/s, 1984)

Private 1 2405627 SPARKS: Armies Of The Night / EVELYN 'CHAMPAGNE' KING: Give It Up (1985)

Curb MCA 52879 Music That You Can Dance To / Shopping Mall Of Love (1986)

MCA/Curb MCA 23640 Music That You Can Dance To (LP Version) / (Mini Version) / (Club Version) (12", 8/86)

MCA/Curb MCA23684 Fingertips (Extended Club Version) / The Scene (Special Club Edit) / Fingertips (Short Version) (12", p/s, 1986)

Fine Art/Rhino RNTW70410 So Important (Extremely Important Mix) / (Incredibly Important Mix) / (Single Version) (12", p/s, 1988)

Fine Art/Rhino PRO2 90006 So Important (Single Version Edit) /So Important (Extremely Important Mix Edit) (CD, promo only, 1988)

Art Of Mix AM 8802 2MEN A DRUM MACHINE AND A TRUMPET: Tired Of Getting Pushed Around / SPARKS: So Important (Dance Edit – Remix By Mr. E) / BOYS FROM BRAZIL: Hot Stuff / JANET JACKSON: Jam It, Janet / MANUFACTURE: Armed Forces (2x12", p/s)

Fine Art/Rhino RNTW70412 Just Got Back From Heaven (Heaven Can Wait Mix) / (Heaven Can Wait Dub) / (Single Version Edit) / (Angels With Dirty Faces Mix) / Heaven Knows Mr. Allison Mix) (12", p/s, 1989)

Fine Art/Rhino R2 70413 Just Got Back From Heaven (Heaven Can Wait Radio Mix) / (Single Version Edit) / (Heaven Can Wait Mix Unedited) (CD, promo, 1989)

Art Of Mix AM 8808 ERASURE: Stop (Extended Dance Mix) / SPARKS: Just Got Back From Heaven (6:24 Reincarnation Mix by Michael Marshall and Steve Smith) / VARIOUS: 123 Medley / SECTION 25: Looking From A Hilltop (2x12", transparent p/s)

Finiflex 8187628271 National Crime Awareness Week (The Radio Mix) / (The Bates Motel Mix) / (The Janet Leigh Mix) / (The Mother's Mix) (12" 1993)

BMG/Logic LGJD59007 When Do I Get To Sing 'My Way'? (Radio Edit) / (Vince Clarke Remix) (p/s, promo-only collector's edition, 1994)

BMG/ Logic 79591590071 When Do I Get To Sing 'My Way'? (The Rapino Brothers Extended Sola Mix) / (Men Behind The Club Mix) / (Microbots Mix) / (The Grid's Ron and Nancy Mix) (12", 1994)

BMG/Logic 79591–590072 When Do I Get To Sing 'My Way'? (Sparks Radio Edit) / (Rapino 7") / (The Grid Radio Edit) / (Men Behind Club Mix) / (Vince Clarke Mix) / (Microbots Mix) (CD, 1995)

BMG/ Logic 79591590231 (When I Kiss You) I Hear Charlie Parker Playing (Red Jerry Remix) / (Color Blind Club Mix) / (DJ Casanova's Saturday Nite At Palladium Vocal Mix) / (DJ Casanova's Saturday Nite At Palladium Dub 1) / (Radio Edit) (12", p/s, 1995)

BMG/ Logic 9591–590232 (When I Kiss You) I Hear Charlie Parker Playing (Radio Edit) / (Bernard Butler's Edit) / (Red Jerry Remix) / 9Colour Blind Club Mix) / DJ Casanova's Saturday Nite At Palladium Vocal Mix) / (DJ Casanova's Saturday Nite At Palladium Dub 1) (CD, 1995)

Oglio 85003–1 The Number One Song In Heaven (Dave Aude's Heavenly Vocal)/ (Tin Tin Out Remix) / (Dave's Rubber Dub) (12", promo, picture label, 1998)

Oglio 9005–85004–2 The Number One Song In Heaven (Plagiarism Album Version) / (Dave Aude's Heavenly Vocal) / (Dave's Rubber Dub) / Hey Skinny / The Number One Song In Heaven (Video) (CD, 1998)

Oglio No Cat No. Plagiarism Radio Sampler: Angst In My Pants/Funny Face/ This Town Ain't Big Enough For Both Of Us (With Faith No More) (1999)

Columbia CAS 42328 SPARKS: Beat The Clock (Wide Mix) / SPARKS: Beat The Clock/ RENEGADE MASTER: Wild Child (Fat Boy Slim Remix) (12", p/s w/green sticker, white label)

Columbia CSK42303 SPARKS: Beat The Clock (Plagiarism Album Version Radio Edit 3:29) / RENEGADE MASTER: Wild Child (Fat Boy Slim Mix) (CD, 1999)

In the Red ITR 137 Dick Around / Hospitality On Parade (Live) (p/s, some white/pink vinyl, 2006)

In The Red 51372 Dick Around / (Baby, Baby) Can I Invade Your Country (Alternate Lyric)/ Happy Hunting Ground (Live Hollywood May 20, 2006) / Bon Voyage (Live Hollywood May 20, 2006) / In The Future (Live Hollywood May 20, 2006) / Interview / video content (CD, 2006)

PART TWO: ALBUMS

HALFNELSON / SPARKS
UK: Bearsville/WEA K45511, UK, 10/74 w/ lyric inner sleeve
US: As *Halfnelson* Bearsville BV2048, US, 10/71; as *Sparks* Bearsville BV 2048, US, 4/72

Wonder Girl / Fa La Fa Lee / Roger / High C / Fletcher Honorama / Simple Ballet / Slowboat / Biology 2 / Saccharin And The War / Big Bands / (No More) Mr Nice Guys

A WOOFER IN TWEETER'S CLOTHING
UK: Bearsville K45510, 4/73, w/lyric inner sleeve.
US: Bearsville 45510, US, 11/72

Girl From Germany / Beaver O'Lindy / Nothing Is Sacred / Here Comes Bob / Moon Over Kentucky / Do Re Mi / Angus Desire / Underground / The Louvre / Batteries Not Included / Whippings And Apologies

KIMONO MY HOUSE
UK: Island ILPS 9272, LP w/lyric inner sleeve, 5/74, No. 4; Island IMCD198, CD, 1994; Island 5240332 with bonus tracks Barbecutie / Lost And Found, CD, 1997; Island / Universal Music Catalogue 984317 (21st Century Edition) with bonus tracks Barbecutie / Lost And Found / Amateur Hour (Live Fairfield Halls 9/11/75), CD, 11/06
US: Island / Antilles AN7044, 1974

This Town Ain't Big Enough For Both Of Us / Amateur Hour / Falling In Love With Myself Again / Here In Heaven / Thank God It's Not

Christmas/ Hasta Mañana Monsieur / Talent Is An Asset / Complaints / In My Family / Equator

PROPAGANDA
UK: Island ILPS 9312, LP w/ lyric inner sleeve, 10/74, No. 9; Island IMCD199, CD, 1994; Island 5240352 with bonus tracks: Alabamy Right/Marry Me, CD 1997; Island / Universal Music Catalogue 9843410 (21st Century Edition) with bonus tracks: Alabamy Right / Marry Me / *Saturday Scene* interview, CD, 11/06.
US: Island ILPS 9312, LP w/ lyric inner sleeve, 1975, No. 63

Propaganda / At Home, At Work, At Play / Reinforcements / B.C / Thanks But No Thanks / Don't Leave Me Alone With Her / Never Turn Your Back On Mother Earth / Something For The Girl With Everything / Achoo / Who Don't Like Kids / Bon Voyage

INDISCREET
UK: Island ILPS 9345, LP w/gatefold sleeve, 9/75, No. 18; Island IMCD 200, CD, 1994; Island 5240322 with bonus tracks Profile / I Want To Hold Your Hand / England, CD, 1997; Island/Universal Music Catalogue 9843411 (21st Century Edition) with bonus tracks Profile / The Wedding Of Jacqueline Kennedy To Russell Mael / Looks, Looks, Looks (Live Fairfield Halls 9/11/75), CD, 11/06
US: Island ILPS 9345, LP w/gatefold sleeve, 10/75

Hospitality On Parade / Happy Hunting Ground / Without Using Hands / Get In The Swing / Under The Table With Her / How Are You Getting Home / Pineapple / T★ts / It Ain't 1918 / The Lady Is Lingering / In The Future / Looks, Looks, Looks / Miss The Start, Miss The End

BIG BEAT
UK: Island ILPS 9445, LP w/lyric inner sleeve, 10/76; Island IMCD 201, CD, 1994; Island 5240342 with bonus tracks Tearing The Place Apart / Gone With The Wind, CD, 1997; Island / Universal Music Catalogue 9843412 (21st Century Edition) with bonus tracks: I Want To Hold Your

Hand / England / Gone With The Wind / Looks Aren't Everything / Intrusion-Confusion, CD, 11/06
US: Columbia PC 34359, LP w/lyric inner sleeve, 10/76.

Big Boy / I Want To Be Like Everybody Else / Nothing To Do / I Bought The Mississippi River / Fill 'Er Up / Everybody's Stupid / Throw Her Away (And Get A New One) / Confusion / Screwed Up / White Women / I Like Girls

INTRODUCING SPARKS
UK: CBS CBS 82284, LP w/inner lyric sleeve, 10/77; Lil' Beethoven LBRCD RON/LBRCDRUSS, CD, 11/07
US: Columbia PC 34901, LP w/inner lyric sleeve, 10/77
Japan: Imperial Record TECI-26546, CD paper sleeve with obi-strip, with bonus tracks: Breathe / Fact Or Fiction / Those Mysteries (Demo Version), 5/09

A Big Surprise / Occupation / Ladies / I'm Not / Forever Young / Goofing Off / Girls On The Brain / Over The Summer / Those Mysteries

NO.1 IN HEAVEN
UK: Virgin V2115, LP, some on yellow vinyl with lyric inner sleeve, 6/79, No. 73
US: Elektra/Asylum 6E186, LP, 1979
Japan: Imperial Record TECI-26547, CD paper sleeve with obi-strip, with bonus tracks: Dancing Is Dangerous / Is There No More To Life Than Dancing / Beat The Clock (Meat Beat Manifesto Remix – Double Bass Remix), 5/09

Tryouts For The Human Race / Academy Award Performance / La Dolce Vita / Beat The Clock / My Other Voice / The Number One Song In Heaven

TERMINAL JIVE
UK: Virgin V2137, LP, w/inner sleeve, 1/80
US: Oglio Records OGL 81600–2, CD, 1998

Japan: Imperial Record TECI-26548, CD paper sleeve with obi-strip, with bonus tracks: The Farmer's Daughter / After Dark / Modesty Plays (Instrumental), 5/09

When I'm With You / Just Because You Love Me / Rock'n'Roll People In A Disco World / When I'm With You (Instrumental) / Young Girls / Noisy Boys / Stereo / The Greatest Show On Earth

WHOMP THAT SUCKER
UK: Why-Fi WHO1, LP, w/lyric inner sleeve, 5/81
US: RCA AFLI – 4091, LP w/lyric inner sleeve, 1981, No. 182; Oglio Records OGL 81601–2, CD 1998
Japan: Imperial Record TECI-26549, CD paper sleeve with obi-strip, with bonus tracks: Love Can Conquer All / The Oblongs / Love Can Conquer All (Smooth Version), 5/09

Tips For Teens / Funny Face / Where's My Girl / Upstairs / I Married A Martian / The Willys / Don't Shoot Me / Suzie Safety / That's Not Nastassia / Wacky Women

ANGST IN MY PANTS
UK: Atlantic K 50888, LP, w/lyric inner sleeve, 6/82
US: Atlantic SD19347, LP w/ lyric inner sleeve, 1982, No. 173; Oglio Records OGL 81602–2, CD, 1998
Japan: Imperial Record TECI-26550, CD paper sleeve with obi-strip, with bonus tracks: Angst In My Pants (Radio Promo Ad) / Kidnap / A Trying Day / Dancing Is Dangerous (I Ought To Know), 5/09

Angst In My Pants / I Predict / Sextown USA / Sherlock Holmes / Nicotina / Mickey Mouse / Moustache / Instant Weight Loss / Tarzan And Jane / The Decline And Fall Of Me / Eaten By The Monster Of Love

SPARKS IN OUTER SPACE
UK: Atlantic 7800551, LP, w/inner lyric sleeve, 6/83
US: Atlantic 80055–1, LP, w/inner lyric sleeve, 1983; Oglio Records OGL 81603–2, CD 1998

Japan: Imperial Record TECI-26551, CD paper sleeve with obi-strip, with bonus tracks: Miniskirted / All You Ever Think About Is Sex (Unreleased Alternate Version) / Sports, 5/09

Cool Places / Popularity / Prayin' For A Party / All You Ever Think About Is Sex / Please Baby Please / Rockin' Girls / I Wish I Looked A Little Better / Lucky Me, Lucky You / A Fun Bunch Of Guys From Outer Space / Dance Godammit

PULLING RABBITS OUT OF A HAT
US: Atlantic 801601, LP w/ inner lyric sleeve, 1984; Oglio Records OGL 81604–2, CD, 1998.

Pulling Rabbits Out Of A Hat / Love Scenes / Pretending To Be Drunk / Progress / With All My Might / Sparks In The Dark (Part One) / Everybody Move / A Song That Sings Itself / Sisters / Kiss Me Quick / Sparks In The Dark (Part Two)

MUSIC THAT YOU CAN DANCE TO
UK: Consolidated TOONLP2, LP, w/inner sleeve, 11/86; Curb/Redhot 4686173, as *The Best Of Sparks*, substituting 'Armies Of The Night' for 'Change', CD, 1990
US: MCA/Curb MCA 5780, LP w/inner sleeve, 1986

Music That You Can Dance To / Rosebud / Fingertips / Armies Of The Night / The Scene / Shopping Mall Of Love / Modesty Plays (New Version) / Let's Get Funky

INTERIOR DESIGN
UK: Fine Art/Rhino R270841, LP, w/inner bag, 1988; Magnum CDTB 141, CD 8/92; Lil' Beethoven LBR CD 014 with bonus tracks: Madonna (French)/Madonna (German)/Madonna (Spanish)/The Big Brass Ring/So Important (Extremely Important Remix), CD, 10/08
US: Fine Art/Rhino R170841, LP w/inner bag, 1988; Fine Art/Rhino R270841, CD, 1988

So Important / Just Got Back From Heaven / Lots Of Reasons / You've Got A Hold Of My Heart / Love-O-Rama / The Toughest Girl In

Town / Let's Make Love/ Stop Me If You've Heard This Before / Walk Down Memory Lane / Madonna

GRATUITOUS SAX & SENSELESS VIOLINS
UK: BMG/Logic 74321232, CD, 11/94; Lil' Beethoven 102, CD reissue, 5/06
US: Logic/BMG 74321232671, LP, 1995

Gratuitous Sax / When Do I Get To Sing 'My Way'? / (When I Kiss You) I Hear Charlie Parker Playing / Frankly, Scarlett, I Don't Give A Damn / I Thought I Told You To Wait In The Car / Hear No Evil, See No Evil, Speak No Evil / Now That I Own The BBC / Tsui Hark / The Ghost Of Liberace / Let's Go Surfing / Senseless Violins

PLAGIARISM
UK: Roadrunner RR 8791–2, CD, 1997
US: Oglio Records OGL 89109–2, CD, 1997

Pulling Rabbits Out Of A Hat (Orchestral Version) / This Town Ain't Big Enough For Both Of Us (Orchestral Version) / The Number One Song In Heaven (Part Two) / Funny Face / When Do I Get To Sing 'My Way'? (Orchestral Version) / Angst In My Pants (New Version) / Change (Orchestral Version) / Popularity / Something For The Girl With Everything (Orchestral Version) / This Town Ain't Big Enough For Both Of Us (w/Faith No More) / Beat The Clock / Big Brass Ring / Amateur Hour (w/Erasure) / Propaganda (Orchestral Version) / When I'm With You (New Version) / Something For The Girl With Everything (w/Faith No More) / Orchestral Collage /The Number One Song In Heaven (w/Jimmy Somerville) (Orchestral Version) / Never Turn Your Back On Mother Earth (Orchestral Version)

BALLS
UK: Recognition CDREC 510, CD, choice of red, blue, yellow or green jewel case, with die-cut silver surround, 8/00; Lil' Beethoven LBRCD 103, plus bonus tracks: Calm Before The Opera / Calm Before The Storm (Full Length Instrumental), 10/08
US: Oglio Records 89119–2, CD, 2000

Balls / More Than A Sex Machine / Scheherazade / Aeroflot / The
Calm Before The Storm / How To Get Your Ass Kicked / Bullet Train /
It's A Knock Off / Irreplaceable / It's Educational / The Angels

LIL' BEETHOVEN
UK: Artful LILBCD 2, CD, in white hardcover wallet, 10/02; Lil'
Beethoven LBRV 001
As 'Deluxe Edition', w/black slipcase, with bonus tracks CD: The
Legend Of Lil' Beethoven / Wunderbar / The Rhythm Of The Thief
(Instrumental Version) / CD-ROM extras, 3/2004
US: Palm Pictures 2126, CD, 2003

The Rhythm Thief / How Do I Get To Carnegie Hall? / What Are All
These Bands So Angry About? / I Married Myself / Ride 'Em Cowboy /
My Baby's Taking Me Home / Your Call Is Very Important To Us. Please
Hold. / Ugly Guys With Beautiful Girls / Suburban Homeboy

HELLO YOUNG LOVERS
UK: Gut GUTCD 53 CD, 2/06, No. 66
US: In The Red ITR 131 LP/ CD In The Red 131, 2006

Dick Around / Perfume / The Very Next Fight / (Baby, Baby) Can I
Invade Your Country / Rock, Rock, Rock / Metaphor / Waterproof /
Here Kitty / There's No Such Thing As Aliens/ As I Sit To Play The
Organ At The Notre Dame Cathedral

EXOTIC CREATURES OF THE DEEP
UK: Lil' Beethoven LBRCD 011, CD, 5/08, No. 54
US: Lil' Beethoven 11, CD, 2008

Intro / Good Morning / Strange Animal / I Can't Believe You Would
Fall For All The Crap In This Song / Let The Monkey Drive /Intro
Reprise / I've Never Been High / (She Got Me) Pregnant / Lighten
Up, Morrissey / This Is The Renaissance / The Director Never Yelled
'Cut' / Photoshop / Likeable

THE SEDUCTION OF INGMAR BERGMAN

UK: Lil' Beethoven LBRV 4, 2-LP w/booklet, 11/09; Lil' Beethoven LBRV 4X, 4-LP/CD set, signed by Ron and Russell w/booklet and lift-off lid box set, 11/09.

US: Lil' Beethoven LBRV 4, 2-LP w/booklet, 12/09; Lil' Beethoven LBRV 4X, 4-LP/CD set, signed by Ron and Russell w/booklet and lift-off lid box set, 12/09.

1956 Cannes Film Festival / "I Am Ingmar Bergman" / Limo Driver (Welcome To Hollywood) / "Here He Is Now" / "Mr. Bergman, How Are You?" / "He'll Come 'Round" / En Route To The Beverly Hills Hotel / Hollywood Welcoming Committee / "I've Got To Contact Sweden" / The Studio Commissary / "I Must Not Be Hasty" / "Quiet On The Set" / "Why Do You Take That Tone With Me?" / Pleasant Hotel Staff / Hollywood Tour Bus / Autograph Hounds / Bergman Ponders Escape / "We've Got To Turn Him 'Round" / Escape (Part 1) / Escape (Part 2) / "Oh My God" / Garbo Sings / Almost A Hollywood Ending / "He's Home"

PART THREE: CHOICE COMPILATIONS

2 ORIGINALS OF SPARKS

UK: Bearsville/WEA K85505, 2-LP, gatefold sleeve, with 12-page booklet, 1975;
Sparks/A Woofer In Tweeter's Clothing, Dojo LOMACD23, CD, 12/93.

Wonder Girl / Fa La Fa Lee / Roger / High C / Fletcher Honorama / Simple Ballet / Slowboat / Biology 2 / Saccharin And The War / Big Bands / (No More) Mr Nice Guys / Girl From Germany /Beaver O'Lindy / Nothing Is Sacred / Here Comes Bob / Moon Over Kentucky / Do Re Mi / Angus Desire / Underground / The Louvre / Batteries Not Included / Whippings and Apologies

THE BEST OF SPARKS

UK: Island ILPS9493, LP, 3/77, reissued 9/79

This Town Ain't Big Enough For Both Of Us / At Home, At Work, At Play / Hasta Mañana Monsieur / Tearing The Place Apart / Never Turn

Your Back On Mother Earth / Get In The Swing / Looks, Looks, Looks /
Amateur Hour / Thanks But No Thanks / Gone With The Wind /
Something For The Girl With Everything / Thank God It's Not Christmas

PROFILE
US: Rhino/Fine Art R270731/2, 2-CD set w/long box, 3/91

DISC ONE: Wonder Girl / (No More) Mr Nice Guys / Girl From
Germany / I Like Girls / This Town Ain't Big Enough For Both Of Us /
Barbecutie / Amateur Hour / Talent Is An Asset / Lost And Found /
Hasta Mañana Monsieur / Propaganda / At Home, At Work, At Play /
Something For The Girl With Everything / Never Turn Your Back On
Mother Earth / Achoo / Get In The Swing / Looks, Looks, Looks /
Happy Hunting Ground / Big Boy / Nothing To Do / Over The
Summer / A Big Surprise

DISC TWO: Beat The Clock / The Number One Song In Heaven /
Tryouts For The Human Race / When I'm With You / Funny Face /
Tips For Teens / Upstairs / Angst In My Pants / Sextown USA / I
Predict / Moustache / Modesty Plays / Cool Places / All You Ever
Think About Is Sex / With All My Might / Change / Music That You
Can Dance To / So Important

**MAEL INTUITION – THE BEST OF SPARKS 1974–76 [IT'S
A MAEL, MAEL, MAEL WORLD]**
UK: Island IMCD88, CD, 5/90

This Town Ain't Big Enough For Both Of Us / Amateur Hour / Here
In Heaven / Thank God It's Not Christmas / Hasta Mañana Monsieur /
Complaints / Never Turn Your Back On Mother Earth / Something
For The Girl With Everything / Achoo / Propaganda / At Home, At
Work, At Play / Reinforcements /BC / Hospitality On Parade / Happy
Hunting Ground / Without Using Hands / Get In The Swing / It Ain't
1918 / In The Future /Looks, Looks, Looks

THE HEAVEN COLLECTION
France: Columbia 4735152, CD, 2/93

This Town Ain't Big Enough For Both Of Us / The Number One Song In Heaven / Beat The Clock / Tryouts for The Human Race / When I'm With You / Young Girls / Funny Face / Tips For Teens / I Predict / Angst In My Pants / Modesty Plays / Cool Places / With All My Might / Change / Music That You Can Dance To / So Important / Singing In The Shower (w/Les Rita Mitsouko) / National Crime Awareness Week

THE HELL COLLECTION
France: Columbia 4735162, CD, 2/93

Shout (Live At The Forest National, Brussels, 1981) / All You Ever Think About Is Sex (Dance Mix) / Get Crazy (Alternate Recording) / Jingle For Brussels Concert / Rosebud (Extended Dance Mix) / Je M'Appelle Russell / 'Nissan' Commercial / Singing In The Shower (Original Demo Version) / Madonna (French Version) / The Japanese Have Come And They Bought My Number One / Just Got Back From Heaven (Heaven Can Wait Mix) / Dance Godammit (Dance Mix) / The Armies Of The Night (Alternate Version) / Breaking Out Of Prison (Alternate Version) / Jingle Announcing 'Magic Mountain' Concert / I Predict (Live At The Palace, Hollywood, 1985) / Sextown USA / Achoo (Life At Fairfield Halls, Croydon UK 1975) / This Town Ain't Big Enough For Both Of Us (Life At Fairfield Halls, Croydon UK 1975)

SPARKS OGLIO CATALOG SAMPLER
US: Oglio Records OGL 81605–2, CD, 1998

Cool Places / All You Ever Think About Is Sex / Angst In My Pants / I Predict / Tips For Teens / Funny Face / When I'm With You / Young Girls / With All My Might / Pretending To Be Drunk

THE 12-INCH COLLECTION
US: Oglio Records OGL 81605–2, CD, 1999

All You Ever Think About Is Sex / Beat The Clock / Young Girls / Cool Places / Dance Godammit / I Predict / Modesty Plays / Kiss Me Quick / Pretending To Be Drunk / The Number One Song In Heaven

THIS ALBUM'S BIG ENOUGH – THE BEST OF SPARKS
UK: Music Club MCCD 503, CD, 2002

This Town Ain't Big Enough For Both Of Us / Amateur Hour / The Number One Song In Heaven / Get In The Swing / Looks, Looks, Looks / Something For The Girl With Everything / Beat The Clock / Young Girls / Cool Places / La Dolce Vita / A Fun Bunch Of Guys From Outer Space / Dance Godammit / Tryouts For The Human Race / Never Turn Your Back On Mother Earth

PART FOUR: DVD

SPARKS LIVE IN LONDON
UK: Lift Off 84001 (DVD, 3/01)

It's A Sparks Show Tonight / Aeroflot / Something For The Girl With Everything / Scheherazade / (When I Kiss You) I Hear Charlie Parker Playing / More Than A Sex Machine / Do-Re-Mi / Angst In My Pants / Ron Performs Waiting For Godot With Rex The Wonderdog / How To Get Your Ass Kicked / Talent Is An Asset / Girl From Germany / Balls / Ron Levitates Baby Leroy / Bullet Train / Beat The Clock / This Town Ain't Big Enough For Both Of Us / The Number One Song In Heaven / Never Turn Your Back On Mother Earth / Amateur Hour / When Do I Get To Sing ' My Way?

LIL' BEETHOVEN LIVE IN STOCKHOLM
UK: Demon Vision DEMONDVD 001 (DVD, 8/04)
US: Standing Room Only (DVD, 4/05)

The Rhythm Thief / How Do I Get To Carnegie Hall? / What Are All These Bands So Angry About? / I Married Myself / Ride 'Em Cowboy / My Baby's Taking Me Home / Your Call Is Very Important To Us. Please Hold. / Ugly Guys With Beautiful Girls /Suburban Homeboy / It's A Sparks Show / National Crime Awareness Week / Here In Heaven / The Number One Song in Heaven / Nothing To Do /The Calm Before The Storm / The Ghost Of Liberace / Talent Is An Asset / Hospitality On Parade / (When I Kiss You) I Hear Charlie Parker Playing / This Town Ain't Big Enough For Both Of Us / When Do I Get To Sing 'My Way'? / Amateur Hour

DEEVEEDEE (LIVE AT THE LONDON FORUM)
UK: Liberation, 6066 (DVD, 11/07)

Rock, Rock, Rock / Dick Around / Perfume / The Very Next Fight / (Baby Baby) Can I Invade Your Country / Metaphor / Waterproof / Here Kitty / There's No Such Thing As Aliens / As I Sit To Play The Organ At The Notre Dame Cathedral / Achoo / Something For The Girl With Everything /Tryouts For The Human Race/ The Number One Song In Heaven / Pineapple / Never Turn Your Back On Mother Earth / When Do I Get To Sing 'My Way'? / This Town Ain't Big Enough For Both Of Us /Amateur Hour / Happy Hunting Ground / Suburban Homeboy / Change / Dick Around (reprise)

PART FIVE: SELECTED COLLABORATIONS
BIJOU
Pas Dormir
Phillips 9120 430, LP, Canada, 1979
Produced By Ron and Russell Mael

CHEAP TRICK
Busted
Epic 466 8761, CD, 1990
Sparks guest on You Drive, I'll Steer

THE GO-GO'S
Talk Show
IRS 7041, US, LP, 1984
Includes Yes Or No (Wiedlin/Mael/Mael)

GRAND POPO FOOTBALL CLUB
Shampoo Victims
Atmospheriques 82876501, CD, 1/2002
Yo Quiero Mas Dinero / La Nuit Est La
Co-written with Ron and Russell, with Russell and Tammy Glover on backing vocals

KRISTIAN HOFFMAN
Kristian Hoffman & ...
Eggbert ER 80032, CD, 6/02
Russell duets on Devil May Care

LES RITA MITSOUKO
Marc Et Robert, Virgin CDV 2572, CD, 1988
Hip Kit / Singing In The Shower / Live In Las Vegas
Featuring Ron and Russell Mael

Re, Virgin CDV 2637, CD, 1990
Hip Kit (Remix) / Singing In The Shower (Remix)
Featuring Ron and Russell Mael

LIO
Suite Sixtine
WEA WE 835, LP, Canada, 1983
I'll Expose You / Marie Antoinette / My Top Twenty / Party For Two /
Housewife Of The Year / Clothes
Lyrics by Ron and Russell Mael

MARC MOULIN
Top Secret
Blue Note 5360342, CD, 2002
Vocals on What? and inter-song comments by Ron Mael, engineered by
Russell Mael

ADRIAN MUNSEY
Virgin VS 226 C'est Sheep (Part 1) / C'est Sheep (Part 2) (7", p/s, 6/79)
Virgin VS 22612 C'est Sheep (Part 1) / C'est Sheep (Part 2) / C'est
Sheep (Part 3) (12", p/s, 6/79)
Written and produced by Ron and Russell Mael

NOEL
Is There More To Life Than Dancing?
Virgin V2126, UK, LP, some picture disc, 4/79

Dancing Is Dangerous / Is There More To Life Than Dancing / The
Night They Invented Love / Au Revoir / I Want A Man

Virgin VS 258 Dancing Is Dangerous / I Want A Man (7", p/s, 4/79)
Virgin VS 258–12 Dancing Is Dangerous / I Want A Man (12", p/s,
4/79)
Virgin VS 286 The Night They Invented Love / Au Revoir (7", 8/79)
Written and produced by Ron and Russell Mael

ORBITAL
The Blue Album
CD ATO 21527, 2004
Sparks collaborate on Acid Pants

PIZZICATO 5
Ca Et La Du Japon
Nippon Columbia COCP 50460, CD, 2001
Includes Kimono

THE RAMONES
Pleasant Dreams
Sire SRK 3571, LP, 7/81
Russell Mael on backing vocals

SALON MUSIC
This Is
Japan, CD, 1987
Special Guest – Russell Mael

O Boy
Moon 32XM-79, CD, Japan, 6/88
Ron: African wood on In My Life / Russell: backing vocals on Say
Hello, Wave Goodbye

TELEX
Sex (Birds And Bees)
Interdisc INTO 1, LP, 1982

Brainwash★ / Drama, Drama★ / Haven't We Met Somewhere Before?★ / Long Holiday / The Man With The Answer★ / Carbon Copy★ / Exercise Is Good For You / Dream-O-Mat★ / Sigmund Freud's Party / Mata Hari / Dummy★ / L'amour Toujours / Loops / Cloches Et Stifflets / Don't Put All Your Dreams In One Basket / I Can't Turn You Loose / Brainwash (long version) / The Look Of Love / Basta
★Lyrics written by Ron and Russell Mael

I (Still) Don't Like Music Volume 2 Remix Collection
CD 1999 (SSR 211CD)
Includes Brainwash (Juan Atkins Mix) Lyrics by Ron and Russell Mael

Bibliography

Bellos, David. *Jacques Tati*. The Harvill Press, London, 1999

Boyer, Paul S., Clifford E. Clark Jr., Joseph F. Kett, Neal Salisbury, Harvard Sitkoff and Nancy Woloch (Eds.) *The Enduring Vision: A History Of The American People* DC Heath, Lexington, Toronto, 1996

Clarke, Donald. *The Penguin Encyclopaedia Of Popular Music* Viking-Penguin, London, 1989

Dickson, Paul. *From Elvis To E-Mail: Trends, Events And Trivia From The Postwar Era To The End Of The Century* Federal Street Press, Springfield, MA, 1999

DeCurtis Anthony and James Henke with Holly George-Warren. *The Rolling Stone Album Guide* Virgin Books, London, 1992

Gross, Michael and Maxim Jakubowski. *The Rock Yearbook 1981.* Virgin Books, London, 1980

Harding, James. *Jacques Tati, Frame By Frame* Secker & Warburg, 1984

Hardy, Phil and Dave Laing. *The Faber Companion To 20th Century Popular Music* Faber & Faber, London, 1990

Jakubowski, Maxim. *The Rock Album* Frederick Muller Limited, London, 1983

Jones, Alan and Jussi Kantonen. *Saturday Night Forever – The Story Of Disco*
Mainstream Publishing, Edinburgh, London, 1999

Kishino, Yukio. *Sparks Guide Book*
Map/Out One Disc, Tokyo, 2006

Knobler, Peter and Greg Mitchell. Editors. *Very Seventies. A Cultural History Of The 1970s, From The Pages Of Crawdaddy*
Simon & Schuster, New York, 1995

Kutner, Jon and Spencer Leigh. *1000 UK Number One Hits*
Omnibus Press, London, 2005

Marcus, Greil. Editor. *Lester Bangs: Psychotic Reactions And Carburetor Dung*
Serpent's Tail, London, 1997

Marsh, Dave. *The Heart Of Rock And Soul: The 1001 Greatest Singles Ever Made*
Penguin, London, 1989

Mendelsohn, John. *I, Caramba: Confessions of An Antkiller*
Rhino Publishing, Los Angeles, 1995

Morley, Paul. *Words And Music – A History Of Pop In the Shape Of A City*
Bloomsbury, London, 2003

Robbins, Ira A. (Ed). *The New Trouser Press Record Guide*
Collier Books, New York, 1989

Quatro, Suzi. *Unzipped*
Hodder and Staughton, London, 2007

Salewicz, Chris (Ed). *Keep On Running. The Story Of Island Records*
Island Records/The Island Trading Co., 2009

Shaar Murray, Charles. *Shots From The Hip*
Penguin, London, 1991

Sounes, Howard. *Seventies: The Sights, Sounds And Ideas Of A Brilliant Decade*
Simon and Schuster, London, 2006

Southall, Brian. *The A-Z Of Record Labels. Second Edition*
Sanctuary Publishing, London, 2003

Strong, Martin C. *The Great Rock Discography, Fifth Edition*
Mojo Books, Edinburgh, 2000

✗ Thompson, Dave. *Sparks – No.1 Songs In Heaven*
Cherry Red Books, London, 2009

Taylor, Derek. *Fifty Years Adrift (In An Open Necked Shirt)*
Genesis Publications, London, 1983

Visconti, Tony. *Bowie, Bolan and the Brooklyn Boy: The Autobiography*
Harper Collins, London, 2007

Newspapers and Magazines:
Many publications including *The Wire; Jackie Magazine; The Word; Daily Record; The Metro; The Times; The Sunday Express; Time Out New York; Muzik; The Independent; Boyz: Rock'N'Reel; Keyboard Player; Scotland On Sunday; The Daily Mirror; Mirabelle; Record Mirror; Record Collector; Q; Mojo; New Musical Express; Melody Maker; Clash Magazine; Trouser Press; National Rockstar; The Guardian; The LA Times; Keyboard Review; Uncut.*

Fleury, Joseph. *Sparks Flashes, Vol. 2, No. 1* 1974

All other publications referenced in text

Websites
The remarkable and ever-informative www.allsparks.com

The entertaining and detailed http://graphikdesigns.free.fr/sparks-mael-site.html – thanks to Xavier Laroate

http://www.experiencefestival.com/a/Martin_Sharp_-_The_Pheasantry/id/5279377

http://www.mother-superior.com/sparks_interview.html

Steven Nistor: http://www.billboard.com/bbcom/tour_diary/article_display.jsp?vnu_content_id=1003805766

Russian fan site: http://www.sparks-alex.narod.ru/SparksE.htm

John Hewlett interview: http://www.geocities.com/martinjjgordon/fish.html

Adrian Fisher and Finnish Sparks fan Petteri Aro: http://www.martingordon.de/old/ade.html

Devo article: http://www.thewire.co.uk/articles/2430/?pageno=3

General Sparks site: http://www.xs4all.nl/~cvbreuke/dispwho.htm

Rocksbackpages.com:
Sparks/1974/Harvey Kubernik/Melody Maker/Sparks: Hometown Heroes At Last/07/07/2009 13:32:17/http://www.rocksbackpages. com/article.html?ArticleID=11323

Sparks/1980/Betty Page/Sounds/Sparks: *Terminal Jive* (Virgin) ★★/16/09/2009 15:04:00/http://www.rocksbackpages.com/article. html?ArticleID=14593

Sparks/1974/Max Bell/NME/Sparks/16/09/2009 15:14:36/http:// www.rocksbackpages.com/article.html?ArticleID=14362

Sparks/1979/Harry Doherty/Melody Maker/Sparks: Too Much Too Soon Again/16/09/2009 15:18:45/http://www.rocksbackpages.com/ article.html?ArticleID=14053

Sparks/1983/Mark Leviton/BAM/Sparks/16/09/2009 15:28:36/ http://www.rocksbackpages.com/article.html?ArticleID=5064

Meyer Mael information: http://vitals.rootsweb.ancestry.com/ca/ death/search.cgi

Interviews
1. Ron and Russell Mael, October 2002/February 2003 for *Record Collector* articles
2. Ronna Frank, November 6, 2008
3. Ian Hampton, November 26, 2008
4. Rupert Holmes, January 2, 2009
5. Martin Gordon, January 27, 2009
6. Karl Stoecker, January 28, 2009
7. Jim Mankey, January 21, 2009
8. Ira Robbins, March 7, 2009

9. Tony Visconti, April 27, 2009
10. David Humphrey, April 27, 2009
11. Jon Savage, May 5, 2009
12. Muff Winwood, May 20, 2009
13. Jim Wilson, May 25, 2009
14. Marcus Blake, May 25, 2009
15. Steve Nistor, May 20, 2009
16. Harley Feinstein, June 29, 2009
17. James Lowe, June 30, 2009
18. Thom Rotella, July 20, 2009
19. Chris Blackwell, July 20, 2009
20. David Betteridge, July 21, 2009
21. Sue Harris, July 24, 2009
22. Gered Mankowitz, July 27, 2009
23. Tony Calder, July 27, 2009
24. John Taylor, July 27, 2009
25. David Sefton, July 27, 2009
26. Tim Clark, July 28, 2009
27. Nick Rhodes, July 28, 2009
28. David Kendrick, August 4, 2009
29. Larry Dupont, August 10, 2009
30. John Hewlett, September 12, 2009
31. Trevor White, September 14, 2009
32. Peter Zumsteg, September 17, 2009
33. Richard Williams, September 21, 2009
34. Larry Vigon, September 21, 2009

Plus also thanks for passing conversations and quick emails from Dave Ball, Eric Blum, Greg Brooks, Roy Carr, Jim Goodwin, Mark Hagen, Mark Lewisohn, Ian Little, Brian May, Paul Morley, Pete Nash, Andy Neill, Chris O'Donnell, Katherine Orloff, Dave Cameron-Pryde, Andy Ross, Snuffy Walden, John Williams, Luke Zamperini

LP/CD notes:
2 Originals Of Sparks (Bearsville, 1975, K 85505) (essay by Joseph Fleury, interviews with Ron and Russell Mael)

Profile: The Ultimate Sparks Collection (Rhino, 1991, R2 70731) (essay by Ira Robbins, interviews with Ron and Russell Mael)

Mael Intuition (The Best Of Sparks 1974–76, It's A Mael, Mael, Mael World) (Island, 1990, IMCD 88) (essay by 'Gummo Mael'[Paul Morley])

The Heaven Collection (Sony, 1993, COL 473515–2) (interviews with Ron and Russell Mael)

Sparks Present Motown Made To Measure (Tamla Motown, 2006, 994 001–5) (interviews with Ron and Russell Mael)

Kimono My House: 21st Century Edition (Island, 2006, 984 341–7) (essay by Paul Lester, interview with Russell Mael)

Propaganda: 21st Century Edition (Island, 2006, 984 341–0) (essay by Martin Aston, interview with Ron Mael)

Indiscreet: 21st Century Edition (Island, 2006, 984 341 -1) (essay by Chris Jones, interview with Russell Mael)

Big Beat: 21st Century Edition (Island, 2006, 984 341–2) (essay by Daryl Easlea, comments by Russell Mael)

Radio:
This Town Ain't Big Enough For Both Of Us – The Story Of Sparks, BBC Radio 2, January 20, 2007

Acknowledgements

Wonder Girls: Darling Jules and my delightful Flo – you are everything and everything is you

No. 1 in Heaven: To all the dear departed Easleas.

To Andrew Johnstone, somewhere in Southchurch, for all those Sunday mornings when you should have been helping me with my French homework, but played me *Big Beat* instead.

To Michelle Bloe (sic) the girl on the waltzer at Maldon Promenade Park in 1975.

To Mr and Mrs Nick Maslen. Thank you very much for the use of your dining room.

Sincere thanks to all the interviewees

To Ron and Russell Mael – ***Talent Is An Asset* is completely unauthorised and no new interviews were conducted with Ron and Russell for this book**. However, I would like to thank them for their courtesy and generosity with their time in all our earlier meetings and communications.

To Sue Harris and Lucy Wigginton

To Auke Lenstra – for services beyond the call of duty

Josie Hudson from Leigh-On-Sea, Greg Brooks, Gary Taylor, Mark Hagen, Steve Hammonds, John Glover, Ted Cummings, Barney Hoskyns, Christine Atkins, Adam White, Lois Wilson, Alan Hodgson, Mark Paytress, Peter Doggett, Chris Jones, Scott Maclachan, Richard England,

Jonathan Parsons, David and Tara Hemingway, Paul Collier, Steven Collins, and the L-O-S groovers, my dear friends at *Mojo*, *RC* and Universal; Phil Alexander, Jenny Bulley, Geoff Brown, Danny Eccleston, Andrew Mame, Mark Blake, Martin Aston, Joel Mciver, Val Cutts, Tim Jones, Alan Lewis, Jason Draper, Hannah Chadwick, BK, Susie Sue Armstrong, Simon Li, CAC, Adam Barker, Jerome Ramsey, Mark Wood, Lutz Stoever, Matt Read, Emma Parrot, both Johnny Cs, Joe Black, Julian Fernandez, Jonny Turner, Andie Daw, Silvia Montello, Brian Rose, anyone I've missed, you know, the whole damn lot. Andreas of the Street, Nigel Reeve, Jason Day, Hik Sasaki, Steve Webbon, Adam Velasco, Paul Lester, Tim Fraser-Harding, Colin Smith, Adam Velasco, Mike Glaspell, Mike Storey, Double A, Dave Clarke, GK Skinner, the good people.

Graham, Wendy, Nathan and Katy Brown; John Jazz, Nicky, Amelia and little green Isaac; Andrew, Ronnie and Harland Branch; Simon, Saskia, Maisy and Lily Dornan; Siôn, Aga and Jonaz, Selvy; Pete n Debs; Larry; Ben, Caroline and Alex.

In my family: Pat, Alan, Chrissie, Stephen, Sharon, Katie, Thom, Beth and Ellie; Win, Liz, Ian, Kate, Ivy, George, Sylvia, Glenn, Mandy, Sienna, Savannah, Craig, Tanya, Zach, Justin, Jane, Jake, Luke and Tom.

The greatest living Englishmen and women, The Wolstanton Cultural Quarter; Barry Pitts, Lisa Walmsley, Nick Maslen, Fiona Dutton, Rob and Aud Ebrey and all joyous children and grandchildren

To Chris Charlesworth, Andy Neill and Jacqui Black

To Joe Devine and Nancy Wallace

Everyone who provided encouragement and to virtually everyone who, when I mentioned what I was doing, talked about seeing Sparks on *Top Of The Pops*. *"Ooh look, there's Hitler on the telly."*

And, Lorcan ...

Famous red pants: "Feels like I'm wearing nothing at all."